W9-BSU-143

400

GARDENER TO GARDENER

WE **INSPIRE** AND **ENABLE** PEOPLE TO IMPROVE
THEIR LIVES AND THE WORLD AROUND THEM

© 2000 by Rodale Inc.
Illustrations © 2000 by Keith Ward

The information in this book has been carefully researched, and all efforts have been made to ensure accuracy. Rodale Inc. assumes no responsibility for any injuries suffered or for damages or losses incurred during the use of or as a result of following this information. It is important to study all directions carefully before taking any action based on the information and advice presented in this book. When using any commercial product, *always* read and follow label directions. Where trade names are used, no discrimination is intended and no endorsement by Rodale Inc. is implied.

Printed in the United States of America on acid-free ∞, recycled ♻ paper

We're always happy to hear from you. For questions or comments concerning the editorial content of this book, please write to

Rodale Book Readers' Service
33 East Minor Street
Emmaus, PA 18098

Look for other Rodale books wherever books are sold. Or call us at (800) 848-4735.

For more information about Rodale Organic Gardening magazine and books, visit us at

www.organicgardening.com

Editors: Vicki Mattern and Fern Marshall Bradley
Cover and Interior Book Designer: Nancy S. Biltcliff
Cover and Interior Illustrator: Keith Ward
Layout Designer: Daniel MacBride
Researchers: Diana Erney and Sarah Wolfgang Heffner
Copy Editor: Stacey Ann Follin
Production Editor: Nancy N. Bailey
Manufacturing Coordinator: Patrick T. Smith
Editorial Assistance: Kerrie A. Cadden and Claudia Curran

RODALE ORGANIC GARDENING BOOKS

Managing Editor: Fern Marshall Bradley
Executive Creative Director: Christin Gangi
Art Director: Patricia Field
Production Manager: Robert V. Anderson Jr.
Studio Manager: Leslie M. Keefe
Associate Copy Manager: Jennifer Hornsby
Manufacturing Manager: Mark Krahforst

Library of Congress Cataloging-in-Publication Data

Gardener to gardener almanac & pest-control primer : a month-by-month guide and journal for planning, planting, and tending your organic garden / edited by Vicki Mattern and Fern Marshall Bradley.
   p. cm.
  Includes bibliographical references and index.
  ISBN 0–87596–864–3 (hardcover : alk. paper)
  ISBN 0–87596–862–7 (paperback : alk. paper)
  1. Organic gardening. 2. Garden pests— Biological control. I. Mattern, Vicki. II. Bradley, Fern Marshall.
  SB453.5 .G33 2000
  635'.0484—dc21   00–009575

Distributed in the book trade by St. Martin's Press

2 4 6 8 10 9 7 5 3 1 hardcover

2 4 6 8 10 9 7 5 3 1 paperback

GARDENER TO GARDENER

Almanac & Pest-Control Primer

A month-by-month guide and journal for planning, planting, and tending your organic garden

Edited by Vicki Mattern and Fern Marshall Bradley

RODALE

RODALE
Organic Gardening Starts Here!

Here at Rodale, we've been gardening organically for over 50 years—ever since my grandfather J. I. Rodale learned about composting and decided that healthy living starts with healthy soil. In 1940 J. I. started the Rodale Organic Farm to test his theories, and today the nonprofit Rodale Institute Experimental Farm is still at the forefront of organic gardening and farming research. In 1942 J. I. founded *Organic Gardening* magazine to share his discoveries with gardeners everywhere. His son, my father, Robert Rodale, headed *Organic Gardening* until 1990, and today a fourth generation of Rodales is growing up with the magazine. Over the years we've shown millions of readers how to grow bountiful crops and beautiful flowers using nature's own techniques.

In this book, you'll find the latest organic methods and the best gardening advice. We know—because all our authors and editors are passionate about gardening! We feel strongly that our gardens should be safe for our children, pets, and the birds and butterflies that add beauty and delight to our lives and landscapes. Our gardens should provide us with fresh, flavorful vegetables, delightful herbs, and gorgeous flowers. And they should be a pleasure to work in as well as to view.

Sharing the secrets of safe, successful gardening is why we publish books. So come visit us at the Rodale Institute Experimental Farm, where you can tour the gardens every day—we're open year-round. And use this book to create your best garden ever.

Happy gardening!

Maria Rodale

Maria Rodale
Rodale Organic Gardening Books

Contents

Welcome to
Gardener to Gardener!

Whether you're new to gardening or have decades of experience, no doubt you've discovered that your gardening activities are closely tied to the seasons. As an organic gardener, you might also have learned that gardening is a kind of partnership between you and the natural world: You can influence what goes on in your garden, but you can't really control it. "Chemical gardeners" never stop trying to control what happens in the garden. But organic gardeners succeed by working with Nature. By learning to read Nature's cues, you begin to know when to give plants a helping hand—maybe a BT spray will do the trick, for example—and when to stand back and let Nature take the lead.

A Handy Garden Almanac

How do you learn to read Nature? One of the best ways is to record your gardening experiences and the natural conditions you observe in your garden (weather, insect and animal activity, plant health, etc.). Gardeners have been taking such notes—in the form of almanacs and journals—for generations, and probably since people first started planting seeds.

That's why we think you'll find this *Gardener to Gardener* almanac especially useful. We've organized it by month, just like a traditional almanac, and included a "Gardener's To-Do List" for each month. We know that your garden activities are very much affected by your local climate, so we've organized these garden checklists according to the USDA Plant Hardiness Zones. (If you don't know what zone your garden is, check the hardiness map on page 246 to find out.) Each chapter also includes more in-depth information about typical garden activities for that month. Plus, some chapters include log sheets for keeping track of important data, such as a Seed Inventory and a Planting Log.

This book is also a primer on organic pest control. In Chapter 6, we take an in-depth look at the most troublesome garden pests and tell you how to get the best of them without chemical sprays. This chapter has great advice and solutions for you—whether you're a novice or a pro at fighting pests.

A special note for Deep South gardeners (especially in Zone 10): You know that your garden is anything but typical! When other gardens are in high gear in August and September, yours is resting. But come October, when other gardens die down, your planting season is in high gear. So if you garden in Zone 10, you'll need to apply some of the seasonal advice according to your own timetable: For instance, instead of reading the planting information in Chapter 4 during the month of April, you probably want refer to it in October.

An Adaptable Garden Journal

Along with a wealth of regional and seasonal advice, we've included plenty of room for you to record your own observations of the weather and your garden's progress in Part 2 of the book, "Your Gardening Journal." We're gardeners ourselves, and we know that, despite good intentions, most gardeners don't get around to taking garden notes every day: Sometimes you'll have plenty to record for one week, then nothing at all for the following week. That's why we haven't restricted this note-taking section to a formal calendar but instead have provided a more flexible journal format.

A Unique Garden Companion

You'll find that one of the special pleasures of reading *Gardener to Gardener* is the feeling that you're talking to a trusted gardening companion. That's because each chapter is filled with advice and tips from hundreds of gardening friends: the readers of *Organic Gardening* magazine. This group of experienced organic gardeners has shared their best ideas on everything from seed starting to organic pest control to attracting birds and butterflies to your garden. Plus, nearly every chapter includes a garden project or technique, also contributed by fellow gardeners.

If you enjoy the reader tips in this book, you may also want to visit a special place online where organic gardeners are meeting friends, sharing gardening secrets, and discussing the issues dear to their hearts. It's the Gardener to Gardener Forum at www.organicgardening.com. Sign on and say hello!

Part 1
The Gardener's Year

From the first days of January to the last weeks of December, there's always something for gardeners to plan or do that involves plants. On snowy winter evenings, there's armchair gardening with seed and nursery catalogs to inspire. There's no better task on a bright spring morning than planting new perennials, and when it's too hot to dig or plant in summer, it's still pleasant to cut a bouquet of annuals for the dining room table. Fall garden pasttimes include harvesting squash, raking leaves, and setting up a bird-feeding station.

In the chapters that follow, you'll find unique ideas from gardeners like you for everything from organizing seed packets to keeping weeds under control and simplifying harvest chores. We've included great how-to advice on planting, propagation, and more. There's a special section on organic methods for keeping pests from pestering your plants. You'll also find log sheets where you can record important information like your inventory of seeds, planting dates for your vegetables and flowers, and what and how much of each crop you preserve.

Chapter 1

January

Getting Started: Planning and Designing the Garden

In spring, summer, and fall, people sort of have an open season on each other; only in the winter, in the country, can you have longer, quiet stretches when you can savor belonging to yourself.

—*Ruth Stout*

Many of us think of spring as the beginning of the gardening year, but the truth is, the first seeds of a garden—the very idea of the garden and all of the planning that goes with it—are planted in winter. In January, when outdoor temperatures are too cold for plant growth in most of North America, the thought of green plants, warm air, and fragrant blooms is more than comforting: It's irresistible.

What gardener doesn't enjoy pouring over garden catalogs and books, plotting new garden beds, and reviewing notes on last season's successes and failures? It's your chance to make a fresh start and create your dream garden.

Whether you're creating your first garden or refining your established garden, planning is an essential step in the process. In temperate climate areas, January is ideal for reviewing notes from last season; taking stock of seed supplies; mapping the location of new beds and borders; reading up on plant choices; and choosing new cultivars for your garden.

Gardener's To-Do List—January

If you don't know what USDA hardiness zone you live in, check the map on page 246 to find out.

Zone 3

- ☐ Check your leftover seeds and make a list of what you need before ordering.
- ☐ Order seeds and plants early to avoid substitution.
- ☐ Take cuttings from fruit trees for grafting in April. Wrap the twigs in a wet paper towel, seal the wrapped twigs in a plastic bag, and store the bag in the freezer until spring.

Zone 4

- ☐ Organize your seeds: Discard those that are too old, then make a list of seeds to order.
- ☐ Order seeds of onions, geraniums, and other slow-growing plants now so you receive them in time to start indoors next month.
- ☐ Draw your garden plan.
- ☐ Check the condition of your gardening equipment.
- ☐ Build a garden trellis.
- ☐ Surprise your friends by harvesting Jerusalem artichokes and parsnips from the garden during a January thaw.

Zone 5

- ☐ Start seeds of pansies, snapdragons, and hardy perennials.
- ☐ Replenish your supplies, including seed-starting mix and organic fertilizers.
- ☐ Where there isn't much snow cover, push back any plants that have "heaved" out of the ground because of freeze-thaw cycles.

- ☐ Start a collection of scented geraniums by taking cuttings from a friend's plants.
- ☐ If you're growing geraniums indoors in pots, cut back leggy stems by about half; repot the plants in fresh soil, then set them in a cool, bright window.

Zone 6

- ☐ Study the "skeleton" of your landscape and decide where to put new structures, such as pathways and arbors.
- ☐ Keep bird feeders well stocked with favorites, such as black oil sunflower seeds.
- ☐ Discard old seeds for the garden; mail orders for new seeds.
- ☐ Create a computer database of your garden plants with notes on performance.
- ☐ Rake heavy snow off shrubs.
- ☐ Start seeds of pansies, dusty miller, browallia, begonias, snapdragons, and delphiniums indoors under lights.
- ☐ At month's end, start seeds of onions, leeks, broccoli, cabbage, and cauliflower indoors under lights.

Zone 7

- ☐ On mild days, remove winter weeds, such as wild onions and chickweed.
- ☐ Sow seeds of Shirley poppies (*Papaver rhoeas*) for bloom in May and June.
- ☐ Sow larkspur seeds directly in flowerbeds where you want them to grow; look for blooms by midspring.

- [ ] Indoors, start seeds of perennials or slow-growing annuals, like coleus and geraniums, beneath lights.
- [ ] Start seeds of cabbage, early lettuce, and at the end of the month, broccoli.
- [ ] When onion and cabbage transplants are available at the garden center, select the best ones, then plant them in the garden beneath a row cover.
- [ ] Near the end of the month, weed the asparagus bed and strawberry plot, then feed the plants and renew the thinning mulches.

Zone 8

- [ ] Shop local nurseries for asparagus roots, strawberry plants, and fruit trees.
- [ ] Cover root crops still in the ground with an extra layer of mulch.
- [ ] When cold temperatures are predicted, protect transplants of onions, cabbage, broccoli, and chard with a row cover.
- [ ] Sow beets, carrots, radishes, cress, bok choy, and garden peas directly in the garden; cover the planting rows with dark compost to warm the soil.
- [ ] Sow seeds of herbs, such as dill and parsley.
- [ ] Sow seeds of annual flowers (delphiniums, snapdragons, and larkspur are good choices) anywhere you want flowers for cutting or as a background for other plants.
- [ ] Top-dress lawns and garden beds with compost.

Zone 9

- [ ] Use the weather to your advantage: Observe the location of standing puddles left by winter rains; note where you need to improve drainage for plants.

- [ ] Finish pruning fruit trees, vines, and bushes.
- [ ] Sow seeds of geraniums, peppers, tomatoes, and eggplant in pots filled with a peat moss/vermiculite mixture; set the pots on a sunny windowsill or beneath lights until it's warm enough to plant them outside.
- [ ] In the garden, "scratch in" wildflower seed mixes and California poppy seeds; plant nasturtium seeds a bit deeper.
- [ ] Set out transplants of pansies, calendulas, and primroses.
- [ ] As the soil warms, plant carrots, broccoli, lettuce, spinach, cilantro, parsley, and Asian greens.
- [ ] Harvest carrots, radishes, and brussels sprouts—sweetened by frost.

Zone 10

- [ ] It's the dry season—water vegetable plants, nondormant tropical plants, and bedding plants regularly.
- [ ] Spray compost tea on roses and bromeliads.
- [ ] Mulch peas to extend the harvest.
- [ ] Sow pumpkins and winter squash directly in the garden; start cucumbers and watermelons in pots.
- [ ] Sow quick-maturing varieties of carrots, broccoli, cabbage, coriander, parsley, and dill.
- [ ] Plant heat-tolerant chicory, lettuce, and Swiss chard in shade so that they stay cool when the weather warms.
- [ ] Snip off flowers of tropical fruit and young citrus to save their strength while they grow; bring the flowers indoors to perfume the house.

Planning a Great Garden

Creating a good plan can be the difference between having a bed full of struggling plants and having a successful garden. The key features of a good garden plan are a list of the plants you want to grow, plus how many of each you need to plant, and a scale drawing that shows where you'll plant each plant. Here are 10 helpful tips to keep in mind as you put together your garden plan:

1. Look on the sunny side. Most garden plants (particularly edibles) need a minimum of 5 hours of full sun each day. Nearly all vegetables produce better with 8 hours of sun per day. If a portion of a bed is shady part of the day, plan to grow sun-loving crops—like tomatoes, peppers, and corn—on the sunny side. Fill in the partly shaded area with those that like a bit of relief from the heat—like lettuce, carrots, and peas. Do the same with flowers.

Don't guess about the location of your sunniest and shadiest spots—determine just where to plant your crops by charting the sun's course over your garden. To map where your garden receives full sun, light shade, and moderate to deep shade, use stakes and string to mark the shady areas in the morning (A), at noon (B), and in late afternoon (C).

"The amount of sun that a plot gets is by far the most important factor to know when planning a garden because it's the one thing you can't change," says Anne Halpin, author of *Year-Round Flower Gardener*. "You can improve your soil's drainage or plant a windbreak fairly easily, but if you have an unalterable lack of sun, your plants will always struggle."

2. Raise high the growing beds.
Very few plants like to sit in constantly damp soil. The loose soil of raised beds, created by the addition of organic matter (such as compost, manure, leaf mold, and straw) to your soil, means good drainage and plenty of room for your plants to put down nice long roots. No matter how old or new your garden is, growing your plants in raised beds will give them a boost.

How high and wide should beds be? About 6 inches to a foot higher than the surrounding soil is the right height, and a width of 3 to 4 feet allows you to reach into the center of the bed from either side. The path between your beds should be wide enough to let your garden cart or wheelbarrow pass through.

3. Choose your lineup.
It's one of the most common mistakes that gardeners make: planting far more than they have room for or than they can reasonably care for.

If you want a steady supply of relatively small amounts of continually fresh produce from early spring into late fall, choose crops that produce throughout the season and avoid planting those that produce all at once. If, on the other hand, you mostly want your garden to feed you during the off-season, select crops like determinate tomatoes—these types bear all their fruit at once and are perfect for those who are growing with freezing and canning in mind. Minimal space, you say? Then switch gears and plan to grow crops you can trellis up—such as cucumbers, squash, peas, beans, and gourds—and add vertical space to your horizontal garden.

4. Hedge your bets.
Some years the weather simply doesn't cooperate with our gardening plans. (OK, maybe that's every year.) Nancy Pierson Farris, who's been growing a garden in Estill, South Carolina, for more than 20 years, has a strategy to compensate for this basic reality of life.

"One side of our property is low, and it stays fairly wet in spring and fall," she explains. The other side is high and stays dry in even the rainiest seasons. So I plant some of everything on both sides; that way I am virtually assured of getting good results no matter what that year's weather is like. You can adapt Nancy's strategy in your planning by planting more than one variety of each important vegetable crop that you grow. (You can do the same with annual flowers.)

Superstars for Shade

Although many popular garden plants do best in full sun, that doesn't mean you can't have a garden in shade. Plenty of beautiful ornamentals thrive in the partial shade. Even some edibles can produce in partial shade, as long as they get 4 to 6 hours of sun per day.

PERENNIALS

Astilbes
Bellflowers
Daylilies
Ferns
Foxgloves
Heucheras
Hostas
Ligularia
Phlox
Primroses

ANNUALS

Begonias
Four o'clocks
Impatiens
Nicotiana
Salvias

EDIBLES

Beans
Beets
Blueberries
Carrots
Leaf lettuce
Peas
Radishes
Raspberries
Swiss chard

*Garden
Cheat Sheets*

*Sometimes I find it difficult
to remember all I need to
know about plants, fertilizers,
garden rotations, and weeds
when I'm out in the garden.
After a couple of years of
running back and forth to the
house to continually check my
notebook, I finally developed a
portable system that lets me
keep the information I need
close at hand.*

*I simply jot the info I know
I'll need onto 4 × 6-inch index
cards, then I put the cards in a
small plastic bag that I keep in
my garden caddy. Later, when
I'm in the garden and can't
remember whether to plant
the dill around my tomatoes or
my broccoli, I just scan my
index cards. (These cards are
becoming smudged with
muddy fingerprints, so I plan
to make some new ones and
cover them with clear
packaging tape, which can be
wiped clean.)*

*Sara Anderson
Arlington, Virginia*

5. *Nix the high-need picks.* Now take your list and "cut out anything that needs a lot of attention," says Farris. "Plants that aren't naturally well suited to your climate, for instance, will demand much more
of your time and attention than they're worth." To ensure the success
that keeps you coming back for more year after year, stay away from exotics your first season or so, too.

6. *Plant to join the rotation club.* Rotating your crops keeps
your soil and plants healthy and productive. If you have a large garden,
it's easy—just move your crops from one section to the next each year. In
a smaller garden, you may have to pass on growing some crops each year.

Think about crop rotations when drawing up this year's plan, and
you'll naturally come up with next year's plan as well. Label your beds
A, B, C, and so on, and see how many years you can go before you have
to plant tomatoes (perhaps the most important crop not to plant over
and over again in the same soil) in a certain spot again. If you can make
it 3 years, you're golden!

7. *Plan for your plate.* Now that you've winnowed your list down
to what you want to grow, you need to figure out how much you need to
plant to get the amount you want. For instance, "a dozen lettuce plants
will be enough for a family of four to have lettuce four times a week
through the season," estimates Jeff Dawson, garden director at Fetzer
Valley Oaks in Hopland, California. (*Note*: Because lettuce plants wear
out, eventually go to seed, and get too bitter-tasting to eat when they do,
you'll need to start several runs of plants during the year. You'll need
about a dozen plants going at any given time, which could mean 48 to 96
plants total in a season, depending on your climate.) "I'd plant about the
same of spinach and radishes, and half as many beans," adds Dawson.

Two to four indeterminate tomato plants and an equal number of
pepper and cucumber plants will provide enough of a harvest to keep
fresh produce (and fill out those salads!) on your table all season long, he
estimates. Two squash plants will yield plenty for summer eating or
winter keeping, he adds.

8. *Sketch it out.* Now you're ready to take all the pieces of this
puzzle and make them fit together. The best way to do this is to take a
pencil and paper (graph paper is especially handy if you have it) and draw
an outline of your garden, as close to scale as you can. Then start filling
in the crops where you want them to go.

"Build around perennials," says Anne Halpin. This goes for both the
flower and the vegetable garden, If you already have or plan to plant
perennial crops—such as asparagus, rhubarb, horseradish, and berries—

put them at the edges of your garden so you won't disturb them when you change plantings in the middle of the season or when you begin digging next spring, Halpin suggests.

Another sensible tactic is to group plants that have similar water needs. You'll be able to give "thirsty" plants a good soaking (with a soaker hose, drip irrigation, or a sprinkler) without wasting stray water on those that require less water.

"If you garden in a very dry area, plan to space your plants a little closer together than the catalog or seed packet recommends to help shade your ground and keep it from drying out," Dawson suggests. "Likewise, in damp regions, plant a little farther apart to allow the plants to dry out better and prevent fungus attacks."

9. Plan for final height. "Be sure to consider the final size of the mature plants," warns Halpin. "Remember that tall, leafy plants will shade out the shorter plants, unless you place them on the north side of the garden." You can use differences in plant heights to your advantage by planting lettuce and spinach where taller crops will cast a shadow over them for part of the day. The shade will help these leafy crops last a little longer into the summer, as both bolt and turn bitter in the heat.

Also, think about using tall crops, such as corn, as a trellis for vining crops, such as pole beans. Or, if a fence or similar structure is already in place, make a plan that will allow you to plant peas, beans, cucumbers, sweet peas, and so on, near it for free support.

10. Be ready to improvise. "I write my plans in pencil," says Nancy Pierson Farris. "A pencil with a good eraser. Every year, something I didn't plan for upsets my plans, so I just erase and add, trying to build on what I've already done that *did* work."

Take advantage of your garden shade. Plant crops that need some relief from summer heat, such as lettuce, in the shelter of trellised melons and other tall crops.

Garden Plotter

Plan for a Full Season of Bloom

As an apartment dweller, my only garden space is a 10 × 3-foot bed. Since I can see my little garden from my living room window, I like to have it constantly filled with flowers. I've found that the way to achieve this constant bloom is to plant bulbs! Even though I plant the bulbs very close together, they don't seem to suffer. Tulips, freesias, and anemones kick off my spring season; gladiolus follow in summer; and cyclamen and fall-blooming crocuses bloom in fall and well into our mild winter. A few geraniums fill in any lulls in the performance. What I really like is that the whole thing is portable: When I'm ready to move, I'll just dig up the bulbs and take them with me.

Hilary Holt
Pacific Grove,
California

Try a Mulch-and-Grow Perennial Garden

Here's a no-fail plan for turning a weedy or barren site into a showplace with minimal effort. (It's especially good for an area where the soil is compacted.) The idea is to bring the area back to life over the course of three years by spreading a thick layer of mulch, planting annuals, and then gradually planting perennials.

This triangular plot covers about 50 square feet. If you have more room to fill, plant four or five of these elegantly simple beds in sequence and you'll fill those empty (or ugly!) square feet beautifully!

The very first step in preparing this garden is to improve your soil. So get the soil surface covered! Spread a 10-inch layer of organic mulch over your future garden site. You can use straw or spoiled hay, mixing in leave or grass clippings if you have them. Then, dig into some fertile soil in another part of your yard—and capture the biggest earthworms you can find. Tuck groups of four to eight earthworms under the mulch in two or three different places. Moisten the mulch lightly if it's dry.

Year One

In the spring, spread a layer of compost 2 to 3 inches thick over the straw mulch covering your garden site.

Wait a few weeks for the compost to settle and the soil to warm, then plant cleome, cosmos, and globe amaranth seeds in the compost. (Plant cleome early in the spring, when the soil is still cool; the cosmos when danger of frost is past; and the glove amaranth when the soil is warm.) If you're in a hurry to see some color, feel free to plug in transplants instead, of course.

In late summer or fall (but before a hard freeze), collect seeds from the cosmos when the flowers dry. Then remove and compost the plants, move the mulch aside in a few spots, and plant some daffodil bulbs.

Cover the entire garden with 3 to 4 inches or more of mulch.

Year Two

In the spring, plant the cosmos seed you saved from the previous fall and the shining coneflower and artemisia plants that you purchased or started inside. Move the mulch aside for planting, then pull it back around the plants to discourage weeds. Be sure you avoid digging up the areas where your daffodils are now emerging.

During the growing season, deadhead your perennials regularly to take advantage of a long bloom period.

After frost, remove and compost the cosmos, cut the coneflower stems back to 4 to 5 inches, and mulch once again. Let the artemisia stand until spring.

Year Three

In the spring, plant salvia, Ozark sundrops, and gold-and-silver chrysanthemum. (Remember to keep removing those spent flowers for a summer-long show!)

In midsummer, let the Ozark sundrops go to seed. After the frost, cut all the plant stems back to 4 to 5 inches, except for the artemisia, which can stand until spring and will provide some winter color.

Plant List

A 'Ruby Queen' cleome (*Cleome hasslerana* 'Ruby Queen'): 5 plants

B 'Early Wonder' cosmos (*Cosmos bipinnatus* 'Early Wonder'): 7 plants

C 'Buddy' globe amaranth (*Gomphrena globosa* 'Buddy'): 3 plants

D 'Goldquelle' shining cone-flower (*Rudbeckia nitida* 'Goldquelle'): 3 plants

E 'Silver King' artemisia (*Artemisia ludoviciana* 'Silver King'): 3 plants

F Daffodils (*Narcissus* hybrids): 3 plants

G 'East Friesland' sage (*Salvia nemorosa* 'East Friesland'): 3 plants

H Gold-and-silver chrysan-themum (*Ajania pacifica*): 3 plants

I Ozark sundrops (*Oenothera missouriensis*): 3 plants

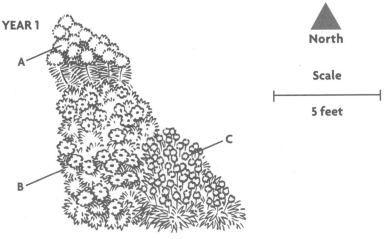

Turn a barren site into a showplace with a mulch-and-grow perennial garden. As your gardens mature, you'll enjoy elegant and colorful flowers and foliage.

Simple Seed Organizer

Last spring I became tired of my usual routine of rummaging through a large box of half-opened seed packages to find what I needed, so I decided it was time to get organized. I took some file folders and taped the sides together about halfway, then put in seed packets of each type of plant, along with pertinent articles and growing tips. On the outside of each file folder, I taped photos and descriptions of the varieties (cut from seed catalogs) inside the folder. Organizing my seeds this way allows me to see at a glance what varieties I have, when to plant them, and how to grow them.

Valerie Curtiss
Coos Bay, Oregon

Seed Catalog Savvy

OK, you've sketched out your plan for the coming season and you've sorted through your leftover seeds. Now you're ready to cozy up with all the seed catalogs you've been stashing away over the past month. You start paging through them. The photos are enticing, but what exactly do all the abbreviations and symbols mean? And why does the information in one catalog conflict with that in another?

Seed companies have to describe each plant in their catalogs in a few short sentences or phrases. The result is a super-compressed lingo, a special language of seed catalogs. Misunderstanding the meaning of this language, which includes phrases like "days to maturity" and "yellows resistant," can mean the difference between delectable success and flat-out failure. Here's how to read the catalogs.

Variety Name

Let's start with the name of a given variety. If you peruse a few catalogs, you'll see that some varieties (often very old ones) go by several different names. Generally, the most common name is listed first, with some of the others afterward.

The mysterious Roman numeral "II" that sometimes appears after a variety name simply indicates that the variety has been significantly improved since its first appearance. 'Oregon Sugar Pod' received its II, for instance, when mildew resistance was added.

Hybrid versus Open-Pollinated

You'll see seeds described as open-pollinated or hybrid. If you want to save your own seeds from your crops, it's important to understand the difference between the two types.

Open-pollinated seed. Open-pollinated varieties are those whose seed comes from pollination that occurs naturally in the field. If you save the seeds from an open-pollinated variety and plant them, the seedlings will look just like the parent plant.

Many open-pollinated varieties get better—more adapted to the local conditions—if you keep saving the seed from the strongest, most productive plants year after year. By continually saving and planting the seed from your best plants, you'll gradually create a strain that's well adapted to the conditions in your own garden.

Hybrid seed. You probably won't be happy with the results if you try to save seed from hybrid varieties. Hybrids are identified in seed catalogs by the symbol F_1 or the word *hybrid*. Hybrids are created by using the pollen of one variety to fertilize the flowers of another variety of the same type of plant. The seeds that result from this mixed marriage produce unique plants that aren't like either parent. If you save seed from hybrid plants and plant it, you never know what you'll get.

Days to Maturity

Most catalogs list the "days to maturity" of their varieties. To use this essential number, you must first figure out whether the number of days cited refers to the time required from seed sown directly in the garden to produce flowering plants or to the time that it will take a 6-week-old transplant to mature or bloom. Seeds that are generally started inside (such as tomatoes and peppers) will need a week or so to sprout plus another 6 weeks to grow to transplant size; only *then* does the "days to maturity" number come into play. Add those 7 weeks (say 50 days) to the listed "days to maturity" to learn the total number of days required for a planted seed to mature to a crop that's ready for harvest.

And whether you start your seeds indoors or outdoors, remember that the "days to maturity" listings in catalogs are loose guidelines at best. Local weather conditions and your garden's sun-to-shade ratio are two of many factors that can greatly affect the actual number of days it will take a plant to reach maturity. (Because of this, the catalogs of regional companies tend to have more locally accurate "days to maturity.")

Descriptive terms. Some catalogs completely avoid the term *days to maturity* and instead simply identify varieties as *early, midseason,* or *late.* Whichever the case, you're safest if you consider these qualifiers mostly

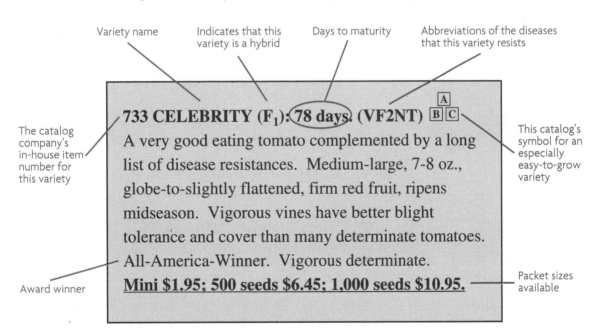

Variety name

Indicates that this variety is a hybrid

Days to maturity

Abbreviations of the diseases that this variety resists

The catalog company's in-house item number for this variety

733 CELEBRITY (F₁): 78 days. (VF2NT)

This catalog's symbol for an especially easy-to-grow variety

A very good eating tomato complemented by a long list of disease resistances. Medium-large, 7-8 oz., globe-to-slightly flattened, firm red fruit, ripens midseason. Vigorous vines have better blight tolerance and cover than many determinate tomatoes. All-America-Winner. Vigorous determinate.
Mini $1.95; 500 seeds $6.45; 1,000 seeds $10.95.

Award winner

Packet sizes available

Seeds or Transplants?

You can buy transplants at nearly every garden center, home center, hardware store, and discount center in spring. So why start your own seeds at all? Many nurseries do a terrific job of producing transplant-size seedlings of common vegetables and flowers. But by starting your own plants from seed, you can choose from an almost unlimited selection of plants. You also have greater control over conditions and timing: Your transplants will be exactly the right size at the right time for *your* conditions. (You won't be stuck with overgrown seedlings that never quite recover in the garden, which commonly happens with garden center seedlings). And, perhaps most important, starting plants from seeds is *fun!* It's a terrific antidote to the late-winter blues.

in relation to each other. If you have a short season, look for the lowest days to maturity numbers in any given catalog. Long season? You're free to try those slow-growing exotics!

Disease Resistance

Catalog descriptions commonly include a variety's ability to tolerate or resist disease. Careful—these two words have distinctly different meanings. *Tolerance* means that the variety probably won't suffer from a disease *as much* as another variety that lacks tolerance—however, disease-tolerant varieties can still get (and suffer from) the disease. *Resistance* means that the variety in question probably won't get the disease at all.

If a variety description lacks the terms *resistant* or *tolerant*, don't assume it's susceptible to disease. Disease resistance ratings are conveyed only after several leading commercial varieties are grown, doused with disease, and compared over time. Those that show little or no infection are labeled "resistant." Those with slightly higher levels of infection are rated "tolerant." Many heirlooms and other varieties sold in small quantities have never been tested, so they can't be rated.

Some catalogs use codes to indicate which diseases a variety is resistant to, especially for tomato varieties. If you see abbreviations such as TMV or LB in the listings, skim the pages in that section of the catalog. Most catalogs include a key to the codes. (For example, TMV could stand for tobacco mosaic virus, and LB for late blight.)

Hardiness

Cold hardy can be a tricky term, too. When cool temperatures suddenly plummet, even supposedly hardy plants can get burned. Many catalogs shy away from hardiness ratings; a few use symbols to designate varieties that are cold tolerant and/or suitable for over-wintering.

Award Winners

Many catalogs note award designations, such as All-America Selections (AAS), in their variety descriptions. Since 1933, the AAS organization has been picking winners annually from among the new varieties of flowers and vegetables offered to North American gardeners.

The AAS folks conduct tests of new varieties at sites throughout the United States and Canada. Unpaid judges rate the new varieties on qualities such as disease resistance, overall appearance, and for vegetables, flavor and yield. The winners are chosen from those evaluations.

Not every great new variety wins an AAS award, however, so some seed companies have devised their own standards. (Burpee, for instance, calls its new super-dependable selections Signature plants.)

Seed Inventory

From season to season it's all too easy to lose track of the seed packets you've ordered and haven't entirely used up. If you store the leftovers from one season's planting in a cool, dry place, most seeds will remain usable for up to 3 years. This worksheet should help you keep track of the odds and ends of various vegetable, herb, and flower seeds you have on hand. Remember to test stored seeds before planting to make sure they'll still germinate.

CULTIVAR	DATE PURCHASED	AMOUNT PURCHASED	SEED SOURCE	AMOUNT LEFT AFTER SOWING	TO BE USED BY	AMOUNT TO REORDER

Seed Inventory—Continued

Cultivar	Date Purchased	Amount Purchased	Seed Source	Amount Left After Sowing	To Be Used By	Amount to Reorder

GARDENER TO GARDENER

Twist-Tie Pruning Trick

Pruning grapes can be tricky when you aren't sure which canes need to be pruned. I've solved the problem in my orchard by using different colored twist ties to secure new canes to the top of the arbor each year. That way, when it's time to prune off one-year-old canes in early spring, I can easily identify the canes I need to remove by looking for the ones that are tied with the color of the year before.

And be sure to save your prunings—you can use them to start new vines for gift giving. I usually take ten of the cuttings, trim them to about 18 inches long, then lay them horizontally in a shallow trench (leaving only a couple of buds protruding outside the trench); then I fill in the trench with soil. Once the cuttings have rooted, I pot them into individual containers and give them away.

Annie McPherson
Nanaimo, British Columbia

Houseplants Flourish in Fishy Water

A few years back, I noticed an oddly familiar aroma—like fertilizer—while cleaning out the goldfish bowl. The question came to me, "Why should I be dumping out all this good organic material when it could be put to better use?"

Now whenever Gillbert, the family fish, gets his bowl cleaned, the houseplants get a feeding. I simply pour the water into their soil. All the plants seem to enjoy the extra nutrients, and Gillbert appears happy with his clean home.

Bob Uptagrafft
Clarkston, Washington

Garden Info at a Glance

Gardeners accumulate a lot of seeds, and I find that it's difficult to recall specifics about each variety at spring planting time each year. To keep the necessary details close at hand, I cut out the catalog information on each variety and paste it onto a piece of paper, keeping each type of flower and vegetable separate. Then I just take the sheets outdoors with me at planting time. The sheets are also helpful for keeping notes about the performance of each variety and for planning next year's purchases.

Toni Heisey
San Diego, California

Yarrow to the Rescue

Yarrow is my top choice for planting on sites that take heavy foot traffic. In the area around my gazebo, most plants would get trampled on by the kids and the dog—until I discovered that yarrow was one plant that could take the abuse.

Here in Texas, yarrow is an evergreen perennial that blooms all summer long and looks great year-round. I planted several varieties of it, and all grew vigorously in our alkaline clay soil. The yarrow also attracts beneficial insects, and the blooms look great in fresh and dried flower arrangements!

Lela Khan
Carrollton, Texas

Homegrown Shower Favors

When brainstorming for ideas for bridal shower favors, I decided to put my green thumb to good use. Last year, I grew 'Micro-Tom' tomatoes, ornamental peppers, oregano, and basil in small pots, and then used them as table centerpieces and favors for the guests.

Tracy Sopko
Wilkes-Barre, Pennsylvania

GARDENER TO GARDENER

Divide and Multiply

During the winter months, many nurseries in north Florida sell their leftover perennials at a 50 percent discount, so I shop around for the best buys and bring home beautiful but potbound African irises (Dietes vegeta), canna lilies, agapanthus, and daylilies. I used to wrestle with spades, forks, and garden knives trying to divide the matted roots, but have since found a method that makes the task much easier. After getting the plants out of their pots—many of which I have to cut down the sides—I attach the power nozzle to my garden hose and shoot a strong, single stream of water through the soil around the roots. It cuts through those stubborn roots like a laser through steel! Afterward, I can easily break those beautiful clean roots apart to form new plants.

Kathy Skirbst
Middleburg, Florida

Scraping By

An old windshield ice scraper can come in handy in the garden. During the muddy spring season, use it to scrape your boots (the scrapers that have brushes are great for this). Later, when the ground dries out, use your scraper as a minihoe for cultivating in tight spaces.

Anne Bingham
Wauwatosa, Wisconsin

Bad Onions Make Good

Don't throw out storage onions when they start to sprout! Pot them up, and you can eat spicy greens all winter long. Last winter, when I planted a couple of sprouted onions in with my houseplants, I was harvesting deliciously crisp and mild onion greens in just a little more than a week. What's more, they thrive in a window with low light, where little else will grow.

Vicki Delph
Jefferson, Oregon

Seeing Is Believing

When I first began gardening, I was skeptical that the plant would really end up looking like the picture on the package. So I saved the pictures from the seed packets, plant markers, and bulb packages, marked the place and date of purchase on each, then placed them in a standard three-ring photo album with self-adhesive pages. When the plant bloomed, I took my own photo of it, then put the photo with the plant's original packaging in the album. Eventually this became a wonderful and easy garden journal and a great winter pick-me-up!

Kathy Cripe
South Bend, Indiana

Chapter 2

February

Warming Up: Starting Seeds and Pruning

There's the almond blossom in February and a few weeks of pre-Spring panic in the garden as we try to do the work we've been talking about all winter.

—*Peter Mayle*

If February freezes make you shiver when you step outside, don't despair. Put your gardening enthusiasm to work indoors. There's much to do! February is prime time for starting seeds inside. In most areas, you can start seeds of cool-loving plants like broccoli, cabbage, onions, pansies, and edging lobelia (*Lobelia erinus*) this month so the seedlings will be ready to plant outdoors a couple of weeks before the last frost. Near the end of the month, gardeners in many regions also can start warm-weather crops, such as tomatoes and peppers, and annual and perennial flowers. Other indoor gardening activities this month could include repotting houseplants and ordering nursery stock for spring planting.

Outdoors this month, focus on the framework of your landscape. Now is your chance to view "the bones" of your property with a critical eye to determine what changes you'll make this year. Consider what trees and shrubs to add or remove; where to put a new perennial bed or arbor; and which branches to prune before buds break and new growth begins.

Gardener's To-Do List—February

**If you don't know what USDA hardiness zone you live in,
check the map on page 246 to find out.**

Zone 3

- [ ] Check for winter sales at your local garden center; you may find good deals on pots, planters, and tools.
- [ ] Replace fluorescent bulbs in grow lights that are more than 2 years old.
- [ ] Organize seed packets according to planting date.
- [ ] Check stored gladiolus and dahlia bulbs; remove any that have deteriorated.
- [ ] Remove geranium and fuchsia plants from cold storage, repot, water, and move them into light to restart their growth.

Zone 4

- [ ] Start seeds of slow growers—such as pansies, onions, leeks, and celery—under lights this month.
- [ ] If snow isn't too deep, prune dead or damaged branches from fruit trees, brambles, and shrubs.
- [ ] Try raising an indoor crop of leaf lettuce beneath lights.
- [ ] Fertilize houseplants that show signs of new growth.

Zone 5

- [ ] Bring geraniums out of storage; cut them back by half, water well, and set them in a bright, cool window.
- [ ] Indoors under lights, start seeds of sun-loving daisies, columbine (*Aquilegia* spp.), stocks (*Matthiola incana*), edging lobelia (*Lobelia erinus*), and shade-seeking impatiens.
- [ ] Start seeds of lettuce, celery, onions, leeks, and early tomatoes indoors under lights.
- [ ] If the ground isn't frozen, sow some spinach and radishes outdoors under cover.
- [ ] Force some indoor blooms! Cut branches or gather prunings from fruit trees, lilacs, and forsythia. Put them in a vase with water, then enjoy the flowers a few weeks later.

Zone 6

- [ ] Under fluorescent lights, start seeds of onions and leeks at the beginning of the month.
- [ ] Near the end of the month, start seeds of broccoli, cabbage, cauliflower, and brussels sprouts indoors under lights.
- [ ] Start slow-growing flowers, such as garden verbena (*Verbena × hybrida*), stocks (*Matthiola incana*), wallflowers (*Cheirianthus cheiri*), and ageratum indoors.
- [ ] If winter has been mild, transplant trees, shrubs, and roses.
- [ ] For the earliest tomatoes, start seeds of 'Early Girl' under lights now. In April, set out the transplants and protect them with Wallo'Waters.
- [ ] Sharpen pruning shears and use them to prune fruit trees, brambles, grapevines, and late summer–blooming shrubs.
- [ ] Rinse houseplants by setting them beneath your shower.

Zone 7

- [ ] When you see the first crocus open, consider it time to set out transplants of lettuce, cabbages, and onions; cover them on cold nights.

- [ ] In the garden, sow seeds of radishes and cold-hardy lettuces.
- [ ] When daffodils "pop," plant seeds of spinach, turnips, and peas.
- [ ] Cover the pea bed with clear plastic until sprouts begin to emerge; then, immediately switch to a floating row cover to protect the seedlings from weather and birds.
- [ ] Start herb seeds indoors under lights.
- [ ] Also indoors, start seeds of annual flowers—such as ageratum, petunia, and snapdragons—that need 8 to 10 weeks to reach transplant size.

Zone 8

- [ ] Feed the soil by applying compost to plantings throughout your landscape: trees, shrubs, lawn, and all garden beds.
- [ ] By the third week of the month, plant potatoes 4 inches deep in warm soil.
- [ ] Begin sowing seeds of leaf lettuces, collards, and other greens outdoors; for continuous harvest, repeat sowings every 2 weeks.
- [ ] On Valentine's Day, prune roses, clean up debris, and then top-dress the shrubs with fresh mulch. No roses? Plant some now!
- [ ] Prune fruit trees, then spray them at their "pink bud" stage with either a copper or lime-sulfur solution if you've had trouble with foliar and fruit diseases.
- [ ] Plant alyssum (*Lobularia maritima*), hollyhocks (*Alcea rosea*), edging lobelia (*Lobelia erinus*), rocket larkspurs (*Consolida ajacis*), and Canterbury bells (*Campanula medium*).

Zone 9

- [ ] Build the soil! During dry spells, dig in composted manure and garden waste; turn under cover crops, such as annual rye, vetch, and clover.

- [ ] Start seeds of indispensable summer veggies—tomatoes, peppers, and eggplants—indoors under lights.
- [ ] Also indoors, start seeds of flowers that are slow to develop, such as lisianthus (*Eustoma grandiflorum*), wax begonias, petunias, and geraniums.
- [ ] Plant perennials, bareroot roses, trees, shrubs, and vines. (Next month could be too hot!)
- [ ] Direct seed radishes, spinach, carrots, peas, onions, and cabbage family vegetables.
- [ ] Continue to plant Iceland poppies (*Papaver nudicaule*), calendulas (*Calendula officinalis*), foxglove, and primroses in flowerbeds.
- [ ] Plant dahlia bulbs and begonia tubers.

Zone 10

- [ ] Celebrate winter's end by filling window boxes and planters with cold-hardy snapdragons and stocks (*Matthiola incana*).
- [ ] Plant seeds of corn and cucumbers in the garden, but be prepared to protect them from a surprise frost.
- [ ] Set out transplants of tomatoes, peppers, and eggplants; be prepared to protect them from frost and, as the weather warms, from intense sunlight.
- [ ] Plant fast-growing varieties of beets, carrots, and radishes so you can harvest a crop before the real heat sets in.
- [ ] Also start southern favorites, such as okra, southern peas, and sweet potatoes.
- [ ] Lubber grasshoppers hatch this month: Spread Semaspore around the perimeter of your property and on their favorite foods—amaryllis (*Hippeastrum* spp.), tuberoses (*Polianthes tuberosa*), rain lilies (*Zephyranthes* spp.), and crinum lilies (*Crinum* spp.).

No Sprouts in Sight?

If you've waited a couple of weeks longer than the normal germination time and you don't see sprouts, one or more of the following conditions could be to blame:

♦ Old or improperly stored (too hot or too damp) seed

♦ Temperatures much higher or lower than seedlings prefer

♦ Seeds planted too deep

♦ Soil kept too dry

13 Steps to Super Seed Starting

When you start your own plants from seed, you'll discover a new world of gardening. You can grow varieties of flowers and vegetables that aren't available as seedlings in local stores—old-fashioned hollyhocks (*Alcea rosea*), heirloom tomatoes, burpless cucumbers, and rare hot peppers, to name a few. You can raise enough flowers to overflow a giant bed for the same cost as a dozen nursery seedlings. You can select the sturdiest seedlings from those that sprout. And you can save your own seed.

Seed starting needn't be time-consuming or complicated. Follow these steps, and you'll be well on your way to a season of plenty.

1. Let them breathe. Seeds contain their own food supply, so they don't need rich soil immediately. What they *do* need is air, so don't plant seeds in muddy dense soil straight from the garden. Instead, choose something loose and light, such as vermiculite or a bagged potting mix from your local garden center.

If you buy bagged mix, stick with the kind sold by your local garden supply center. Some potting soils sold in general retail outlets may be too heavy and dense to allow for good root growth.

2. Provide good drainage. Choose containers that have drainage holes on the bottom so seedling roots don't get waterlogged. Shallow (2- to 3-inch deep) flats work well for plants that you'll set out in bulk, like strawberries. Recycled plastic cell packs (the kind prestarted plants are sold in at the garden center) are fine too; just be sure you clean them thoroughly with soapy water before using. If you use household cast-offs, such as milk cartons, poke some drainage holes in the bottom with an ice pick or a hammer and nail.

3. Moisten the medium before you sow. If possible, use warm water to wet seed-starting mix; the mix will absorb it more quickly. Fill your planting containers with the moist mix, but don't pack it down. Water the container thoroughly to finish wetting the soil before you plant your seeds. (If you water after planting seeds, you may wash them all to one corner of the flat or bury them too deeply under the soil.)

4. Sow sparingly. Crowded seedlings develop long, weak stems in their search for light and space.

5. Cover wisely. Covering the seeds calls for some restraint, too; it's easy to bury them too deeply. Here's the general rule of thumb: Cover the seed with an amount of soil equal to three times its thickness. Some flowers—such as ageratum, impatiens, alyssum, and snapdragons—need light to germinate and shouldn't be covered with *any* soil. When in doubt, check the seed packet directions.

6. *Keep it warm . . .* Warmth and moisture kick the seeds' slumbering metabolism into high gear. Most garden seeds germinate best roughly between 70° and 90°F. For fastest germination, get to know your seeds' preferred temperature for sprouting; see the chart on page 28 for the temperature needs of many common garden seeds.

7. *. . . and wet—but not too wet.* Seedlings need an even supply of water. The best approach is to bottom-water, as shown in the illustration below. If your system doesn't allow for this technique, use a sprinkling can with a spray head to gently distribute the droplets over the soil surface.

8. *Hug the light.* Check your containers frequently. At the first sign of a sprout nudging above the soil, pop the containers under lights or put them in a sunny window. Fast-germinating seeds should sprout in a few days, but slower ones can take 4 to 6 weeks to germinate.

If you're using fluorescent lights, place the young seedlings as close as you can to the light—2 to 4 inches from the tubes.

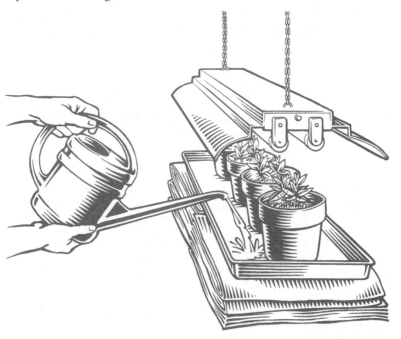

Set up indoor seedlings for bottom watering by arranging cell packs or individual pots in a shallow plastic tray. Use newspapers or boxes under the trays to boost the seedlings up close to lights.

GARDENER TO GARDENER

More Efficient Seed Sowing

Like many gardeners, I really dislike thinning seedlings. Not only do I feel that I've wasted seed, but I also feel like a murderer! I decided that in order to sow fewer seeds, I needed to better see what I was doing. The dark seeds simply didn't show up against the dark soil well enough to let me see how many were there.

The solution was to cover the prepared seedbed with light-colored sand. Now, when I scatter seeds, I can quickly see when there are too many too close together. Using tweezers, I move the extras to bare spots, then cover them with soil. This method works especially well for small seeds, such as onions, which I now never have to thin!

*Sharon Carlson
Union Star, Missouri*

Saving Sad Seedlings

Try these tips to prevent or correct some common seedling problems.

Shriveled seedlings. If your seedlings shrivel and collapse at the soil, the likely culprit is damping-off. If some seedlings are OK, move them to a flat of clean potting soil. To prevent this, use clean flats with drainage and new potting soil. Avoid over-watering.

Tall, spindly seedlings. Plants grow leggy in low light and sometimes when they're crowded or kept too warm. Move them closer to light, thin them, and if conditions are too warm, move them to a cooler place.

Unhealthy-looking leaves. Nitrogen deficiencies can cause plant leaves to pale or turn yellow. To correct, apply diluted fish emulsion. Yellowing of *lower* leaves can be a sign of magnesium deficiency; to prevent this, add a pinch of dolomitic lime to the potting soil.

Purplish or reddish purple leaf undersides may indicate a phosphorus deficiency. Try watering plants with diluted fish emulsion.

9. Pot them up early.

When your seedlings have their first true leaves (the second set, with leaf veins), transplant them to larger pots or space them out in flats. If they've been growing in vermiculite, now is also the time to switch to regular potting soil, which contains more nutrients.

First, fill the new container about two-thirds full with potting soil. Then prick out the growing seedlings one plant at a time, using a slim fork handle, a Popsicle stick, or a similar tool. Set a seedling in a container, and add more potting soil around the seedling until you have at least matched the depth of the old soil. Always cover each seedling's roots before you dig up another one! Select the sturdiest, strongest-rooted seedlings; grit your teeth and toss the rest.

When moving seedlings from a small flat to a larger one, space them about 2 inches apart in their new homes. Water them well, and keep them out of direct light for a day to let the roots recover.

10. Lower the heat (maybe).

Most seedlings don't need as much warmth as germinating seeds. Tomatoes and peppers, for instance, become sturdier and less leggy if kept about 10° cooler than their preferred germinating temperature. (Melons, eggplants, and okra, on the other hand, do best if they're kept a bit warmer than that.)

11. Feed often, but go easy.

After seedlings develop their *second* set of true leaves, give them dilute feedings of plant food every week or two. Fish emulsion is organic, widely available, and easy to use. For the first few weeks, dilute it to half the recommended strength.

12. Prepare them for the move.

Toughen up your seedlings before you move them outdoors so they won't be helpless in the wind, cooler air, and brighter light. Stop fertilizing them about 2 to 3 weeks before you plan to plant them in the garden.

About a week later, begin the next stage: Set the seedlings outside during the day, preferably in a spot where they'll receive direct sun in the morning and bright, but indirect, light in the afternoon. Bring them inside each night. After about a week, leave them out at night as well. Frost-hardy vegetables like lettuce and broccoli won't need to be protected from light frost, but be prepared to protect tomatoes, peppers, and other frost-tender crops.

13. Plant the seedlings outdoors.

After your seedlings become accustomed to the outside world, gently settle them into their garden rows or beds. Try not to disturb their roots as you transplant. Pour water in each planting hole before your plant, or sprinkle the entire bed after you've finished.

The Right Light: Key to Strong Starts

For the strong light and steady warmth that seedlings need, your best bet is to use standard fluorescent lights. Most hardware stores sell the perfect starter set: 4-foot long, two-, four-, or six-tube units. A two-tube unit provides enough light to germinate two 21 × 11-inch flats, which can hold about 120 plants.

If you already have a fluorescent light fixture, buy new tubes for seed starting. Fluorescent tubes last 12,000 hours or more, but they lose about 20 percent of their light intensity after 2,000 hours of use, and up to 50 percent after 5,000 hours. To help you know when to replace them next time, write the date you install the tubes on one of their ends.

You can buy cool white or warm white fluorescent tubes. T. W. Tibbitts, Ph.D., a specialist in lighting and controlled environments for plants at the University of Wisconsin, says the difference between cool white and warm white tubes is too small to give any real advantage. He recommends using all cool white bulbs.

How to Set Up Lights

Suspend your fixture from the ceiling over a table or bench. To protect the table or bench from water, cover it with a plastic cloth. If your floor or table space is limited, attach adjustable metal bookshelf brackets to an available wall. The long, narrow lights will fit nicely on the shelf brackets.

Make sure the area is warm enough for germination. Also, make sure that you can lower the flats or raise the lights as the plants grow so that the seedlings stay close to the lights.

How to Use Lights

Keeping plants as close as possible to the lights is extremely important. Although fluorescent lights look very bright, they actually are only one-tenth as intense as sunlight. They provide just enough light to grow small seedlings. And the lights' intensity drops off very fast as you move away from them. (That's why you can't grow full-size tomato or other sun-loving plants under standard fluorescent lights—as the plants grow, the lower leaves are too far away from the lights to thrive.)

Seedlings need every bit of fluorescent light you can give them, so leave the lights on day and night. Contrary to popular belief, most seedlings don't require a daily period of darkness, says Dr. Tibbitts. Light intensity and duration both affect plant growth. "Because fluorescent lights are only one-tenth as bright as sunlight, your seedlings will grow better if you increase the duration by leaving the lights on continuously."

Plant Light Lowdown

Here's how to sort out your lighting options.

Incandescent lightbulbs. Includes "grow lights." These lights generally aren't suitable for seed starting.

Standard fluorescent tubes. Good for starting seeds and for growing small, low-light plants. Plants must be kept very close to them. These lights aren't bright enough to grow most kinds of larger, flowering or fruiting plants.

Very-high-output fluorescent tubes. More than twice as bright as standard fluorescents. These lights cost more, but they're excellent for growing sturdy, healthy seedlings and larger plants.

Wide-spectrum fluorescent tubes. Designed to provide a spectrum of light that most closely matches natural sunlight. Although these lights are good for growing mature plants, they aren't necessary for starting seeds. They cost more than standard fluorescent lights.

High-intensity discharge lights. Use them for everything from starting seeds to full-scale growing. They're brighter, more efficient, and pricier than fluorescents; types include high-pressure sodium and metal halide lamps.

Germinating and Transplanting Key

	WEEKS BEFORE LAST FROST TO START SEEDS INDOORS	BEST SOIL TEMPERATURE (°F) FOR GERMINATION	SEED PLANTING DEPTH (IN INCHES)	AVERAGE DAYS TO GERMINATION	COMMENTS
FOR POPULAR FLOWERS					
FLOWER					
Annuals					
Ageratum	6–8	70–80	Surface	5–10	Set plants out or direct-seed after last frost.
Alyssum, sweet	6–8	60–75	Surface	8–15	Set plants out around last frost. Or, direct-seed 2–3 weeks before last frost. Often self-sows.
Cleome	4–6	Prechill seeds in refrigerator 1–2 weeks; then 70–85.	Surface	10–14	Set plants out or direct-seed just after last frost. Often self-sows.
Coleus	8–10	70–75	Surface; place pot in plastic bag until seedlings appear.	10–12	Tender perennials grown as annuals. Set plants out after last frost.
Impatiens (*I. wallerana*)	8–10	70–80	Surface; place pot in plastic bag until seedlings appear.	7–20	Set plants out 1–2 weeks after last frost. Susceptible to soilborne diseases; use sterile equipment.
Marigold	6–8. Start triploids and African marigolds indoors.	70–75	⅛–¼	5–7	Set plants out after last frost. Start French and signet marigolds indoors or direct-seed after last frost.
Nasturtium	4–6. Does not transplant well; use peat pots.	65	¼	7–12	Set plants out after last frost. Or, direct-seed 1–2 weeks before last frost.
Petunia	8–10	70–80	Surface; place pot in plastic bag until seedlings appear.	7–20	Set plants out after last frost.
Snapdragon	6–8	70–75	Surface	10–20	Set plants out after last frost. In cool climates, direct-seed a few weeks before last frost.
Sunflower	4–6	70–85	½	5–14	Set plants out or direct-seed after last frost.
Zinnia	4–6. Does not transplant well; use peat pots.	70–80	¼	5–7	In warm climates, direct-seed after danger of frost has passed
Perennials					
Aster	8–10	Prechill seeds in refrigerator for 2 weeks; then 70–75.	⅛; place pot in plastic bag until seedlings appear.	14–36	Set plants out after last frost. Or, direct-seed in early spring or late fall.
Astilbe	6–8	60–70	Surface	14-28	Set plants out after last frost. Or, direct-seed in early spring or fall.
Bee balm	4-8	60–70	⅛	14–21	Set plants out about 1 week before last frost. Or, direct-seed 2–4 weeks before last frost.
Black-eyed Susan	6–8	70–75. Prechill seeds of *R. fulgida* 2 weeks before sowing.	⅛	7–21	Set plants out after last frost, or direct-seed 2 weeks before last frost.

FLOWER		WEEKS BEFORE LAST FROST TO START SEEDS INDOORS	BEST SOIL TEMPERATURE (°F) FOR GERMINATION	SEED PLANTING DEPTH (IN INCHES)	AVERAGE DAYS TO GERMINATION	COMMENTS
Perennials—Continued	Chrysan-themum	6–10 before planting out.	60–70	Surface	7–28	Set plants out after last frost. Or, direct-seed in spring or summer.
	Coreopsis	6–10	55–70	Surface	14–25	Set plants out after last frost. Or, direct-seed in spring or summer.
	Daylily	8–10 before planting out.	Refrigerate in moist growing medium in plastic bag for 6 weeks; then 60–70.	⅛	21–49	Set plants out after last frost. Or, direct-seed in late fall or early spring. Takes 2–3 years from seed to bloom.
	Delphinium	8–10	Prechill seeds in refrigerator for 1 week. Thereafter, many species prefer 65–75.	¼	7–21	Set plants out after last frost. Or, direct-seed in summer for flowers next year.
	Dianthus	4	60–70	⅛	14–21	Set plants out or direct-seed in early spring.
	Poppy	6–10. Does not transplant well; use peat pots.	55	⅛ (most species); surface sow P. orientale.	10–20	Set plants out after last frost. Or, direct-seed in late fall or early spring.
	Yarrow	8–10 before planting out.	60–70	Surface	10–15	Set plants out or direct-seed in early spring.

FOR POPULAR VEGETABLES

VEGETABLE	BEST SOIL TEMPERATURE (°F) FOR GERMINATION	AVERAGE DAYS TO GERMINATION	WEEKS TO TRANSPLANT SIZE (FROM SOWING)	SPRING SETTING-OUT DATES (RELATIVE TO FROST-FREE DATE)		COMMENTS
				WEEKS BEFORE	WEEKS AFTER*	*Indicates latest commonly observed setting-out date. With adequate protection from heat, insect pests, drought, and such, the dates may be extended.
Beans, snap	75–80	7	3–4	—	8	Treat roots gently when transplanting.
Beets	75	7–14	4	4	—	Disturb roots as little as possible.
Broccoli	60–75	5–10	6–8	4	2–3	Transplants well.
Brussels sprouts	68–75	5–10	6–8	4	2–3	Transplants well.
Cabbage	68–75	5–10	6–8	5	2–3	Direct-seed mid- and late-season varieties.
Cauliflower	68–86	5–10	6–8	4	2	Direct-seed fall and winter crops.
Cucumbers	70–86	7–10	4	—	8	Often direct-seeded; transplants shorten time to harvest.
Eggplants	70–86	10	6–8	—	2–3	Transplant well.
Lettuce (all kinds)	68–70	7–10	4–6	2	3	Direct-seed some, too, to stagger harvest.
Melons	80–86	4–10	4	—	2–3	Often direct-seeded; transplants shorten time to harvest.
Onions (from seed)	68–70	10–14	4–6	6	2	Plant onion sets at same time seedlings are set out.
Peppers	75–85	10	6–8	—	2–3	Transplant well.
Squash, summer	70–95	7–10	4	—	4	Often direct-seeded; transplants shorten time to harvest.
Squash, winter	70–95	7–10	4	—	3–4	Often direct-seeded; transplants shorten time to harvest.
Swiss chard	50–85	7–10	4	3–6	—	Disturb roots as little as possible.
Tomatoes	75–80	7–14	6–10	—	4	Can plant earlier with protection.

Pruning Ornamental Shrubs

Right now—late winter to early spring, before new growth begins—is the best time to prune most garden plants, including ornamental shrubs, shade trees, and roses. Proper pruning—shaping a plant rather than trying to control it—helps maintain plant health, strength, and beauty.

Always use sharp tools and practice good sanitation to prevent spreading disease: Don't prune wet plants; otherwise you invite rot or mildew. Always cut well below any visible sign of disease, and clean up prunings as soon as you finish.

To properly prune an ornamental shrub, first decide what the shrub's natural habit is. This will help you determine how—and how much—to cut. If a shrub is overgrown, cut the worst branches first, but leave most of the less-than-perfect branches for another year. It's always better to gradually prune an overgrown shrub back into shape than give it a radical "haircut" in 1 year—which could leave you with few or no branches at all!

There are three basic habits of ornamental shrubs: cane, mounding, and treelike. Use a different pruning approach for each type of habit.

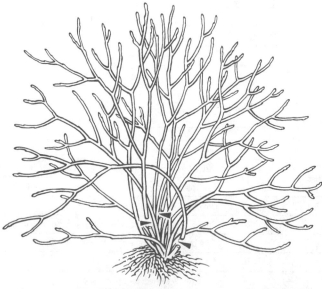

When you prune a shrub with long canes, remove some of the tallest canes and thin out the canes at the center. Also, prune out canes that are growing through the center.

Cane Habit

Cane shrubs renew themselves by sending up new branches, called canes, from the base. Here's how to effectively prune these shrubs.

1. Remove all dead wood from both the center and the outer edges of the shrub.

2. Shorten the shrub by sawing or lopping out some of the tallest canes at or near ground level.

3. Thin out canes that crowd the center of the shrub and ones that cross and rub others. Cut out some of the "wrong-way" canes that start at one side, grow through the center, and continue out the other side of the shrub.

Cane shrubs are very forgiving of being overpruned. You can remove up to one-third of the canes without seriously harming the plant. You can even radically renovate your shrubs by cutting them entirely to the ground in the spring and letting them regrow for a couple of years. More often than not, severe cane pruning will result in resilient and vigorous stem and cane growth.

Mounding Habit

Mounding shrubs have soft, supple stems with small leaves. They're the easiest type of shrubs to keep small. Pruning them is easy, too.

1. Locate the longest, most unruly branch, and grab it with one hand. Follow it down inside the shrub, and cut it off at a point deep inside.

2. Repeat this procedure with the next longest branch, and continue until the shrub is the size your want. You can reduce the size by one-quarter to one-third.

Reducing the size of a mounding shrub is easy to do. Just cut off some of the longest branches from deep inside the plant.

Shrubs by Habit

It helps to know what the habit of a shrub is before you prune. Here's a rundown on many common landscape shrubs.

CANE HABIT
Forsythia (*Forsythia* spp.)

Hydrangea (*Hydrangea* spp.)

Japanese kerria
(*Kerria japonica*)

Oregon grape
(*Mahonia aquifolium*)

Weigela
(*Weigela florida*)

MOUNDING HABIT
Abelia
(*Abelia* spp.)

Barberry
(*Berberis* spp.)

Choisya
(*Choisya* spp.)

Escallonia
(*Escallonia* spp.)

Evergreen azaleas
(*Rhododendron* spp.)

Japanese holly (*Ilex crenata*)

Spirea (*Spiraea* spp.)

TREELIKE HABIT
Camellia
(*Camellia* spp.)

Cotoneaster
(*Cotoneaster* spp.)

Deciduous azaleas
(*Rhododendron* spp.)

Pieris (*Pieris* spp.)

Rhododendrons
(*Rhododendron* spp.)

Witch hazel (*Hamamelis* spp.)

Pruning Cuts You Need to Know

Thinning cut. Remove the branch entirely, cutting it away at the point of origin from the parent branch. Thinning moderately doesn't stimulate regrowth, so it can reduce the bulk of a plant.

Nonselective heading cut. Cut back the branch at any point along its length. This stimulates rapid regrowth, making plants fuller and bushier.

Selective heading cut. Cut back the branch to a side branch or bud. The remaining side branch should generally be at least half the diameter of the stem that you remove. This is the best way to reduce the height of a shrub while maintaining a natural form.

Treelike Habit

Treelike shrubs are stiffer and harder to shorten than mounding or cane. As you prune them, start from the bottom and work up and out. On larger plants, move in a spiral as you work; don't make all your cuts in one place or the plant will look too sparse.

1. Cut out all dead wood. This will be about 80 percent of what you cut.

2. Remove a few of the worst rubbing or crossing branches. Leave the healthiest and best-placed branches in place.

3. Prune to open up the center of the plant. Leave branches that head up and out from the center or that fill an otherwise empty space.

4. Cut out any branches that are growing the wrong way, as long as they're not too big.

5. Prune out any branches that touch the ground, and remove suckers coming up from the roots.

6. Take off branches that head too far up or too far down from their point of origin.

7. Make any heading cuts that you believe are needed.

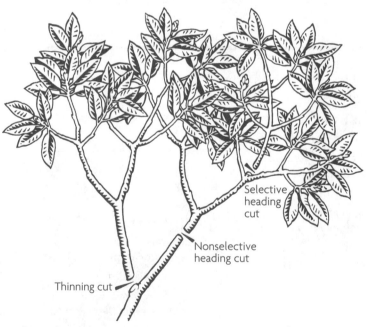

Pruning a shrub with a treelike habit requires three types of cuts: thinning cuts, nonselective heading cuts, and selective heading cuts.

GARDENER TO GARDENER

Brush Up on Seed Starting

I prefer to start my own plants from seed so that I can grow more unusual varieties. But some seeds are very tiny; and no matter how carefully you try to shake them out of the packet or pinch them between your fingers, you end up with a forest of seedlings in each pot. Now I have a better way to plant tiny seeds, using an ordinary paintbrush (the kind that comes in children's watercolor sets).

I simply dip the brush into the seeds in the packet until the bristles bend. Those bristles neatly grab just a few seeds. I then carefully lift the brush out of the packet and tap or stroke the bristles into a cell of my planting tray to release the seeds. The brush gives me more control over how many seeds are planted and where they land.

Nancy Whitehead
Hebo, Oregon

Not Eggsactly a Peat Pot

My husband came up with a great alternative to peat pots for starting seeds of early peas and corn: cardboard egg cartons. First, we poke a hole in the bottom of each egg holder, then we fill the holders halfway with seed-starting mix. Next we sprinkle the seeds over the mix, then cover the seeds with additional mix. We set the cartons on large plastic trays so the seedlings can be watered from the bottom.

When it's warm enough to plant the seedlings outside, we cut the carton into individual pots and plant them.

Debbie Blake
North Canton, Ohio

Zippy Seed Starter

I get impatient with seeds that take a long time to germinate—they take up room that I could be using to start other seeds. To speed things along, I start my pokey seeds in a resealable storage bag.

I put a couple inches of damp potting soil inside the bag, plant my seeds inside the soil, zip the bag closed, and then set it on a windowsill. These freezer-type bags even have a strip on them for labeling, so I write the variety and date on it. After the seeds sprout and begin to grow, I transplant them directly into the garden.

Sue LeMontre
San Diego, California

Perfect Seed-Starting Cups

Many gardeners use paper cups for starting seeds, but here are a couple of ways to improve the performance of paper potting cups. First, make the bottom drainage holes from the inside—the resulting jagged paper should protrude outside the cup. (If you poke the holes the other way and the jagged edges are on the inside, the weight of the potting mix will push the edges back down into the holes and block drainage.)

Also, make sure the drainage holes are near the outside of the bottom rather than at the center. Why? Most paper cups rest on a ridge that holds the bottom of the cup a fraction of an inch above the tabletop. Eventually the damp soil inside the cup will cause the bottom to sag in the middle and touch the table, so any holes there will drain poorly. Because the outside edge is supported by the ridge, drainage holes there stay open.

Carol Pruitt
Columbus, Indiana

GARDENER TO GARDENER

Small Space Seed Starting

If you're short on space but want to start your own seeds this winter, here's an idea that will save you time and space. It requires no drilling or nailing and is ideal for apartment dwellers who can't install permanent fixtures.

Start with a freestanding, coated-wire shelf unit that has adjustable shelves (the kind designed to fit around a washer and dryer). Hang a fluorescent light unit from the upper shelf using the S-hooks and chains that come with the fixture. Put seed trays on the lower shelf, and store seed-starting supplies on the very top of the unit.

Tape aluminum foil to the wall behind the shelf to reflect light onto the plants and protect the wall from moisture caused by misting the seedlings. When seed-starting time is over, simply disassemble the setup and put it away or use the light and shelf for other purposes.

Lila Ralston
Athens, Georgia

Soil Cubes for Starting Seeds

Soil blocks (freestanding blocks of soil formed by a soil-block maker) are great for starting many seeds. But I find them too big for very small seeds, such as alyssum, ageratum, and edging lobelia. So I make soil cubes, instead. For small, delicate seedlings, these cubes are much easier to manage than flats. Here's what to do:

1. Press a moist potting soil/vermiculite mixture into a plastic ice cube tray, then place it in the freezer.

2. When the soil is frozen, pop out the cubes by twisting the tray. (You can make the job even easier by running a little warm water over the bottom of the tray.) Then, set the cubes in a shallow tray.

3. When the cubes have thawed, pick up a few seeds at a time with the dampened end of a toothpick. Transfer them onto each cube. Water the tray, not the cubes, to keep the cubes intact. Cover the cubes loosely with plastic to retain humidity.

4. When the first seedlings emerge, set the whole thing under fluorescent lights.

5. When the seedlings have two or three leaves, cut back on watering and allow the cubes to dry out a bit. Plant the cubes into larger pots or plant them directly in the garden.

Jonna Flicker
Kansas City, Missouri

Dryer Lint Wicks Water to Seedlings

The best way to water seed flats is from the bottom (pouring water into a holding tray below the flat), because there's less chance of washing away tiny seedlings. I've found that I can improve the wicking (upward movement) of water into the soil by lining the bottom of the flat with sheets of lint that I collect from my clothes dryer! A piece of lint about $1/4$ to $1/2$ inch thick is just about perfect; lay it on the bottom of the flat before you put in your soil.

Linda Tamblyn
Merriam, Kansas

Chapter 3

March

Groundwork: Making Compost and Building Beds

Being happy is [having] dirt under your fingernails, wearing old clothes, having a good idea get better the longer you work at it, starting a new bed, giving plants away, and listening to rain.

—*Geoffrey B. Charlesworth*

At last: The earth has softened and begun to warm—enough to allow you to scoop up a handful, squeeze it gently, and watch it crumble into smaller pieces. Although you can't see it, your soil is teeming with life.

Soon the soil will be just the right texture and temperature for planting. Until then, you can prepare. Gather together organic materials to make compost, the ideal organic amendment for soil. You can never have too much of it: Not only does compost feed the soil and, in turn, the plants, but it also protects plants from disease, buffers soil imbalances, and retains moisture.

March is also the time to build new beds, according to the plan you devised in January, and replenish existing garden areas. Raised beds, as we'll soon discuss, offer many advantages, including better drainage, earlier planting, and easier maintenance.

For those who garden in a warmer zone, the garden will need to be prepared early in the month. Unlike those in the rest of the country who must wait a bit longer to plant most crops, you can begin planting and transplanting spring veggies and flowers in the garden at or near the last expected frost.

Gardener's To-Do List—March

**If you don't know what USDA hardiness zone you live in,
check the map on page 246 to find out.**

Zone 3

- ☐ Prune overgrown nonspring-flowering shrubs.
- ☐ Start seeds of onions, tomatoes, edging lobelia (*Lobelia erinus*), asters, marigolds, cauliflower, cabbage, and brussels sprouts indoors under lights. When seedlings have their second pair of true leaves, transplant them to larger pots.
- ☐ Pot up stored bulbs, such as hybrid tuberous begonias, dahlias, canna (*Canna × generalis*), and calla lilies (*Zantedeschia aethiopica*). Set them in the light.
- ☐ Water evergreens growing near the house foundation if the soil is dry. Also, mist the foliage—needles will absorb the much-needed moisture.

Zone 4

- ☐ On apple and mountain ash trees, prune away branches killed by fire blight to prevent further spread of the disease; also prune black knots off of cherries. Make cuts 1 foot below the diseased area. Disinfect pruners with a 10 percent bleach solution between cuts.
- ☐ Start pepper and eggplant seeds indoors under lights.
- ☐ Start seeds of zinnias, salvia, petunias, and nicotiana indoors under lights.
- ☐ Pot up seedlings started last month and potbound houseplants.
- ☐ Don't rush to remove mulch from perennials: The sun could heat the soil and stimulate new growth, which the hard freezes still to come could damage.

Zone 5

- ☐ Start warmth-loving crops—such as tomatoes, peppers, and eggplants—indoors under lights.
- ☐ Transplant early tomatoes into larger pots, planting the stem deeper into the soil for additional root growth.
- ☐ Start annual flowers, such as marigolds and zinnias, indoors under lights.
- ☐ Tie up ornamental grasses, and use a serrated bread knife to cut them back to a few inches above ground level.
- ☐ Trim dead or damaged branches from trees, shrubs, and roses.
- ☐ In the vegetable garden, begin to plant potatoes, peas, lettuce, radishes, and carrots.
- ☐ Late in the month, transplant pansies outdoors; also, sow seeds of nasturtiums and sweet peas.
- ☐ At month's end, transplant an early tomato outdoors, protected by a Wallo'Water. Before you plant, fill the planting hole with warm water.
- ☐ Start seeds of perennials—such as columbine (*Aquilegia* spp.), campanula, bellflower (*Campanula* spp.), blanket flower (*Gaillardia* spp.), globeflowers (*Trollius* spp.), and pyrethrum (*Tanacetum coccineum*)—indoors under lights.

Zone 6

- ☐ If you've had a mild winter, look for hosta shoots poking up through the soil. Dig up clumps that need to be divided, split them apart, and replant them. Water generously.
- ☐ Free the foliage from spring-blooming bulbs that are tangled in mulch.

- ☐ If the weather's mild, plant roses, trees, and shrubs.
- ☐ Move cool-loving broccoli, cabbage, and cauliflower outdoors to a coldframe or protected spot.
- ☐ Start seeds of tomatoes, peppers, eggplants, perennials, and annual flowers indoors under lights.
- ☐ As soon the garden soil is workable, plant peas, potatoes, sweet peas (*Lathyrus odoratus*), poppies (*Papaver* spp.), rocket larkspur (*Consolida ajacis*), and mignonette (*Reseda odorata*).
- ☐ If there's no snow, top-dress the lawn with compost. Fill in low spots and reseed.

Zone 7

- ☐ In the middle of the month, plant a row of Swiss chard. Tender stalks will be ready to harvest in mid-May—and the plants will keep producing all summer.
- ☐ Also in midmonth, sow other hardy vegetables, such as carrots, beets, kohlrabi, radishes, leaf lettuces, and turnips.
- ☐ Transplant onions, shallots, broccoli, cabbage, cauliflower, collards, white potatoes and asparagus crowns to the garden.
- ☐ Set out herbs, such as rosemary, chives, and thyme—but not tender basil!

Zone 8

- ☐ Get cool-season crops into the garden now. Don't wait—soon the weather will be too hot for them. Have row covers or homemade windbreaks handy to protect plants on chilly nights.
- ☐ Early this month, sow the last plantings of spinach, turnips, mustard, beets, carrots, and broccoli.
- ☐ In mid- to late March, plant corn, tomatoes, squash, peppers, and cucumbers. Nourish young plants with liquid organic fertilizer.

- ☐ Pull mulch away from perennials, shrubs, and trees to allow the soil to warm around them.
- ☐ Plant carnations (*Dianthus* spp.), daisies, marigolds, petunias, and snapdragons.
- ☐ At the end of the month, fertilize the lawn.

Zone 9

- ☐ Feed roses with an organic blend of cottonseed meal, alfalfa meal, and composted manure.
- ☐ Plant cool-loving vegetables, such as cabbage, broccoli, spinach, radishes, Asian greens, lettuce, and parsley. It may be too late to plant peas, however, if temperatures usually turn hot in your area by April or May.
- ☐ Harden-off tomatoes, peppers, and eggplants by moving them outside, beneath a plastic cover or inside a cold frame. Plant them in the garden after the last possible frost.
- ☐ Prune away frost-damaged areas on citrus.

Zone 10

- ☐ Plant okra, sweet potatoes, mustard, collards, cucumbers, and melons.
- ☐ Plant flowers that will tolerate heat: petunias, zinnias, cockscomb (*Celosia cristata*), and caladium (*Caladium × hortulanum*).
- ☐ Start papaya (*Carica papaya*), chayote (*Sechium edule*), roselle (*Hibiscus sabdariffa*), and jelly melon (*Cucumis metuliferus*).
- ☐ If your holiday poinsettia is leggy, cut it back and plant it outdoors in a spot that doesn't receive artificial light at night.
- ☐ Prune tabebuias (*Tabebuia* spp.) as soon as blooming stops.
- ☐ At month's end, use a micronutrient spray to fertilize everything.
- ☐ Dig compost into the soil near new plants and around the dripline of established trees and shrubs.

Get Your Soil Tested

Do you pile a lot of fertilizers onto your garden soil each spring, hoping to supercharge it? Or have you been largely ignoring your soil?

Well, it's time to get serious about your soil—and to take advantage of one of the best kept secrets in gardening: Soil testing is inexpensive and widely available to most American and Canadian gardeners and farmers through their local cooperative extension office or similar system. Most gardeners can get a pretty comprehensive test done for between $5 and $10—less than you'd probably spend for a bag of fertilizer.

Getting Tested

How you go about getting your soil tested depends on where you live. In most states, your local county extension service will sell you an inexpensive soil-testing kit, or tell you how to get one. In Canada, soil testing labs are listed either in the yellow or blue pages of the directory.

When submitting your soil sample for testing, ask the lab to tailor any recommendations they make to a small garden (unless you happen to "garden" in acres). Lab recommendations are designed to serve farmers, so they're generally given in terms of pounds per acre, unless you request otherwise. (If your recommendations are in "pounds per acre," just divide those figures by 43 to get "pounds per 1,000 square feet.")

Also, be sure to mention that you would like any remedies they propose to be in the form of organic soil amendments. (But don't be disappointed if they ignore you—not all labs are willing or able to give organic recommendations.)

A few weeks after you send your sample to the lab, you should receive your test results in the mail.

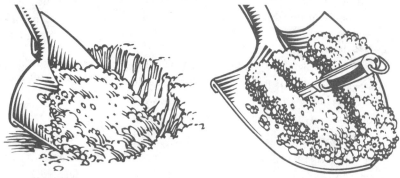

When you collect soil samples for testing, you'll dig a small hole in your garden, take a slice of soil from the side of the hole, and then save just the core of that soil slice. By combining several cores from different areas of your garden, you'll create a sample that represents your whole garden.

Reading the Results

Labs will test for some or all of the following factors and present the results in a chart or graph.

pH. pH is a measure of your soil's acidity or alkalinity. A pH reading of 7.0 is neutral; numbers higher than 7.0 indicate that your soil is alkaline, and numbers below 7.0 indicate that your soil is acidic. If a soil is extremely alkaline, nutrients will be "tied up" and your growing plants won't be able to absorb them. Most crops perform well at a pH between 6.2 and 7.0, which means that they grow best in neutral to slightly acid soil. At this range, nutrients are more available to plants.

If you garden in the East, your soil may be too acidic. The East's heavy rains wash away the calcium and magnesium that would otherwise keep the soil's pH above an acidic level. Western soils tend to be too alkaline because low rainfall levels allow alkaline elements to build up in the soil instead of washing away.

If your soil is too acidic, your soil test report will probably tell you to add lime—either calcitic lime (if soil magnesium levels are OK) or dolomitic lime (if soil magnesium levels are low).

If your soil is too alkaline, your report might tell you to add sulfur to lower the pH. But don't just pile it on! Follow the specific recommended amounts if they were included in your report, or check with your extension agent or the lab.

Phosphorus (P). Phosphorus is crucial to the health and growth of plants, "especially in the seedling stage," explains Stanley Chapman Ph.D., extension soils specialist with the University of Arkansas. If your soil is deficient in phosphorus, the growth of your plants could be stunted. Plants with small or shallow root systems and root crops like turnips, radishes, and beets are usually affected.

Sandy or shaley soils that don't contain much organic matter—a common occurrence in the South and parts of the West—are generally low in phosphorus.

You can raise a "low" phosphorus reading by adding bonemeal or rock phosphate to your soil any time of the year. Phosphorus isn't leached out by rain like some other nutrients; once you apply it, it stays there. For that reason, don't add too much—an overload could upset your soil chemistry for a long, long time. Always mix phosphorus-rich soil amendments thoroughly into the top 6 to 8 inches of your soil. In the spring, when cold soil causes microbial activity and exchanges that take place in the soil to slow down, it's difficult for plants to absorb phosphorus from the soil. An early spring feeding of fish emulsion will supply phosphorus to transplants (especially tomatoes) in your garden—

Telltale Weeds

According to gardening folklore, weeds can offer clues to soil health. "Reading" the weeds in your garden isn't a substitute for a soil test, but it's fun to do, and it may help you figure out what your soil needs.

Chickweed, lamb's quarters, and **pigweed** indicate soil that is fertile and is tilled frequently.

Common yarrow indicates soil that's low in potassium.

Dandelions indicate compacted soil or acid soil.

Docks indicate poor drainage or acid soil.

Field bindweed indicates a hardpan, compacted soil and low organic matter.

Mustards indicate a hardpan or crusty surface and acid soil.

Quackgrass indicates compacted soil and low organic matter.

Conduct an Earthworm Survey

Do you know how many earthworms are in your garden? Taking a earthworm count is a quick way to estimate soil fertility, explains Bill Wolf, former president of the Necessary Trading Company, a Virginia company that manufactures and sells organic fertilizers.

Spring is the ideal time to check for earthworm activity. Wait until the soil temperature is at least 50°F and the soil moisture content at the surface is 20 percent or more. Using a shovel or spade, dig a cube of soil measuring roughly 1 foot on each side, and lay it on the ground. Break it apart and look for earthworms. "You'll find at least ten earthworms per cubic foot in a healthy soil," says Wolf. Repeat the procedure at several locations in your garden. If your soil's average is fewer than ten worms per cubic foot, it's time to add more organic matter to your soil.

that way you'll know your young plants are getting a nutrient they need at a critical development stage!

Potassium (K). Potassium helps plants resist disease, strengthens their stalks, and improves the quality of their fruits and seeds. "Potassium has been called the antifreeze of plants," says Dr. Chapman, "because it circulates throughout the plant's entire system, keeping all the parts healthy and running."

Lack of potassium can cause the older leaves on a plant to have a burned appearance, the growth of the plant itself to be stunted, and the fruit to be of poor quality.

Sandy soils that contain little organic matter are commonly low in potassium, and a potassium deficiency can be aggravated during dry weather because roots can't move as freely through dry soil to find the scarce amounts of potassium that are present.

If you need to add potassium to your soil, do it before you plant in spring. Good sources include seaweed meal, Sul-Po-Mag (that natural sulfur-potassium-magnesium combo), and greensand.

Calcium (Ca). Calcium is a major component of a plant's cell walls. "A lack of calcium in garden soil can first show up (commonly during dry periods) as blossom end rot (a black, decayed spot on the end of the fruit opposite the stem side) on tomatoes," explains Dr. Chapman. "Lack of calcium can also cause spindly plant growth and can cause leaves to stick together and not open up."

Acid, sandy soils along the seacoasts are generally low in calcium. Adding limestone to these soils raises the pH and adds calcium.

Sulfur (S). Sulfur is a major component of all living organic matter, so it's no surprise that soils that are low in organic matter are also generally low in sulfur—which is bad because your growing plants need sulfur to form amino acids and proteins. Also, nitrogen needs to have enough sulfur around to do its job of feeding your plants. That's why having adequate amounts of sulfur in your soil is very important if you're growing sweet corn. "Corn uses lots of nitrogen, and therefore the soil it's planted in needs to have enough sulfur to help the corn take up and use all that nitrogen," explains Dr. Chapman. Good sources of sulfur are gypsum and Sul-Po-Mag.

Magnesium (Mg). Magnesium is an essential component of chlorophyll, which gives plants their green color and allows them to turn sunlight into energy via photosynthesis. When the amount of magnesium in your soil is in short supply, your plants will take this nutrient from their older leaves and move it to their newer ones, which need it most.

"When this happens, the oldest leaves show interveinal yellowing and may permanently dry up and fall off, especially in tomatoes," explains Dr. Chapman. "That's why a magnesium deficiency is commonly mistaken for a foliar disease," he continues. "Both start on the older leaves and gradually move up the plant."

Magnesium can be deficient in sandy soils with an acid pH. Adding dolomitic limestone (also called magnesium lime) raises the pH and provides the needed magnesium as well. Sul-Po-Mag is also a good source of this important nutrient.

Nitrogen (N). Nitrogen is very important to your plants, and the amount they get can make a huge difference in how much they yield. (Insufficient nitrogen in soil can decrease tomato production by 50 to 75 percent!) And yet, most soil labs don't include nitrogen as part of their basic test. That's because the nitrogen content of soil can change dramatically from day to day and from season to season. If you want a reading on the nitrogen level of your soil, you usually have to request it and pay a few dollars more.

When nitrogen is measured, labs can indicate the level a couple of different ways. For organic gardeners, the percentage of organic matter in your soil is a good long-term indicator of how much nitrogen will eventually be available to your plants. As that organic matter breaks down, it releases nitrogen in a plant-edible form.

If your soil doesn't have enough nitrogen, you can add more organic matter in the form of compost (an inch or so a year in the North and a couple of inches in the South), or appropriate amounts of nitrogen-rich fertilizers like bloodmeal or alfalfa meal.

But the odds are better that the reading will indicate your soil has too much nitrogen. Too much nitrogen will give you big lush plants but with few fruits. And those overfertilized plants are more susceptible to insect and disease problems. If your soil has too much nitrogen, simply cut back on the organic matter, grow lots of nitrogen-hungry crops—like sweet corn, potatoes, and lettuce—and let the rain take care of the problem.

Salts (Na). If your garden is in an area where excess salts can be a problem (usually the West, where there isn't enough rain to wash naturally occurring salts away), the labs will test for something called "electrical conductivity." Dr. Chapman warns, "Excess salts absorb the water in the soil that plant roots are trying to take up. Those salts can also injure or destroy those plant roots directly."

If the reading is high (indicating a high level of salt), you can correct the problem by adding gypsum in the amount that the lab recommends.

Soil Savior

A single teaspoon of fertile soil that has had compost added to it regularly contains an amazing 100 million bacteria, an astonishing 400 to 800 feet of fungal threads (called hyphae), and millions of other microbes. Soils that have received only conventional chemical fertilizers typically contain drastically lower numbers of these beneficial living creatures, explains Elaine Ingham, Ph.D., a soil ecologist who measures the amount of microcritters present in soil samples.

"We've tested some chemically farmed soils in California that were almost totally dead," she reports. "We could find only about 100 bacteria per teaspoon—that's absolutely nothing."

But compost can restore the fertility of even such severely damaged soils—and quickly too. Dr. Ingham relates a case where growers were convinced to stop using the highly toxic fungicide methyl bromide to control disease in their strawberry fields and to instead apply compost. The result: Their strawberry yields increased 600 pounds per acre the very first year!

The Scoop on Compost

Compost is the gardener's rendition of humus, Nature's age-old fertilizer for forests and fields. Compost is an excellent fertilizer and a superb soil conditioner. What's more, it protects plants from drought and disease. This fabulous substance—essential to any organic garden—is guaranteed to give you healthy, beautiful, and productive plants.

And one of the best times to apply compost is now—about 2 to 4 weeks before you begin planting, "so that the compost has time to stabilize in the soil," explains Garn Wallace, Ph.D., of Wallace Laboratories in El Segundo, California.

But how should you make and use this miraculous stuff? Well, relax—it's much easier than you might think. Here are the basics.

How to Make Compost

It's true: "If you pile it, it will rot!" Some gardeners simply pile organic materials—kitchen scraps (other than meat or bones), garden prunings, grass clippings, leaves, and so on—in an out-of-the-way corner of their yard, or inside a bin. Even if you don't bother to water the pile or to turn it, you'll still get sweet-smelling, crumbly brown compost in about a year.

But if you pay a bit more attention to your compost pile, you'll be rewarded with finished compost in as little as 2 to 3

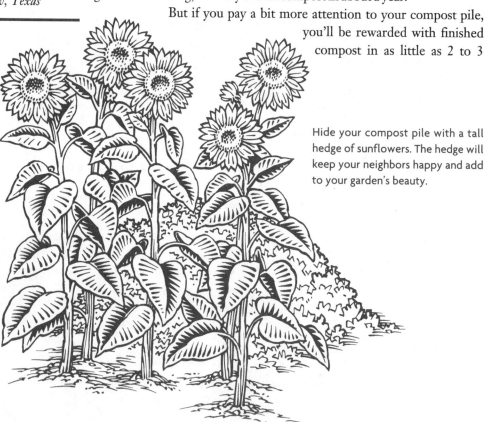

Hide your compost pile with a tall hedge of sunflowers. The hedge will keep your neighbors happy and add to your garden's beauty.

weeks. There are four keys to turning your garden waste into garden gold in a short period of time:

1. Start with the right blend. To make compost, you need to mix carbon-rich materials with nitrogen-rich materials. Carbon-rich materials include leaves, hay, and straw. Nitrogen-rich materials include grass clippings, kitchen scraps, and garden plant waste. Go heavier on the carbon materials and lighter on the nitrogen materials. Use grass clippings sparingly and mix them thoroughly with other ingredients so they don't mat down.

2. Shred materials into small pieces. Before you assemble your compost pile, run fall leaves through a chipper/shredder or run over them with a lawn mower. Also, cut up kitchen scraps: Dice broccoli stalks, chop spoiled potatoes, and so on. (Coffee grounds and eggshells—already in small pieces—are excellent additions to the compost pile!)

3. Help the materials get air. Once a week or so, use a pitchfork to move the materials around, or move the entire pile over a couple of feet, layer by layer. Try to move the materials that were on the inside of the original pile to the outside of the new pile. Or, use a compost tumbler—a container that moves the materials for you when you turn the crank or tip the barrel. Turning the pile allows air to circulate between the small pieces. (A passive alternative is to place "chimneys"—sections of plastic pipe that are 2 to 3 inches in diameter—in the center of the pile to open air holes.)

Here's a simple formula that puts it all together. Mix about two to four buckets of fresh grass clippings into every ten buckets of leaves. Spray everything with a hose as you add it to the pile so that the mix feels wet but not soggy. Also, add a few shovelfuls of garden soil to introduce friendly bacteria, which will help break down the materials.

Check the pile a couple of days later. It should be hot in the middle—a sign that the microbial decomposers are doing their job. After about a week, turn the pile with a pitchfork, and add more water if it's dry. Repeat the turning and watering, if necessary, a week or two later. In about a month, you should have beautiful, rich, finished compost.

Occasionally, you may notice an off smell as the materials decompose. Usually, it means the pile is too wet, lacks air, or contains too much nitrogen. To remedy this, spread out the ingredients to allow them to dry; fluff them up a bit to improve air circulation; or add more dry carbon materials, such as straw, or leaves to balance an excess of nitrogen. When the pile develops that good, earthy aroma, your compost is ready to use.

Use lattice, snow fence, or pallets to fashion a simple bin to contain your garden gold. The slatted material will allow air to reach the pile.

4. Keep the pile moist. Keep your compost pile about as moist as a wrung out, wet sponge. Don't saturate it with water. If you live in a dry region, make a shallow depression on the top of the pile to serve as a catch basin. Covering the pile with a plastic tarp will also help retain moisture.

How to Use Compost

To improve fertility and soil structure in new beds, mix compost deep into the soil. In established gardens, apply compost as a mulch around your plants, or work it into the soil each spring or fall when you till or dig the bed.

But if you're fighting disease in your vegetable beds, apply the compost to the surface of the soil only—don't dig it in. Dug-in compost feeds plants and fluffs up the soil but doesn't provide as much disease protection as surface-applied compost does. Extensive research shows that compost has the power to prevent many common plant diseases while it feeds garden plants. In fact, plant disease expert Harry Hoitink, Ph.D., of Ohio State University, says that just an inch of compost on the surface of the soil will prevent plant disease better than anything else available—including chemical fungicides! To get maximum disease-preventing power from your compost, mulch the surface of garden beds with *slightly immature* compost, if you have it, adds Dr. Hoitink.

Compost Creature Collective

If you could take a very close look at compost, you'd see that it's filled with living organisms. Here are some typical compost inhabitants:

Bacteria. These 10 millionth of an inch long, single-celled organisms are neither plant nor animal—scientists have created a third kingdom just for them. Bacteria "glue" soil particles together, improving soil structure, making nutrients more available, holding plant-feeding nitrogen in place, and even degrading pollutants.

Actinomycetes. Bacteria that grow in long, thin chains in the soil. They produce the unique, earthy smell that's a sure sign of good compost and rich soil—and they actively suppress many plant diseases.

Thermophilic bacteria. This type of bacteria thrives in the heat of a cooking compost pile.

Earthworms. Like tiny plows, earthworms feed on soil microbes and soil organic matter and release nitrogen as they tunnel through and mix up the soil. Their castings make great fertilizer, too.

Fungi. Decomposers that help to break down the organic matter in the soil.

Mites, pillbugs, springtails. These and other soil-dwelling insects and arthropods feed on fungi, release plant-feeding nitrogen, and help bacteria, organic matter, and fungal hyphae increase the water-holding capacity of your soil.

Nematodes. Microscopic worm-like soil-dwelling creatures. Most species are beneficial, eating bacteria and fungi and releasing plant-feeding nitrogen into the soil. Some species are destructive, but in compost-rich soils, the beneficial nematodes will help keep the destructive type in check.

Besides fighting diseases and supplying nutrients, compost has a remarkable effect on the condition of the soil. As bacteria feed on compost, they produce carbohydrates that "glue" the soil's tiniest mineral particles together into larger pieces, called "aggregates." The more aggregates there are, the more porous the soil becomes, allowing vital air and water to reach plant roots.

The earthworms that thrive in compost-enriched soil create tunnels that further aerate the soil, and their castings also help bind together soil particles. All this activity improves both heavy clay and sandy soils, allowing them to hold the maximum possible amounts of air, nutrients, and water and making them much more resistant to erosion caused by wind and water.

When to Use Compost

If you plan to *mix* the compost into your garden soil, the best time to do so is two to four weeks before you plant. This gives the compost time to stabilize in the soil.

If you plan to *spread* the compost on the surface of your soil as a mulch (the best way to protect the soil against disease), you have two choices. You can either do so several weeks before you plant, or wait until after seeds have sprouted and the young plants are up and growing. The germination of some seeds—especially beans, carrots, and onions—can be inhibited if these seeds are planted directly into fresh, nutrient-rich compost. (This is especially true in dry regions.)

How Much Compost to Use

For new garden beds, mix 1 to 2 inches of finished compost into the soil, about 4 to 6 inches deep. After that first year, mix in a ½-inch layer each spring if you garden in a moderate climate with a 5- to 7-month growing season.

You'll need more compost than those in hot climates (the deep South), areas with longer growing seasons (the South or along the coasts), areas that receive heavy rainfall (the Pacific Northwest), and areas with sandy soil (along the coasts).

If you garden in any of these conditions, double the initial application to 2 to 4 inches. Also double the annual maintenance amount to 1 inch. For an added boost, sidedress heavy-feeding vegetables (such as corn, tomatoes, and cucurbits), annual flowers, and late-blooming perennials with more compost in midseason. (Although side-dressing isn't critical in more moderate regions, it can benefit plants there, too.)

In any region, apply compost when you plant a succession crop. An ⅛- to ¼-inch layer on top of the soil will help plants get a strong start.

Creative Composting

Gardeners will make compost bins out of almost anything. Here are some more creative bin ideas.

Dog kennels. Some large compost bins can result by taking apart old dog boarding kennels. Use wire to tie the components of the kennels together into the desired pile shape. You can even use a hinged door for the front!

Leaves. Convince your neighbors to unload their bagged leaves at your house. Then, heap them in a small circle around a low compost pile. The bags will insulate the pile so the center of your pile will remain unfrozen. You can compost your kitchen scraps all winter.

Double-duty pallets. When you fashion a bin out of wooden pallets, instead of positioning the pallets with the end boards horizontal and the open ends sideways, try placing them with the open ends facing up. It's a perfect place to store garden stakes, long-handled tools, or row-cover hoops.

Turn Your Lawn into a Garden

Looking for an easy way to remove sod for a new garden bed? Here's one that requires no ripping, straining, or heavy lifting! The trick is to use a linoleum (or carpet) knife to slice the sod, just like you would a piece of carpet, then roll it. The grass comes up so cleanly that you can transfer it to bare spots, water and wait for it to re-root. Or, run the grass mat through a shredder, add it to your compost pile, then watch the steam rise from the heat of the decomposing greens.

If you don't already have a linoleum (or carpet) knife, you can buy one at almost any hardware store. This tool has a special, L-shaped blade that's sharp on both inside edges and at the point.

Here's how the technique works:

1. Plunge the point of the linoleum knife into the grass, and pull the knife back toward you, about 4 feet. (*Be careful not to pull too fast*—you want to cut the sod, not yourself.)
2. Cut a parallel line about 2 feet away from the first one.
3. Make a connecting cut at one end of the lines to form three sides of a rectangle.
4. Loosen the sod by working your fingers down and into the connecting cut. If you gently but firmly tug at the rectangle of grass, you'll feel it begin to pry loose from the soil. If the mat of grass doesn't come up right away, run the blade just under the grass along the connecting cut to slice through the roots at the edge. This will loosen enough of the sod to give you leverage to start pulling.

Needing more room for vegetables or flowers? To transform part of your lawn into a new garden bed, start by carefully cutting a rectangle in your lawn grass using an L-shaped linoleum or carpet knife.

5. When you have 2 to 3 inches loose, roll back the sod with your hands—just as though you were rolling carpet. Use your fingers or the knife to sever any stubborn grass or weed roots.

6. To prepare the area for planting, simply dig a little compost into the exposed soil.

If the area you're transforming from lawn to garden received lots of foot traffic, it may be compacted. In that case, you may need to till or deeply dig the area by hand to loosen the soil. Then you can work in some compost and plant.

After cutting through the grass, loosen the sod with your fingers and gently tug on the end of the rectangle. If the mat doesn't lift up, run the knife under the mat edge to slice the roots. Try pulling again and roll the sod back like a carpet. You may need to clip stubborn grass or weed roots.

Not Enough Compost?

Truth be told, many of us don't have the room, materials, or time to make all of the compost we need for our garden. And so, we turn to other sources, such as the bagged composts sold at garden centers or bulk composts available at municipal composting sites.

Before you use one of these composts, however, inspect it carefully. Look for compost that's dark and crumbly and that has a pleasant, earthy smell, with no hint of ammonia or sourness. That wonderful earthy aroma is produced by a specific group of bacteria called "actinomycetes," which grow only in mature compost and fertile soils, explains soil ecologist Elaine Ingham, Ph.D. (Large numbers of actinomycetes sometimes show up as a white powder on the compost—nothing to worry about.)

If you live in an arid region, where salts can build up to harmful levels in the soil, make sure you see a dependable analysis before you buy large quantities of compost. Commercial composts sometimes are made with lots of manure, which can be high in salt. And adding salty compost to already salty soil will simply aggravate the problem. If you garden in soil prone to high salt levels, look for compost with an ECe (a measure of salts) of less than 10 millimho/cm.

Wherever you garden, avoid composts that contain sewage sludge (sometimes called biosolids). Although the EPA regulates sludge composts, many experts feel the EPA regulations aren't strict enough. These composts may often contain toxic contaminants that can build up in soil.

GARDENER TO GARDENER

Weekend Compost

The secret to good, fast compost, I believe, is to cut up the raw materials into fine pieces before you pile them together. A pile of unshredded leaves, for instance, takes a year or more to decompose, while shredded and moistened leaves will decompose in a week.

Here's my shred-and-layer method of composting. Usually, I have two to three piles going at once in successive stages, and I maintain them on the weekends.

Each weekend when I clean up my lawn and gardens, I collect about three to four wheelbarrow loads of weeds, prunings, and spent vines and about a bushel of grass clippings and leaves. I also collect and save about 5 gallons of kitchen waste each week. Because I have plenty of green plant waste, no animal manure is necessary to supply nitrogen.

After I collect the materials, I run everything through my chipper/shredder to chop it up. If the mix is very dry, I moisten it with water, and then rake it together to form a pile about 2 feet high and 3 feet wide, in a location that gets morning sun and afternoon shade. I then cover the whole thing with black plastic to help retain moisture and warmth. Presto—the next morning the pile is hot!

The following weekend, I add a similar batch of stuff to the pile and mix it in well. Sometimes, I harvest "rough compost" from a pile after just two weeks, then till it into the soil or use it as mulch. Usually, though, I add more raw material to the pile on a third weekend, making it about 2 cubic yards in size.

By the fourth weekend, the pile has cooled. I uncover it, dig into it, spread it out to dry for a couple of days, and then run it through the chipper/shredder again. The compost that comes out looks and feels like fluffy, moist peat moss.

Howard Rathlesberger
Woodside, California

Composting by the (Dog) Yard

We've been composting for 30 years or so. We always put all our compost materials into two large bins, but when the bins rotted out for the second time, we looked for something quick and easy to replace them. When I saw that the local Agway was having a sale on dog yards, I decided I'd found our replacement. I set it up in about an hour. I didn't get it quite even, but the worms don't seem to mind.

Dorothy Fidler
Gettysburg, Pennsylvania

Poultry Turners

Organic Gardening magazine helped us start our first compost pile 22 years ago. Our birds (turkeys and chickens) have always been active in turning the pile. They scratch through it, mixing it, adding nitrogen, and sometimes finding tidbits for themselves. It may not be the most efficient way to do this job, but it's the most enjoyable for us. Our hard clay soil here in northwest Tennessee has shown improvement.

Mark and Padi Hewitt
Palmersville, Tennessee

GARDENER TO GARDENER

Cook Up Some Seaweed Soup

Seaweed is rich in potash, trace elements and substances that help protect crops in cold weather. I've found that it's also a favorite of worms—since I started using seaweed as fertilizer, my soil has become so aerated by the earthworm activity that I don't even need a trowel to dig. I just use my hands!

I'm fortunate to live along the coast, where I can easily get seaweed. Every spring after a big storm, I go to the beach and fill several plastic garbage bags with seaweed that has washed ashore. (The rain conveniently washes all the salt off of it for me.) I don't worry about what type of seaweed I collect, but I do try to find some that's already starting to decompose.

When I get home, I half-fill large containers (10 to 15 gallons) with the seaweed, then fill them the rest of the way with rainwater. Two weeks later, a thick soup has formed at the tops of the containers, while the seaweed stays below. I scoop out the "soup" and put it into gallon containers. Later, when I'm transplanting my seedlings to the garden, I feed them with my special seaweed tea: about 1 cup of the soup diluted in a bucket of water.

Later, I work the rotting seaweed mass at the bottom of the containers into my garden soil, and layer some of it into the compost pile.

Sue Le Montre
San Diego, California

A Neighborly Affair

I'm always in need of more compost and mulch, so I distribute a flyer to nearby homes to let them know that they can drop off their bagged leaves or clippings in our driveway. I point out that burning leaves pollutes the air and that composting is a better option. Our neighbors respond by bringing us dozens of bagfuls. It's a win-win situation for everybody.

Hannelore "Honey" Huisman
Rock Island, Illinois

Today's Garbage, Tomorrow's Garden

Twice a week, before trash pickup day, I separate materials for our municipal recycling program and compost the rest (minus meat scraps and citrus peels), the easy way: right in the garden. I choose a spot in my garden that won't be used for a few months, then dig a hole deep enough to hold my biweekly supply of kitchen waste and sometimes shredded newspapers.

I mix the organic materials with some soil, wet the mixture, then cover it with about 6 inches of soil. Next, I cover the surface with a 4 × 6-foot piece of hardware cloth to keep animals at bay. In a few weeks, the organic wastes have decomposed enough for me to move the hardware cloth to a new spot along the burial row.

John Bunicci
Shoreham, New York

GARDENER TO GARDENER

Rodent-Proof Bins

Saint Francis of Assisi is the patron saint of ecology, so we Fransican friars at the Saint Camillus parish in Silver Spring, Maryland, have tried to do our part by composting leaves, trimmings, and kitchen scraps. We'd been composting for 5 years when the kitchen scraps started attracting rodents. I asked one of our parishioners if he could design a rodent-proof compost bin to replace the containers we were using. The new bin is constructed with 2 × 4-inch lumber, galvanized hardware cloth with ½-inch openings, and hinged top and front panels. We've been using the new bin for several months now. It's full of kitchen scraps—and critters haven't found a way in yet!

> Fr. Jud Weiksnar
> Silver Spring, Maryland

Compost Tea Leaves

When I began saving kitchen scraps for the compost pile, I tried to remember to empty my under-the-sink scrap bucket every few days. But sometimes, especially in winter, I forgot. The result was usually a moldy mess. Then, I discovered that adding tea leaves to the bucket kept the other materials (potato peels, carrot tops, and so on) fresh for weeks at a time!

My theory is that the acidic tea leaves—like peat in a bog—inhibit bacterial growth. Note: Wet tea bags can be messy to empty, so I squeeze out the excess water and let them air dry for a couple of days before I cut them open and add the contents to the bucket.

> Anne Bingham
> Wauwatosa, Wisconsin

Mothproof Organic Fertilizers

Meal moths and larvae used to infest my bags of organic fertilizers until I began storing them in sealed containers. Instead of buying jars and tubs, I go to our local recycling bin and recover large liquid detergent jugs with caps and spouts. I remove the spouts with pliers, empty the bagged fertilizer into the jugs, then replace the spouts. This produces a sealed container that allows me to pour out the amount of plant food I need, while keeping the contents safe from insects.

> Victoria Price
> Silver Spring, Maryland

Chapter 4

April

Digging In: Planting and Transplanting

Early in April, as I was vigorously hoeing in a corner, I unearthed a huge toad, to my perfect delight and satisfaction; he had lived all winter, he had doubtless fed on slugs all the autumn. I could have kissed him on the spot!

—*Celia Thaxter*

Who needs a calendar to know it's spring? With magnolias, forsythia, daffodils, and fruit trees in full bloom, nature makes it abundantly clear that spring has arrived and, with it, planting time.

With plans made and beds prepared, you can start planting. Take advantage of increased daylight hours by setting out transplants in the evening. With a good soaking, the plants will settle in during the cool nighttime hours before the bright sun returns. Keep the plants semishaded for at least the first several days, until they adjust. (Also keep plastic or other coverings handy to protect plants from frost, when it threatens.) This is also the time to stock up on mulch. Check with local tree-pruning firms, who might be able to deliver their chipped branches and bark to your home for free.

Don't be surprised if you find yourself with a flat of bargain bedding plants or a discounted rose that isn't part of your plan! Until you figure out where to put your adoptees, stick them in a "nursery" bed (a bed designated for temporarily homeless plants) to keep them from becoming more potbound.

Gardener's To-Do List—April

If you don't know what USDA hardiness zone you live in,
check the map on page 246 to find out.

Zone 3

- ☐ Dig up and enjoy parsnips still left in the garden from last fall.
- ☐ Dig compost into beds as soon as the soil can be worked.
- ☐ Fertilize established lawns.
- ☐ If weather allows, plant onion sets, lettuce, spinach, peas, sweet peas (*Lathyrus odoratus*), carrots, and parsnips in the garden.
- ☐ Indoors, continue to start seeds of squash, melons, and corn.
- ☐ Start gladiolus corms indoors.
- ☐ Sprout seed potatoes by moving them from cold storage into room temperature.
- ☐ In the last week of the month, remove winter covering from tender roses, perennials, and strawberries.

Zone 4

- ☐ When the soil has warmed and dried, plant cold-tolerant crops, such as peas, spinach, lettuce, radishes, and onion.
- ☐ In flowerbeds, plant lilies, primroses, and lilies-of-the-valley.
- ☐ Plant raspberries as soon as possible, but wait until the soil has begun to warm before planting strawberries.
- ☐ Dig and divide perennials, such as daylilies and irises.
- ☐ Indoors, start tomato seeds if you plan to set them out under protective covering next month.
- ☐ Start broccoli seeds indoors for an early crop—but don't delay; soon it will be too warm.

Zone 5

- ☐ If the ground has thawed, divide and replant perennials, such as asters, bee balm, and hostas.
- ☐ Plant roses and lily bulbs.
- ☐ When the ground is warm and dry, transplant early tomatoes outdoors, inside protective Wallo'Waters.
- ☐ Seed a second crop of lettuce (start the seeds indoors or sow them directly in the garden).
- ☐ Sow spinach in the garden to get tender leaves before the weather warms.

Zone 6

- ☐ Clean up the garden in preparation for the season ahead: Remove last year's dead plants, rake back winter mulches, and top-dress beds with compost.
- ☐ After you've finished preparing your beds, plant potatoes, peas, spinach, and other leafy greens as well as beets, turnips, and carrots.
- ☐ Put up a trellis for tall varieties of peas as soon as they sprout.
- ☐ Dig, divide, and replant perennials, such as helenium, fall asters, Shasta daisies, chrysanthemums, and phlox.
- ☐ As soon as the weather settles, plant transplants of pansies, forget-me-nots (*Myosotis* spp.), foxglove (*Digitalis* spp.), and other cool-weather flowers.
- ☐ Sow seeds of sweet peas, bachelor's buttons (*Centaurea cyanus*), and larkspur (*Consolida ajacis*) in flowerbeds.

Zone 7

- ☐ Pass by broccoli and cabbage on sale at garden centers—hot weather will soon arrive, causing plants to go to seed instead of forming edible heads.
- ☐ Thin crowded carrots, chard, and lettuce.
- ☐ Remove floating row covers from peas early in the month. Drive tall, twiggy branches into the ground next to the plants for support.
- ☐ Mulch around the base of cool season crops to keep their roots cool and moist.
- ☐ Select new azalea and rhododendron bushes while they're in bloom to make sure that the color complements your landscape.

Zone 8

- ☐ Give flowers and vegetables a foliar feeding of liquid seaweed or compost tea; spray the liquid nutrients on foliage early in the day before it gets too hot.
- ☐ Plant black-eyed, purple hull and crowder peas, okra, peanuts, sweet potatoes, squash, melons, cucumbers, and corn—all can withstand the heat that will arrive in less than 2 months.
- ☐ Keep planting basil—it loves the warm weather.
- ☐ Plant "bulbs" of caladium, calla, gladiolus, and water lily.
- ☐ Keep adding kitchen scraps and grass clippings to your compost pile.
- ☐ Replenish your mulch!

Zone 9

- ☐ If slugs and snails are decimating your plants, collect them in the evening, when you're most likely to spot them.
- ☐ Plant pumpkins, summer squash, melons, and other vegetables that thrive in heat.

- ☐ Every 2 weeks from now until late summer, plant small blocks of bush beans and sweet corn to extend the harvest until frost.
- ☐ Thin fruits on fruit trees to increase their size and keep branches from breaking.
- ☐ Plant summer bedding plants, such as petunias, lisianthus (*Eustoma grandiflorum*), wax begonias, and impatiens.
- ☐ Sow seeds of nasturtiums, marigolds, portulaca, amaranthus, salvias, vinca (*Catharanthus roseus*), sunflowers, and zinnias.
- ☐ Plant perennials like ornamental alliums, bellflowers (*Campanula* spp.), daisies, yarrow, daylilies, coreopsis, penstemon, perennial geraniums (*Geraniums* spp.), iris, and statice.

Zone 10

- ☐ Plant perennials so they can settle in before the summer heat arrives; give them plenty of water.
- ☐ Plant heat-loving bedding plants, such as vinca (*Catharanthus roseus*), strawflowers (*Helichrysum bracteatum*), blanket flowers (*Gaillardia* spp.), and gazanias.
- ☐ Plant roselle (*Hibiscus sabdariffa*), amaranth, and Malabar spinach (*Basella alba*) now through August; make sure you give the Malabar spinach some shade and extra water.
- ☐ Try some tropical edibles: Buy malanga, gingerroot, and others at the market. Cut them into pieces at least ½ inch long, and plant. Harvest from October through December.
- ☐ Trellis tropical cucurbits (luffa, chayote, Tahitian squash, and so on) on a fence, and reap the rewards this fall.

Enlist Volunteer Violas

When I buy violas in spring to set out in my flower and herb beds, I also buy old-fashioned Johnny-jump-ups to plant with them. The violas rarely set viable seed, but they do cross freely with the Johnny-jump-ups. By the following spring, I've got hundreds of vividly colored hybrids blooming in my beds.

Freddie Lynn Bass
Columbia, Mississippi

Be a Smart Plant Shopper

If you want to shop wisely for plants, start by doing your homework. Study your site. Is it sunny or shady? What's the pH (acidity or alkalinity) of your soil? Does it tend toward clay or sand? What's your plant hardiness zone? Also, think about what you want plants for—windbreak, shade, fragrance, or color?

Once you're sized up your site, you're ready to head to the nursery or garden center. Follow these 10 tips for making the best choices.

1. Shop early and often. If there's a special plant you want, don't wait until the last minute to ask for it. With enough advance warning, the staff at your local garden center will be happy to either order it or grow it in their greenhouse for you.

2. Get good advice. Get to know the garden centers and nurseries in your area. Visit them during nonpeak hours, when workers have time to answer your questions.

3. Buy healthy plants. They have a rich, green color; compact growth; an even shape; and a size proportionate to their container. Unhealthy plants may be lopsided and have weak stems or insects. Yellow leaves could mean poor care, and purple foliage can indicate cold damage.

4. Buy buds, not blooms. Look for plants with lots of new growth and buds. Often smaller plants with buds will perform better than larger plants with blooms. Smaller plants tend to adjust to transplanting better than larger plants, and they'll grow faster. A perennial in full bloom in a pot may not bloom again until the next year in your garden.

5. Hold that plant! Most bedding plants and vegetables are available for sale a month or more before it's safe to plant them outside. If you find healthy selections that you want to buy, take them home and hold until the conditions are right for planting. To keep the plants from getting leggy, give them as much light as possible. Place them outside on a sunny porch during the day, but bring them indoors at night.

6. Buy bargains with caution. Cheap plants may not be the bargains you're hoping for. Poor-quality plants may die prematurely, and rootbound plants are slow to establish themselves. Misshapen plants may never outgrow their bad structure.

7. *See the root system.* With the help of a clerk, take the plant out of its pot and check its roots. The soil mass should retain its shape. Look for white growing tips on the roots; they're healthy and actively growing. If a plant is rootbound, you'll see masses of roots all over the surface of the rootball, and very little soil mix. If they're not too severely stunted, rootbound perennials might be saved by scoring the roots, as shown in the illustration below.

8. *Read the label.* You can learn a lot from plant tags: a plant's name (both common and botanical), the amount of sun or shade it needs to grow well, its hardiness zone and, perhaps, its heat zone, a new system of rating plants on the amount of summer heat they can withstand.

9. *Buy plants that resist pests and diseases.* Only about 38 percent of the trees and shrubs now sold are naturally pest and disease resistant, says Brian Maynard, Ph.D., assistant professor of urban forestry at the University of Rhode Island and head of a project to increase the availability of care-free plants. Dr. Maynard recommends: western hemlock (*Tsuga heterophylla*) instead of Canadian hemlock; 'Heritage' river birch (*Betula nigra* 'Heritage') instead of paper or European white birch; and kousa dogwoods (*Cornus kousa*) instead of native flowering dogwoods. A knowledgeable nursery should be able to suggest others.

10. *Check out the guarantee policy.* Some stores will replace plants that don't survive. Follow our advice, and they won't need to!

Use a sharp knife to cut through dense roots of potbound plants in several places (*left*). Cutting the roots prompts new root growth. But keep in mind that rootbound bedding plants and vegetables may never bounce back, even if you score the roots (*right*).

Seeds Stay Put

Heavy spring rains can wash away a garden in minutes, taking newly planted seeds along with it. To keep seeds protected and help germination, I use large mesh onion bags that I get from a local grocer.

After I plant my seeds, I lay the mesh bags end to end on top of the row, then pin the bags in place with row-cover pins, or something similar. The mesh covers allow the rains to soak through without disturbing the soil. When the tiny seedlings emerge, I remove the covers. I've used this method successfully to germinate seeds as small as spinach and radishes to larger ones like beans and corn.

Bill Anderson
Platte City, Missouri

Planting Your Veggie Garden

After a long, cold winter, it's tempting to get out into the garden on the first warm day and start planting. But remember that even though the weather feels warm to you, it may not be warm enough for your crops. Both soil and air temperatures have to be right for seedlings and transplants to get off to a good start.

Knowing what conditions your crops need will help you pick the best time to begin planting. Seed packets and seedling labels usually give general guidelines on the best planting times. You'll also find planting guidelines on page 59.

You can plant some cold-tolerant crops, such as peas and lettuce, as soon as you can work the soil in the spring. Depending on your climate, this can be as early as late February or as late as early May. When your soil has thawed and dried out enough to be worked, start sowing or setting out transplants of these early crops.

Other crops need warmer soil for germination and good growth. For instance, you can plant bean seeds and squash transplants around the last frost date (the average date of the last spring frost in your area; see the zone map on page 246). About 2 weeks after the last frost date for your area, you can plant tender crops such as corn, tomatoes, and melons. Be prepared to protect tender plants if weather reports predict a late frost.

There are a couple of exceptions to these general planting instructions. One is the West Coast, where soil may not be warm enough to plant summer crops, even though the danger of frost has passed. And in mountain areas, spring frosts may continue long after the soil temperature is adequate for planting.

Use a soil thermometer to accurately gauge soil temperature (you can buy soil thermometers at some garden centers or from mail-order garden-supply companies). Plant when the soil conditions are ideal. Then be prepared to protect your plantings if weather forecasters predict a cold spell.

Picking Plant Spacings

Every plant needs a certain amount of sun and root space to develop and produce properly. Whether you plant in rows, hills, or beds, be sure to allow adequate spacing between seeds or transplants. Look for spacing guidelines on the seed packet or on the plant label if you're planting transplants that you bought at a garden center.

Where two different crops meet in rows, hills, or beds, you need to decide how close to plant them. Calculate this spacing by adding the correct distance between two plants of each crop and dividing it by two. For example, if lettuce should be 6 to 8 inches apart and broccoli 18 to 24 inches apart, then lettuce and broccoli should be 12 to 16 inches apart.

Sowing Seeds Outdoors

Nearly every gardener develops a favorite method for sowing seeds easily. Here are the basics—with time, you'll come up with your own innovations (see the tips at the end of this chapter for some great hints from gardeners like you!)

Sow in rows. Sowing seeds individually in rows allows you to walk between the rows to cultivate or tend individual plants. Large-scale growers prefer rows because they allow for the use of large equipment. Use the corner of a rake or hoe to open a shallow furrow. Drop individual seeds by hand into the prepared furrow at the proper spacing. To cover the seeds, pick up handfuls of soil and sift it through your fingers over the row. This will screen out stones, sticks, soil clumps, and other debris.

Sow in beds. By planting in beds rather than in rows, you can grow more plants in the same amount of space, because you don't have to allow for paths between rows. Set seeds or transplants evenly over the bed at the standard spacing. Large seeds—like peas, beans, and squash—are easy to plant individually at the correct spacing.

You may find it easier to broadcast smaller seeds. To broadcast, mark the area in the bed that you want to cover. Scatter the seed evenly over the prepared soil. Gently rake the seed in or cover it with soil to get the correct planting depth. Once you see the seedlings emerge, thin them as needed.

Sow in hills. With hill planting, you group three to five seeds or so together, then allow wide spaces between the groups. The "hills" aren't necessarily actual mounds, although planting on low mounds can improve drainage and reduce the chance of seed decay. Vining crops—like melons, squash, and pumpkins—are common choices for hill planting. Use rocks or stakes to lay out the spacing of your hills before you plant your seeds.

After you've covered the seeds with soil, pat the planted area with your fingers or the back of a rake to get good contact between the seed and the soil. Label the area, and water gently (so you don't wash the soil away). Keep the soil moist until you see stems and leaves popping out of the ground.

The Perfect Planting Grid

If you're frustrated with the lopsided results you get from eyeballing the right spacing between plants, use a planting grid made from concrete reinforcing wire. Each square in the grid is 6 inches on a side. Lay the grid on the bed, and plant with it in place. Then lift the grid away.

The squares also provide a frame of reference to help you broadcast seeds more easily. For instance, instead of scattering carrot seeds over a large garden bed, just broadcast them over one individual square of the grid. You'll still have to thin the seedlings, but you're less likely to have clumps of carrots in some spots and bare patches in others.

You can store the grid in your shed, garage, or basement and use it year after year.

A board or shingle angled to the southwest works well for shade.

Planting Transplants

The same planting schemes that you use for seeds also work for planting transplants: rows, beds, or hills. Once you've prepared the soil, use stakes and string to mark rows or beds, or use pebbles to mark hills. Then set out the plants at the correct spacing. Dig a hole at least as wide and deep as the container in which the transplant is growing. Remove the transplant from its container by placing one hand over the soil, with the plant's stem between two fingers. Turn the plant over gently, and use your other hand to gently squeeze the rootball loose (from flexible containers like plastic six-packs) or to pull off a rigid container like a plastic pot. If the pot won't come off easily, tap it few times on a hard surface to loosen the rootball.

Set the transplant in the center of the hole. Steady the loosened rootball with one hand, and use your other hand to fill in the soil around it. Pat the soil down firmly around the base—but not too firmly. Some transplants, like lettuce, should be set at the same depth as they were growing in their container. Others, like tomatoes and cabbage, will do well if you dig a deeper hole and bury them up to their seed leaves (the first leaves that appear after germination).

Use your fingers to shape a low circular ridge a few inches out from the plant stem. This ridge will catch and hold water and direct it right to the plant's roots. Water as soon as you can after planting. Apply about 1 quart of water per plant.

Keep transplants well watered until you see new growth, then gradually cut back. If you plan to set in stakes or a trellis, do it soon after planting to avoid injuring growing roots.

Harsh weather after transplanting can damage even hardened-off seedlings. You may need to protect transplants from sun, winds, or cold temperatures for a few days or even up to a week. You can use floating row covers or other commercial products, or make your own devices like the ones shown here.

Shelter your transplants from cold and wind by using halved milk jugs as temporary windbreaks.

Cut a milk carton in half and place it so that the carton blocks the transplant from cold or wind.

Use a newspaper to protect your transplants from sun and wind. Fold the paper edges flat and hold them down with dirt or stones.

Direct Seeding Dates

This table serves as a general timetable to help you schedule plantings out in the garden. But first, call your local extension agent to find out the frost-free date in your area. Use this date as your point of reference as you add or subtract weeks, depending on the hardiness of the crops you're planting. *Hardy* plants can withstand subfreezing temperatures. *Half-hardy* plants can withstand only some light freezing. The fruit and leaves of *tender* crops are injured by light frost, while *very tender* plants need warm temperatures (above 70°F) to grow. Any exposure to temperatures just above freezing will damage fruit and leaves.

FROST-FREE DATE _____

COOL-SEASON CROPS		WARM-SEASON CROPS	
HARDY: PLANT 4–6 WEEKS BEFORE FROST-FREE DATE	HALF-HARDY: PLANT 2–4 WEEKS BEFORE FROST-FREE DATE	TENDER: PLANT ON FROST-FREE DATE	VERY TENDER: PLANT 1 WEEK OR MORE AFTER FROST-FREE DATE
Asparagus	Beets	Beans, snap	Corn (depending
Broccoli	Carrots*	Corn (depending	on variety)
Brussels sprouts	Cauliflower	on variety)	Cucumbers
Cabbage	Lettuce*	Okra	Eggplants
Collards	Potatoes	Tomatoes	Melons
Onions	Radishes*		Peppers
Peas	Swiss chard		Squash, summer
Spinach			Squash, winter

*These particular half-hardy plants can be planted outdoors at the same time as hardy crops if they are protected from extreme cold.

How to Figure the Last Planting Date

	VEGETABLE	DAYS TO MATURITY[1]	+	DAYS TO GERMI-NATION[2]	+	DAYS TO TRANS-PLANTING	+	2 WEEKS SHORT-DAY FACTOR[3]	+	BEFORE FIRST FROST[4]	=	DAYS TO COUNT BACK FROM FIRST FROST DATE
FROST-TENDER	Beans, snap	50		7		direct seed		14		14		85
	Corn	65		4		direct seed		14		14		97
	Cucumbers	55		3		direct seed		14		14		86
	Squash, summer	50		3		direct seed		14		14		81
	Tomatoes	55		6		21		14		14		110
SURVIVE LIGHT FROST	Beets	55		5		direct seed		14		—		74
	Cauliflower	50		5		21		14		—		90
	Lettuce, head	65		3		14		14		—		96
	Lettuce, leaf	45		3		14		14		—		76
	Peas	50		6		direct seed		14		—		70
SURVIVE HEAVY FROST	Broccoli	55		5		21		14		—		95
	Brussels sprouts	80		5		21		14		—		120
	Cabbage	60		4		21		14		—		99
	Carrots	65		6		direct seed		14		—		85
	Collards	55		4		21		14		—		94
	Radishes	25		3		direct seed		14		—		42
	Spinach	45		5		direct seed		14		—		64
	Swiss chard	50		5		direct seed		14		—		69

[1] These figures are for the fastest-maturing varieties we could find. Fast-maturing cultivars are best for fall crops. But for the variety you have, get the correct number of days from your seed catalog.

[2] These figures for days to germination assume a soil temperature of 80°F.

[3] The short-day factor is necessary because the time to maturity in seed catalogs always assumes the long days and warm temperatures of early summer. Crops always take longer in late summer and fall.

[4] Frost-tender vegetables must mature at least 2 weeks before frost if they are to produce a substantial harvest.

Vegetable, Flower, and Herb Log

PLANT NAME	DATE PLANTED	NOTES

Vegetable, Flower, and Herb Log

PLANT NAME	DATE PLANTED	NOTES

Vegetable, Flower, and Herb Log

PLANT NAME	DATE PLANTED	NOTES

How to Plant a Tree

The first step in planting a tree is deciding what tree to plant. Do you want summer shade, evergreen foliage, showy flowers, or attractive fruit? Be sure to match the tree to your site. If you're going to plant close to a building or under overhead wires, choose a tree that will stay compact even at maturity; large shade trees like oaks are better suited to more open sites. If the site is poorly drained (water puddles in the area longer than a few hours after a rain), you'll need a tree that can thrive in those conditions, such as a willow.

Once you have a perfect match of tree and site, you're ready to get growing. Early spring or early fall is a good time to plant (in areas where the ground doesn't freeze, you can even plant in winter). In spring and fall, the air is cool and rainfall is more dependable—so you probably won't need to water as much, and your tree will have time to grow some roots before it needs to produce new leaves.

Follow this procedure when you plant a tree or shrub to ensure it will have a long, healthy life.

Use a shovel or a mattock to dig a hole for your tree or shrub and place the dirt on a tarp for easy clean up. Make sure the hole isn't deeper than the rootball.

1. Mark your chosen planting site with a stake. To figure out how big you need to dig the hole, measure the width and depth of the rootball. Using flour or garden lime, draw a circle that's two to three times wider than the rootball, with the stake as a center point.

2. Cut along the circle with a shovel, and then start digging the hole. Pile the soil on a tarp for easy clean up later.

3. As you dig, keep checking the depth of the hole. You want the hole to be only as deep as the rootball so the ball will sit on solid ground. (This prevents settling.) Once the hole is the right depth, use your shovel blade to chop gently at the sides of the hole. This loosens the soil and makes it easier for new roots to grow out into the surrounding soil.

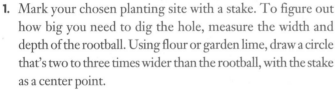

Less Is More

When it comes to planting a tree, sometimes doing less is more.

Don't dig deeply. Digging a shallow but wide planting hole encourages the tree to send its roots outward for better anchoring and prevents it from sinking when the soil settles.

Add nothing to the planting hole. In most cases, adding amendments such as fertilizers and peat moss to the planting hole only interferes with normal water drainage, thus promoting root rot. (One exception: In very sandy soil, adding some compost or other organic matter to the soil you replace can help retain needed moisture around the developing roots.)

Don't bother to stake. The only time you might want to stake a newly planted tree is if the site is very windy. In that case, use a short stake (only 2 feet or so should be above ground level), and place it slightly off center, angled into the prevailing wind. Whenever possible, add the stake to the hole before you add the tree. The combination of a short stake and flexible tie will provide support but still allow the trunk to sway in the wind. In the long run, your tree will develop a sturdy, self-supporting trunk. Remove any stake after the second year.

4. Place the tree in the center of the hole; adjust until it's straight. Add a few shovelfuls of soil to the hole to support the rootball. Take a good look at the tree to make sure it's placed the way you want it. For balled-and-burlapped trees, remove as much burlap, twine, and wire as you can without disturbing the rootball.

5. Fill around the roots with the soil you removed from the hole. Add enough soil to fill the hole about halfway, then use the handle end of your shovel to tamp down the soil. Step gently on the soil. Fill the rest of the hole, tamping the soil again with the shovel handle, and then your foot. This helps prevent large air pockets, which can harm the tree or cause it to shift, from forming.

6. With the leftover soil, construct a 3- to 6-inch-high ridge around the edge of the planting area. The ridge catches water and directs it to the roots. Water the soil thoroughly with a garden hose—let it flow gently for about an hour.

7. Cover the soil with about 2 inches of mulch, such as shredded bark, to help keep the soil moist and encourage good root growth. Keep the mulch away from the trunk of the tree to prevent pest and disease problems.

For the first 4 to 6 weeks after you plant, water the tree twice a week. Gradually reduce the frequency to once a week for the next year or two. Each spring, rake off the previous year's mulch and add a 2-inch layer of compost to provide a small but steady supply of nutrients and to suppress weeds.

Once you've planted your tree, water it well. Then, keeping a few inches bare around the trunk, spread shredded bark.

GARDENER TO GARDENER

Plant Flowers the Easy Way

Last year I decided it was time for a change. Instead of planting my usual neat, straight rows, I broadcasted the seeds of my cutting flowers.

The results were wonderful! I ended up with a variety of heights and colors in a single area, resembling a miniature wildflower meadow. And because of the fullness of the flowers' growth, the garden seemed larger than it actually is. Weeds were minimal: When the flowers were 3 to 4 inches tall, I plucked weeds by hand just once. By late August there was only one new weed in the entire planting.

Here's what I did. After digging up the sod to create the planting site, I worked compost into the exposed, clay soil. Then I framed the area with old, untreated 2 × 4s to make mowing easier and to keep grass out of the bed.

Next, I mixed together seeds of dwarf zinnia, cosmos, bachelor's buttons, and various marigolds in a single jar, then sprinkled them by hand over the prepared soil. I covered the seeds with about 1/4 inch of soil by broadcasting the soil in the same way. Then I watered the bed gently with the spray mist attachment on the garden hose—just enough to moisten the top of the soil. I repeated the watering every afternoon for a week, until the seeds germinated.

A. Guiliani
Green Bay, Wisconsin

Bounty, the Better Broadcaster!

I had trouble broadcasting tiny seeds evenly. Invariably, the sprouts would be sparse in some areas and crowded everywhere else. I decided that the problem was that I couldn't see where the seeds landed. Then I found a solution to this problem, and I've used it successfully ever since then, with terrific results! Here's what to do.

First, prepare the garden bed you want to plant, then cover the "target area" where you will be sowing the seeds with sheets of plain white paper towels (the cheapest, thinnest type you can find). Dampen the area and the towels with water. Next, carefully scatter the seeds onto the towels. After you've spread the seed evenly, cover the seeds with another layer of towels, then cover that with a thin layer of soil or compost. Water the entire area.

The paper towels hold the seeds in place so they don't wash away. Doing this also helps keep the area around the seeds evenly moist, which aids germination. Within a week or two, all that remains are perfectly spaced, happily thriving baby seedlings!

Deb Graham
Mount Vernon, Washington

Use Baskets to Protect Bulbs

Two years ago I planted gladiolus. They bloomed well, but when it came time to dig up the corms in the fall, I kept digging into them by accident. I severed so many that less than half of them were suitable for replanting the next spring. Then I thought of using plastic strawberry baskets as protectors. Last year I put my corms inside the baskets, then planted the baskets in the garden. The roots grew right through the bottom of the baskets, and I was able to dig up the corms without digging into them.

Farelle Flores
Cabello, New Mexico

GARDENER TO GARDENER

Leek Planting Made Easy

Avoid the hassle of digging a trench to plant leeks by using a bulb planter instead. Just prepare the bed before planting, then make individual planting holes, about 6 inches apart, with the bulb planter. Drop the leek seedlings into the holes. You don't even need to bother to fill in the holes—rain will do the job for you! As the leeks grow larger, mound compost around the stems to keep them white and feed the plants.

Irene Esser
Watertown, South Dakota

Can Aloe Help Root Growth?

In my California garden, I grow a lot of trees and a lot of aloe vera. Why the aloe? I believe it contains something that stimulates root growth. Whenever I use liquid from inside the aloe on the roots of transplants (of any kind), the plants seem to recover quickly and suffer no setback. When planting or transplanting trees, I put an entire aloe plant (or two or three) into the planting hole, then chop it all up with a shovel before planting.

Brad Nye
Ontario, California

Cagey Rotation

In the interest of crop rotation, I used to spend several days moving tomato cages, bean trellises, and the like to different locations to get ready for spring planting. Finally I thought, "Why not plant the peas, beans, and cucumbers in cages, just like the tomatoes and make the location of the cages permanent?" Now I just rotate my crops instead of the cages! With this system in place, my tomatoes are planted in a 5-year rotation, instead of landing in the same spot every other year like they used to.

Alan G. Hanson
Sonoma, California

Plant Parsnips in Any Soil

If your soil is too heavy or contains too many rocks to grow good parsnips, try this technique! Prepare your soil by digging in compost or other organic amendments, then use a tool-handle to make long, narrow planting holes about a foot deep, spaced 4 inches apart. (If you're planting more than one row, space the rows about 6 inches apart.) Now fill the holes with ordinary sand—the kind that's used in children's sandboxes. Don't be tempted to use your precious sifted compost—parsnips prefer soil that isn't too rich.

Put two or three parsnip seeds on top of the sand in each hole, cover the seeds with a bit more sand, then keep them moist until they germinate. Once they germinate, thin the sprouts to one seedling per hole—cut, don't pull out, the extra seedlings so you don't disturb the remaining plant. At harvest, you'll get wonderfully straight and delicious parsnips!

Jim Lowe
Red Hook, New York

Portable Potting Station

I enjoy having containers filled with summer annuals and herbs on my deck each year. But filling all those containers requires a lot of potting mix. To make large amounts of my special soil mix and keep potting easy, I use a wheelbarrow as a portable potting station. In it, I mix together compost, loam, vermiculite, peat moss, lime, rock phosphate, and greensand. Then I lay plywood over the handles to create a work surface for filling the containers and planting.

Carol Hanby
Waterford, Connecticut

Chapter 5

May

Garden Favorites: Cultivating Tomatoes Organically

Gardening is more than just digging, planting, pulling weeds, and picking vegetables and fruits. It is also the savoring and cultivation of life.

—*Robert Rodale*

Some plants are so universally loved that it's hard to imagine a garden without them. Take tomatoes, for instance. Nearly everyone's favorite garden vegetable, tomatoes are one of the last things you give up when you can't grow much else. Even the smallest gardens—on a city rooftop or an apartment balcony or in a courtyard—usually will include at least one potted cherry or slicing tomato plant.

And when it comes to growing these garden icons—whether a single plant or hundreds—we gardeners can never learn enough, it seems. There's always another tip, technique, or secret to glean from a fellow aficionado. We figure that one of those secrets is bound to be the one that will make this year's crop the very best ever.

For organic gardeners, the prospect of growing the best tomatoes is even more thrilling. Yes, some of our neighbors still scoff and say it can't be done organically. All the more reason to prove how wrong they are—and perhaps convert them along the way!

Gardener's To-Do List—May

**If you don't know what USDA hardiness zone you live in,
check the map on page 246 to find out.**

Zone 3

- ☐ Remove winter protection from hybrid tea roses, but have those jute sacks ready in case of a freeze.
- ☐ Begin hardening-off annual flowers by exposing them to cooler temperatures for longer periods each day.
- ☐ Seed cold weather crops.
- ☐ Give perennials and fruit trees a generous feeding of compost, and if it has been dry, water them deeply to boost their growth.
- ☐ Toward the end of the month, plant potatoes and seeds of warm-season crops.
- ☐ Protect cauliflower and broccoli transplants from root maggots with 4 × 4-inch collars made of heavy paper, placed on the soil around the base of the plants.

Zone 4

- ☐ In the flowerbed, divide overgrown perennials, and establish new beds with the divisions.
- ☐ Sow seeds of annual flowers such as bachelor's buttons, marigolds, and zinnias.
- ☐ Start melon, cucumber, and squash seeds indoors or in a coldframe.
- ☐ Plant frost-sensitive veggies—such as tomatoes, beans, and summer squash—at the end of the month.
- ☐ Prune lilacs, azaleas, spirea, and other spring-flowering shrubs after they bloom.

Zone 5

- ☐ After the soil has warmed to 60°F, transplant out tomatoes, peppers, eggplants, melons, cucumbers, and sweet potatoes.
- ☐ Small, 3-foot-tall "tomato" cages work for peppers and eggplants; for tomatoes, use sturdier, 6-foot-tall rings made from 4-inch-square chicken wire.
- ☐ Squeeze some last runs of cool-season crops into the garden; try some mâche (corn salad), a tasty cool-weather green.
- ☐ Protect cucumbers, melons, and squash from pests by using row covers. (Be sure to remove them when plants blossom, though.)
- ☐ Divide and replant summer and fall-blooming perennials.
- ☐ Transplant evergreen shrubs and trees, and pop annual flowers into beds.

Zone 6

- ☐ Plant out tomato transplants early in the month and those of peppers and eggplants by the end of the month.
- ☐ Direct seed squash, beans, corn, and okra.
- ☐ Plant a few more runs of leafy greens.
- ☐ Sow sunflowers, zinnias, marigolds. and cosmos wherever you need an extra splash of color.
- ☐ Mulch roses with a 1-inch layer of compost.

Zone 7

- ☐ Plant moonflower (*Ipomoea alba*), caladium, coleus, zinnia, and other heat-tolerant flowers.
- ☐ Don't be too quick to give up on tender perennials and tubers, such as datura, Mexican bush sage (*Salvia leucantha*), cannas, and dahlias. You still may see new leaves by the end of the month.
- ☐ Plant okra, tomatoes, eggplant, peppers, sweet potatoes, southern peas, and other heat-loving veggies.
- ☐ Mulch peas and cole crops to keep the soil cool; water them regularly.
- ☐ Thin peaches, plums, pears, and apples to about 6 inches apart.

Zone 8

- ☐ Harvest spring crops daily to keep them producing for as long as possible.
- ☐ Continue to plant heat-tolerant tomatoes, such as 'Heatwave', 'Sunchaser', and 'Sweet 100'.
- ☐ Plant eggplant, peppers, cucumbers, squash, okra, beans, sweet potatoes, melons, and southern peas this month.
- ☐ Plant caladiums in shaded sites. Try narrow-leaved zinnia (*Zinnia angustifolia*) for hot spots. Give new plantings plenty of water.
- ☐ Continue planting daisies, asters, coreopsis, marigolds, and sunflowers—they nourish the beneficial insects, which will help keep pests in check.
- ☐ Check your drip irrigation system—you'll be depending on it soon.

Zone 9

- ☐ Plant last runs of lettuce, choosing heat-tolerant varieties that are slow to go to seed.
- ☐ Start new plantings of melons, squash, dried beans, okra, and southern peas that thrive in heat.
- ☐ Set out heat-loving petunias, moss rose (*Portulaca grandiflora*), amaranth, vinca (*Catharanthus roseus*), nicotiana, marigolds, and sunflowers.
- ☐ Pull out and compost primula, viola, calendula, and pansy plants that are no longer flowering well.
- ☐ Use drip irrigation to provide a constant supply of moisture to beds; also mulch with organic materials, such as dried grass clippings, pine needles, or leaves.

Zone 10

- ☐ Plant heat-loving veggies, such as sweet potatoes, okra, and southern peas.
- ☐ Keep heat-tolerant herbs, such as lemongrass, going strong by feeding them with fish emulsion and seaweed spray.
- ☐ If thyme, basil, and curry leaf show signs of mildew, spray them with a solution made from 1 tablespoon of baking soda and 1 gallon of water; repeat every few days.
- ☐ Solarize empty garden beds: Cover them with clear plastic for a month or two to kill nematodes and weed seeds and pathogens in the soil.
- ☐ Mulch all plants heavily.
- ☐ Stop whitefly and mealybugs with insecticidal soap.

A Bonemeal Boost

When tomato seedlings seem to be suffering from phosphorus deficiency (which gives the undersides of the leaves a telltale purplish tinge), adding bonemeal to the soil mix that you use to pot up the transplants should remedy the problem, according to Jill Jesiolowski Cebenko, former senior editor for *Organic Gardening* magazine. Add 1 tablespoon of bonemeal per gallon of mix. "This is just enough bonemeal to give the plant a healthy green color," Jill says.

If the young leaves on your tomato plants are small and yellowish-green, your plants may not be getting another nutrient they need: nitrogen. Give your plants a nitrogen boost by watering them with a dilute solution of fish emulsion to keep them green and growing.

Expert Tips for Terrific Tomatoes

Most gardeners can grow a respectable crop of tomatoes without too much trouble. But why settle for a respectable crop when you can grow a bumper crop of blue-ribbon beauties? Here are 13 tomato success secrets gleaned from four master tomato growers. (Hint: Lots of little things can add up to make a big difference in your level of tomato-growing mastery!)

1. Give them light. "I've grown my tomato seedlings under expensive grow lights and under standard fluorescent shop lights, and I've seen no difference whatsoever between the plants," says Steve Draper, who tends 70 to 80 varieties of tasty tomatoes in his gardens in Salt Lake City and Seattle.

2. Keep them close. The usual advice is to set tomato seedlings about 4 inches away from a bank of fluorescent lights. But Amy Goldman, a blue-ribbon tomato grower in Rhinebeck, N.Y., makes sure her plants are no more than 2 to 3 inches from their fluorescent lights. "My seedlings always grow up stockier and bushier when I remember to keep them close to the lights."

3. Use maximum medium. A soggy seedling is a sorry seedling, reminds Steve Draper. He makes sure his seed-starting medium is exceptionally light and well drained by mixing extra vermiculite into the mixes he buys. "Since I started making my mixes almost half vermiculite, I never have damping-off problems," says Draper.

4. Keep them cool. Tomato seeds will germinate most reliably at about 80°F, but tomato seedlings grow best at around 55° to 65°F. "At higher temperatures, a tomato plant will grow too quickly and become spindly and weak," warns Craig LeHoullier, Ph.D., who grows 250 tomato varieties in Raleigh, N.C. "When temps are cooler, the plants grow more slowly, become stockier, and seem better prepared for their eventual move into the garden." LeHoullier keeps his seedlings under fluorescent lights in his garage in early spring.

5. Give the roots room. Your tomato seedlings really pick up steam as they grow, developing faster at each successive stage of their growth. The last thing you want to do is stop that marvelous momentum, says Bill McDorman, owner of High Altitude Gardens/Seeds Trust in Hailey, Idaho. "If you allow a seedling's roots to reach the edge of the container it's growing in, it will immediately slow the pace of its growth," warns McDorman. "And once that happens, it won't start growing quickly again—even when you transplant it outside." He prevents his transplants from becoming rootbound by starting them a little later than most short-season gardeners. "I usually don't start my seeds until about 6 weeks before I plan to set out the plants," he says. "And if I think a plant is getting too large for its container, I move it into a bigger one right away." To keep her transplants from becoming potbound, Amy Goldman transplants all of her seedlings at least three times into successively larger containers before she brings them outside and plants them in the garden.

6. *Feed plants first, then the soil.* All of these tomato experts begin feeding their seedlings a dilute liquid fertilizer (like fish emulsion) once a week after the first couple of true leaves appear on the plants. But *none* feed the plants once they're out in the garden. Bill McDorman layers his beds with lots of kelp meal and compost each fall. "Kelp and compost are both full of minerals essential for tomato plants to produce healthy, well-formed fruit," he explains. "And I've observed that tomato plants grown in kelp-amended soil seem to have an extra 3° to 4° of frost protection," which can be essential when you garden at nearly 10,000 feet altitude, as McDorman does!

7. *Back off if leaves turn brown.* Brown leaf tips are a sign that you are overfeeding your tomato plants—a common mistake, says Craig LeHoullier. But don't despair, he advises; just stop feeding, give your plants some extra water (and time), and the leaves should regenerate shortly.

> **2-Liter Irrigation**
>
> Here's a great way to supply water efficiently to the roots of your prize tomato plants.
>
> Use a nail or awl to punch 8 to 12 holes in a 2-liter soda bottle. (Leave the cap on the bottle.) Cut a hole about ½ inch from the bottom of the bottle. The hole should be just large enough for a garden hose to fit through.
>
> Bury the bottle upsidedown in the soil near a tomato plant. Submerge about two-thirds of the bottle. Fill it with water once or twice a week.

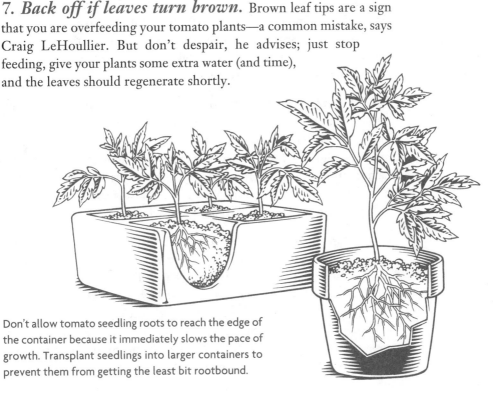

Don't allow tomato seedling roots to reach the edge of the container because it immediately slows the pace of growth. Transplant seedlings into larger containers to prevent them from getting the least bit rootbound.

Treasure the Taste

Once the tomato harvest gains momentum, those big, juicy tomatoes are practically rolling off the vines and into your kitchen. What's the best way to enjoy their vine-ripened flavor? Don't cut them open until right before you plan to eat them. Three minutes after slicing, the wonderful tomato aroma and flavor start to fade. And don't store extra tomatoes in the refrigerator: They lose their aroma and flavor that way, too.

8. Wait for 50°. Wait until nighttime temperatures stay above 50°F to plant your tomatoes outside, says Steve Draper. "Cool nights will slow the growth of your tomato plants too much," he warns. "No matter what the daytime temperature is, if the nights drop below 50°F, the plants will almost stop growing altogether."

9. Consider basic black. Amy Goldman swears by black plastic for growing tomatoes in her cool upstate New York garden. "It warms the soil in the spring, and in the summer it keeps the soil cooler, prevents weeds from coming up, and helps the soil stay moist," she explains. Steve Draper says he covers his beds with it early in the season and places his transplants in the ground through slits in the plastic. "I get good-sized tomatoes earlier than any of my neighbors in Utah, and I'm sure that the black plastic is one of the key reasons," Draper says.

10. Add walls for warmth. Like many tomato growers, Bill McDorman puts Wallo'Water around each of his tomato plants when he sets them out in the garden to keep them warm. What's different is McDorman then leaves the walls in place all season to keep the plants cool when temperatures rise. "The water helps moderate both types of temperature extremes," he explains.

11. Bury your treasures. You can help your young transplants achieve that all-important maximum root growth by covering their stems with soil. Plant transplants as deeply as possible—up to the first set of true leaves, says Craig LeHoullier. Make sure at least two sets of leaves are above the soil. Press the soil gently and water.

12. Be a flower picker. Amy Goldman adds that you shouldn't allow your tomato plant to grow anything but roots and leaves early in life. "I pull off all the flowers on my plants until they reach at least 1 foot tall. I also pull off all the suckers (those strong shoots at the base of the main stem) that appear before the plant starts to set fruit," she says. Either pinch suckers off right above a leaf or flush against a main stem. Only pinch on dry days to prevent unwanted disease problems.

13. Keep 'em up. Every tomato fanatic has a favorite support system. Craig LeHoullier and Steve Draper like to tie their growing vines to stakes, Bill McDorman confines his fruit within cages, and Amy Goldman uses both techniques—supporting her cages with stakes. "We've found that you get more fruit if you just let the plants sprawl a bit inside of big roomy cages," says McDorman. "But you can plant closer together if you stake," argues Draper. "That means more fruit per square foot." We'll leave that one for you to decide.

Specialized Techniques for Tomatoes

Are you hoping that this year you'll finally grow the tomato you've always dreamed of? Are you struggling with inadequate cages or poor growing conditions? Here are some specialized techniques you can use to make your tomato crop be the best it can be.

Tomatoes—the Ph.D. Course

Still trying to grow that mammoth red-ripe beauty that will set records or win you a blue ribbon? Here's some advice from a few who have succeeded in that noble horticultural endeavor.

First, choose a variety that's genetically predisposed to gargantuan growth: 'Delicious', 'Abraham Lincoln', 'Brandywine', 'German Johnson', and 'Giant Belgium' are all known to produce extra-large fruits, regardless of growing conditions. (Fruits of 'Delicious' have won Guinness World Records several times.)

Next, reduce the number of fruits per plant. Go ahead and remove all of the very young, developing fruits at the top of the vine. Leave just a few of the older fruits at the bottom of the plant.

Also remove the fruits that are most distant from the stems, advises Jay Scott, Ph.D., who tests tomatoes at the University of Florida. "You'll always get a bigger size from the fruits closest to the stems, especially if you prune off all the others in that cluster," he says.

For truly king-sized tomatoes, remove all suckers too, allowing only one main stem to develop. Just be aware that a few big tomato varieties ('Suncoast', for instance) grow on determinate vines—ones that reach a certain point and then stop growing—and these shouldn't be pruned. Also, keep in mind that excessive pruning of foliage can cause the fruits to crack.

Pruning extra fruits and supporting the plant stems and fruits with pantyhose ties will lead to a harvest of king-sized tomatoes.

The primary source of food for your tomatoes should be the soil—it should contain plenty of organic matter and have a 6 to 6.5 pH. But to keep your plants growing strong through stressful conditions, feed them diluted fish emulsion or seaweed mix fertilizers every couple of weeks, suggests Gordon Graham, a Guinness World Record holder. And don't forget the benefits of rich compost!

Finally, offer them support. Big tomato growers will stake or cage their plants to keep them off the ground. This keeps the plants away from slimy slugs and soil-borne diseases (like fusarium wilt or verticillium wilt).

Build a Super Tomato Trellis

Linda Barton of Blairstown, New Jersey, stumbled upon a staking technique that allowed her to grow tomatoes, despite a minimal water supply and sustained heat. Her staking system combines the stake-and-weave trellis method with the benefits of intensive planting and allows for the use of row covers. The system is much more efficient and sturdy than conventional cages or trellises. You can also use it to support crops of peas or cucumbers. Here's how to set up a system like Linda's.

1. Construct a raised bed that is 3 feet wide and 13 feet long. Linda framed her raised garden bed with 2 × 9-foot rough spruce planks.

2. Build an A-frame over the raised bed, using six 6-foot-long spruce stakes for the side supports and a 12-foot-long piece of lumber for the ridge beam. To secure the tops of the side supporting poles, thread galvanized wire through holes drilled into the ridge beam and sidepoles (as shown in the illustration, on the opposite page). By securing the poles with wire instead of nailing or screwing them together, the structure can be easily taken apart and stored at the end of the growing season. The galvanized wire makes the structure stable but still flexible enough to sway (instead of blowing over) in a strong wind.

3. Cover the frame with twine. For additional stability and support for vining plants, drill two holes in the ridge beam and run baling twine from the bed ends up to the beam holes, securing the twine to the bed's frame with an eye hook. Use a

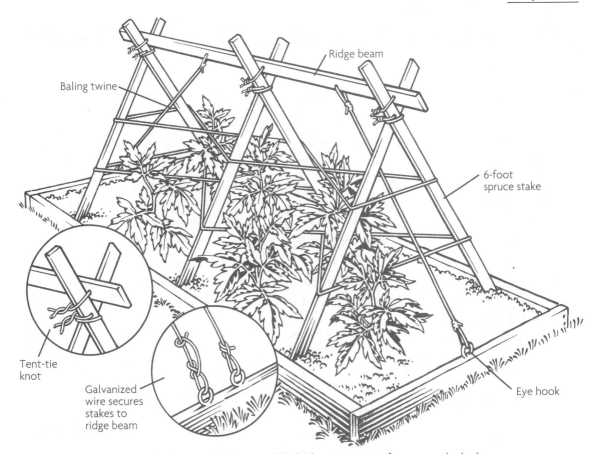

Ridge beam

Baling twine

6-foot
spruce stake

Tent-tie
knot

Galvanized
wire secures
stakes to
ridge beam

Eye hook

To build a super tomato trellis, first construct a raised bed. Then, erect an A-frame over the bed using spruce stakes for side supports and a piece of lumber for the ridge beam. Secure the stakes and beam together with wire. Connect the ridge beam to the edge of the bed using an eye hook and baling twine. Weave bailing twine around the frame. Plant your tomatoes. As they grow, they'll vine up the twined frame.

tent-tie knot (a type of knot that can be adjusted for greater or less slack) to attach the twine to the eye hook. This will allow you to make adjustments as the plants grow.

4. Add more support as needed by zigzagging baling twine between the poles, about 8 inches above the ground, where you'll plant your tomatoes. As the plants grow, weave more of the baling twine back and forth, at 12-inch intervals up the poles, to support the vines and fruit.

GARDENER TO GARDENER

Early Setback Boosts Productivity?

Last year I inadvertently discovered a way to boost tomato productivity. In spring, I set out a few 12-inch-tall 'Delicious' tomato plants, covering them on cold nights. One night it was supposed to be warm, so I left the plants uncovered. Something completely defoliated one of the plants so only a stem was left.

I decided to see if it would recover. I watered it, covered it with a cut-off 2-liter plastic soda bottle, and left the cover on day and night. The plant began to grow new leaves. I fertilized it weekly and, when the temperatures began to warm up, I removed the plastic cover. Eventually that plant went on to produce 74 tomatoes—many more than my undamaged plants. This year, I plan to repeat the "experiment"—strip a plant in early spring—and see whether that plant will be equally productive.

Andrew Shaffer
Houston,
Pennsylvania

Tomatoes from Cuttings

My family loves tomatoes. Each year we grow 10 to 12 varieties from seed, resulting in three to four dozen plants for us to transplant to the garden. But we always lose several of these precious seedlings to birds or cutworms—the top of the plant is severed so that only a stump remains in the ground.

We discovered that we can save these severed plants by rooting the tops. If the top is still in good condition, we remove the leaves around the bottom of the stem and place the cutting in a cup of water. In just about a week, new roots begin forming around the stem. We carefully replant the rooted plant back in the garden. For the first week or so, we keep the plant shaded and keep the soil around it moist. By the time the other plants start bearing, the restarted ones are nearly caught up.

Kathy Bagioni
Newington, Connecticut

Lattice Works for Southern Tomatoes

When the temperatures reach the mid-90s in mid-July here in Valdosta, Georgia, tomatoes usually decide to call it quits for the summer, regardless of variety. I've discovered that the secret to growing tomatoes in these conditions is giving the plants some protection. Now my tomatoes keep producing much longer—no splitting, cracking, or sunscald!

To protect my plants, I erected a lattice structure that keeps out the hottest rays of the sun but allows enough sunlight so the plants keep growing. For my 10 × 12-foot shelter, I put up six poles (made from 10-foot 2 × 4s) on the two long sides of the tomato patch, three poles per side. Then I laid two 12-foot 1 × 3s across the top and nailed them to the poles. Lattice is available in several sizes at many lumberyards and home centers—for my project. I used three 4 × 8-foot pieces. I laid the pieces of lattice across the top and secured them with nails. The entire structure cost about $40.

Clark Edwards
Valdosta, Georgia

GARDENER TO GARDENER

Tomatoes from Small Spaces

I've developed a strategy for raising lots of tomatoes in a small space, while making compost at the same time. This method works well in any garden, but I especially recommend it to those with limited space.

I start by taking pieces of 5-foot-wide woven fence wire and cutting them into 8-foot lengths that, when folded, form 30-inch-diameter cylinders. In fall, I set two of these cylinders in my garden, using steel posts to secure them in place. I then fill the cylinders with leaves, grass clippings, and other organic materials to a height of about 4 feet and allow the materials to compost over the winter.

After danger of frost has passed in spring, I set out my tomatoes, spacing four plants evenly around the outside of each cylinder, close to the wire. As the plants grow, I tie them to the cages, leaving the first sucker that flowers on the plants, but removing all others, so I end up with two main stems on each plant. At least once a week, I water the center of the cylinders—that way, the water runs through the compost to feed the roots of the plants.

When the plants reach the top of the cylinders, I attach a second set of cylinders to the tops of the first ones. The plants eventually reach 10 to 12 feet tall—I usually need a stepladder to harvest the last of the crop! Last year I picked 480 ripe tomatoes from just eight plants. When the season ends, I tear down the cages and spread the compost on my garden.

Cecil Prosser
Altamont, Illinois

High Stakes for Tomatoes

Here's a new take on companion planting: tomatoes and sunflowers. Last year I planted some 'Giant Greystripe' sunflower seeds too thickly and had to thin the seedlings. Because I hate to throw anything away, I decided to plant the extras outside each of my tomato cages and tie them to the cages. It was the best thing I ever did for both the sunflowers and tomatoes. By the end of the summer, the tomatoes had outgrown the cages but didn't fall over because they were supported by the sunflowers.

Ruth E. Smith
Sellersville, Pennsylvania

Hay Bale Tomato System

A coldframe made from hay bales has helped me grow great tomatoes. Since I've been using this system, I haven't had to water, fertilize, or stake my plants! Here's what I do:

First, I form a long, narrow rectangular cold frame by making two rows of hay bales—about 18 inches apart—the entire length of my tomato row. I also connect both ends. In spring, I set the young tomato plants inside the hay bale bed, and then I lay plastic or old storm windows across the top, supported by the bales.

When lawn-mowing season gets underway, I gather up our grass clippings and place them in the bed around the plants, as thick as possible, without covering the plants. When the weather turns warm, I raise and eventually remove the covers, and I continue to mulch the plants with more clippings. As the plants grow tall, the bales act as supports for the vines, keeping the fruits high, dry, and disease-free!

Edgar Wagner
Montgomery, Pennsylvania

GARDENER TO GARDENER

Short Season Tomato Bounty

Do you have a short season or cool summer temps that make it difficult to grow tomatoes? If so, you should try my "undercover" system. Here in Santa Fe (7,000 feet altitude), frosts linger till late May and return by early September. Summer nighttime temps often drop down into the 50s. So anyone who wants to pick ripe tomatoes must set their plants out early (before the last frost) and protect them from cool nights, from spring through fall. The key to my success has been using Wallo'Water to keep plants toasty warm—all season long. The protected plants grow faster, bear earlier and produce higher-quality tomatoes.

Here's what I do: About May 20 (three weeks before our last frost), I set up the 6-foot-long stakes I use to support the Wallo'Water. Using a 1-foot-square template as a guide, I drive one stake into the soil at each of the four corners of the template. To keep the stakes from collapsing inward, I wire two wooden crosspieces to the tops of the stakes where they're out of the way, secure them, and plant my tomatoes. I then slip an empty Wallo'Water over each plant and its group of four stakes, and fill it with water.

As the plants grow, I wrap twine around the stakes to control the plants. And in fall, when frost threatens, I wrap bubble wrap or black plastic garbage bags over groups of two to four plants and their Wallo'Water—this provides enough extra warmth to ripen a few more of the green tomatoes.

Dolores L. Pierson
Santa Fe, New Mexico

Attachable Plant Tags

In the past when I transplanted my tomatoes to the garden, I placed the tag with the name of each variety into the soil around the plant. But by the end of the season, I could barely see the label let alone read it, because of all the foliage and dirt covering it. Now I take those same plastic tags, and punch a hole into one end with a standard hole puncher. Then I cut a slit into the hole from one side of the tag. The tag slips easily onto the cage at the top, where it doesn't get dirty. It's also the perfect solution for those of us with bad backs.

Richard Darby
Merlin, Oregon

Black Plastic Bags for the North

The erratic temps, high winds, and short season of Michigan's Upper Peninsula make it tough to get ripe tomatoes. You have to get the seedlings out early—before the last frost. Trouble was I couldn't find any plant protectors that worked well in my tough climate. Finally, I discovered one that did: black plastic and tomato cages.

Simply place a wire cage over the tomato seedling for support; then cut the bottom out of a black plastic garbage bag and slip it over the cage. Mound a little soil around the bottom of the bag to hold it in place; then secure the top of the bag to the cage with clothespins. Leave the top of the bag open to let in air and sunlight. When the temperatures stabilize, remove the plastic, but leave the cage to support the plant.

Neil Moran
Sault Ste. Marie,
Michigan

Chapter 6

June

Solving Problems: Organic Pest Control

Don't get hysterical about bugs. A successful garden will have plenty of good insects and a few bad ones, too. And just because some bugs are nibbling at your plants, you shouldn't conclude that they're killing or even hurting them. Picking off some troublesome bugs by hand is often all that a small garden needs.

—*Robert Rodale*

Sometime this month, insect pests will discover your garden. Your plants can tolerate some damage. Besides, beneficial insects like lady beetles and parasitic wasps should soon arrive to keep the pests in check. However, when flower, fruit, or veggie damage seems to be getting out of hand, you can control pests effectively with nonchemical methods, such as hand-picking, using sticky traps, and applying *Bacillus thuringiensis*.

Also, remember that healthy plants are much less susceptible to insects. To keep your plants strong and healthy, fertilize them with compost. Applying just ½ to 1 inch of it to your beds will help to keep plants healthy. Test your soil every few years to find out whether you need to add an amendment and, if so, how much. Provide plenty of water. If your garden hasn't been getting at least an inch of rain each week, you'll need to water to ensure that plants don't suffer from drought stress. Usually, taking these steps is all that's needed. But for the times when you need special solutions to problems, read on.

Gardener's To-Do List—June

**If you don't know what USDA hardiness zone you live in,
check the map on page 246 to find out.**

Zone 3

☐ Harden-off, and then set out transplants of melons, tomatoes, peppers, cucumbers, eggplant, and squash.

☐ For a continuous crop of lettuce, radishes, and spinach, sow more seeds midmonth.

☐ Fertilize and water any potted vegetables regularly.

☐ Enjoy asparagus right in the garden—even uncooked, it's delicious.

☐ Plant tender fuchsias, begonias, dahlias, and asters.

Zone 4

☐ Early in the month, finish setting out transplants of vegetables and flowers.

☐ Plant seeds of warm weather crops, such as melons and squash.

☐ Sow more lettuce so you can keep harvesting leaves, even after the first crop goes to seed.

☐ Near month's end, plant cilantro to put in the salsa you'll make later.

☐ Stake or cage tomatoes and other veggies and flowers that tend to sprawl.

☐ Plant asters and pansies for fall bloom.

☐ Spray *Bacillis thuringiensis* on brassicas as soon as you spot cabbage moths.

☐ Mulch beds as soon as the soil warms up.

Zone 5

☐ Stake dahlias and gladiolas when you plant them to keep from damaging their roots later in the season.

☐ Pinch back foliage ends of mums, ½ inch every 2 weeks.

☐ Fertilize roses now: To supply potassium, whiz banana peels in a blender, then plop the stuff beneath the mulch around your roses.

☐ Harvest daily from asparagus plants in patches at least 3 years old.

☐ For autumn harvest, plant bush beans, brussels sprouts, and late cabbage.

☐ Spray tomato plants with compost tea (made by steeping an old pillowcase filled with compost in a bucket of water) to prevent diseases.

Zone 6

☐ Place supports for lanky perennials.

☐ Pinch back chrysanthemums to keep them bushy—½ inch from the growing tips, every 2 weeks until the middle of next month.

☐ Prune spring-flowering shrubs after they've finished blooming.

☐ Cage tomatoes, peppers, and eggplant.

☐ Replace finished lettuce with okra or a late crop of summer squash.

☐ Plant a few more runs of corn, beans, and cucumbers.

☐ Plant sweet potato slips early in the month.

☐ Inventory seeds for the fall garden.

Zone 7

- ☐ Plant pole, lima, and bush beans; winter squash; and luffa gourds.
- ☐ Start seeds for fall crops of eggplants, peppers, and tomatoes to set out in July.
- ☐ Cut and dry thyme, oregano, and mint.
- ☐ Replace bolted lettuce with corn, malabar spinach (*Basella alba*), winged beans (*Psophocarpus tertragonolobus*), and southern peas.
- ☐ Trap slugs with containers of fresh beer.
- ☐ Mulch to reduce weeds and watering later.

Zone 8

- ☐ Plant mums, balsam, cockscomb, wax begonias, salvia, dusty miller, blanket flower (*Gaillardia* spp.), geraniums, marigolds, verbena, and vinca (*Catharanthus roseus*).
- ☐ Plant bulbs or tubers of iris, cannas, water lilies, dahlias, and daylilies.
- ☐ Replenish mulches around plants to keep weeds down and conserve moisture.
- ☐ Plant a cover crop in vacant beds.
- ☐ Plant mustard and turnips for harvesting tender, baby leaves.
- ☐ Work compost into beds, then plant fall crops of peppers and eggplant.
- ☐ Direct seed collards and tomatoes for fall harvest.
- ☐ Continue planting cantaloupes, corn, cucumbers, okra, peanuts, southern peas, summer squash, sweet potatoes, and bush beans.
- ☐ Thin fruit trees early in the month; mulch root area with a thin layer of compost, topped with 3 inches of organic mulch.

Zone 9

- ☐ Look for slow-moving bugs in the cool of the morning; hand-pick them, then dust below the plants with diatomaceous earth (be sure to use a dust mask so you don't inhale the dust) and/or spray plants with insecticidal soap.
- ☐ Last chance to plant sweet potato slips and peanuts this season.
- ☐ Continue planting sweet corn in small blocks, every 2 weeks for continuous harvest through fall.
- ☐ Start more zinnias, marigolds, and sunflowers to replenish tired flowers in late summer.
- ☐ Water plants in the morning so they don't become susceptible to fungus and insect infestation.
- ☐ Plant more heat-tolerant veggies: Replace spinach with Swiss chard and potatoes with taro (*Colocasia esculenta*).

Zone 10

- ☐ Feed fast-growing bananas and summer-flowering perennials, such as hibiscus and ixora, with compost to prepare them for upcoming bloom.
- ☐ Clean up debris beneath mangoes to prevent anthracnose disease; for bad infections, spray with copper solution.
- ☐ Prune cassia trees, royal poinciana, bougainvillea, and jasmine after they bloom.
- ☐ Prune tropical fruits after the harvest this month.
- ☐ Kill pests and disease in vacant beds by covering moist soil with clear plastic for several weeks.

Secrets of Professional Pest Spotters

Now that summer's here, all sorts of insects are discovering the wonderful world of your garden—some are beneficial and will consume your problem pests. But some are bad bugs that want to beat you to the harvest. Where are these insect pests hiding and what can you do to stop them?

Here's the inside track on spotting and managing the most troublesome garden pests, courtesy of several professional insect scouts.

Tomato Trashers

The primary pest of summer tomatoes is the tomato hornworm—a big, bright green worm with diagonal white stripes on its sides. Tomato hornworms eat mostly leaves. Mother moths usually scatter their eggs on the undersides of leaves, where they are hidden from predators, parasites, and angry tomato growers.

In its caterpillar stage, though, the hornworm is often the target of tiny braconid wasps, a type of parasitic wasp. You'll know that the braconid has parasitized the hornworm if you spot little white bumps that resemble grains of rice stuck on the hornworm—these are the wasp's pupae. If you find braconid-beseiged hornworms, don't kill them! Move them away from your best plants and feed them tomato leaves until the baby wasps emerge. The hornworm will die and all those new wasps will seek out more caterpillar pests to parasitize.

If you don't see signs of beneficial wasps helping to control the hornworms, good old hand-picking is your best control, says Geoff Zehnder, Ph.D., an entomology professor and extension specialist at Auburn University in Alabama. To find hornworms early, check often around the center of each tomato plant, where the vegetation is thickest. If you see dark green pebble-like frass (hornworm manure), follow the trail! It will probably lead you to a fat, juicy hornworm. Pick it off and drown it in a jar of soapy water.

TOMATO HORNWORM

Bean Bandits

The Mexican bean beetle is ⅓ inch long and mustard brown in color with black spots. It lays clusters of 40 to 60 yellow eggs on the undersides of bean leaves. When scouting for these eggs, start with the lowest leaves and move upward. Hand-pick and destroy any you find. But if you see single (not clustered) eggs that are pale orange and opaque, leave them alone! They probably belong to the bean beetle's beneficial cousin, the aphid-eating lady beetle.

If you overlook some Mexican bean beetle eggs, you won't miss signs of the larvae. "The damage caused by these larvae really stands out," says Ricardo Bessin, extension entomologist at the University of Kentucky. He suggests you "flip over the leaf, pick off the larvae, and throw them in some soapy water."

Luckily, time is on your side—it takes several weeks for Mexican bean beetle damage to become serious. "Beans can take a lot of defoliation—up to 30 to 40 percent—before yield is hurt," explains Bessin. Weekly monitoring and hand-picking should keep things under control.

In the upper Midwest, the bean leaf beetle is an even more serious bean pest, says Purdue entomologist Rick Foster. Look for ¼-inch reddish or yellow beetles, sometimes with "spots on their backs, but always with a black triangle behind their heads where their wings come together," Foster says. Bean leaf beetles make clean round holes as they feed on both the upper and lower sides of bean leaves and pods. Sometimes more damage is done below the ground—when larvae feed on roots, the plants appear weak and chronically thirsty.

If you spot bean leaf beetles, sneak out early on a cool morning, lay a sheet beneath your beans, shake the beetles down, then drown them in soapy water. In warm weather, you can nab them in a net. For a severe problem, treat the soil with beneficial nematodes—microscopic animals sold in garden supply stores or catalogs—which will feed on the beetle larvae. The nematodes only work in warm weather. To apply them, mix them in water and spray the solution on the soil where the pests are feeding, then wash them in with more water. Because bright light kills nematodes, you should do this very early in the morning or in the evening when light levels are low.

A Winning Combination

"Everybody should plant rows of potatoes alternating with wide rows of bush beans," says Sally Cunningham, author of *Great Garden Companions*. If you try this, you'll find that you have fewer problems with both Mexican bean beetles and Colorado potato beetles. Because of the mix of plants, "the pests just don't find their targets," Sally explains.

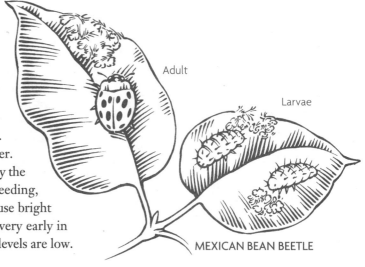

Adult

Larvae

MEXICAN BEAN BEETLE

Stick It to Whiteflies

I have an easy way to control whiteflies on tomatoes. First, I support the plants with 6-foot stakes. Then I put an empty 48-ounce juice can (one end removed) on top of the stake and slip a yellow plastic bag (the kind our newspaper comes in on rainy days) over the can. Next I smear the entire bag with Vaseline. Attracted to the color yellow, whiteflies land on the bag and become stuck! It isn't long before the entire bag is covered with them. When the flies get too thick, I remove the bag, replace it with another, and cover that with Vaseline. It takes four cans—and two or three bag replacements per can—to protect my 20 × 30-foot plot from whiteflies for an entire season. If you don't have yellow plastic bags, just paint the cans yellow and slip clear plastic bags over them.

*Katherine Jarmusik
Brooklyn, Ohio*

Potato Pests

The worst insect pest of the potato is the Colorado potato beetle. Both adults and larvae will chew on the plant's leaves and stems. Early detection of these yellowish orange and black striped monsters is essential to the health of your plant—and your garden. First, keep an eye out for adult beetles that will fly or walk into your patch in spring, after overwintering nearby. "Look on the edges of your garden," advises Judy Hough-Goldstein, chairperson of entomology and applied ecology at the University of Delaware. Catch and smash any adult beetles you see, then look for their eggs.

Colorado potato beetles lay clusters of eggs, almost always on the undersides of leaves. If conditions are favorable, there are up to three egg-laying cycles each year. "The average number of eggs per cluster is 30, and they're a very bright yellow," explains Hough-Goldstein. "Crush them when you find them." (Wear gloves for this duty.)

If you miss a bunch of eggs and hungry larvae start eating your potato leaves, generously spray your potatoes with *Bacillus thuringiensis* var. *san diego* (sold as M-One and Safer Leaf Beetle Attack). Apply it right after the eggs hatch, when the larvae are most vulnerable. Cover the plants well with the spray. As the larvae ingest the *Bacillus thuringiensis*, they'll quickly lose the ability to eat and will soon die. Hand-pick or shake any adult survivors off of the potato plants, and drop them in a container of soapy water (to drown them).

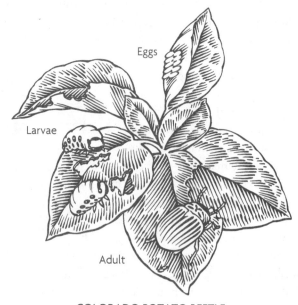

COLORADO POTATO BEETLE

If the edges of potato foliage look scorched and curled, you're probably looking at leafhopper damage. Plants may have tipburn (called "hopper burn" on potatoes) and white spots on the undersides of their leaves. Both leafhopper larvae and adults suck juices from potato leaves, but you won't see larvae because they're hidden inside the leaves. You can spot the fast moving adults, though. The ¼-inch-long, gray (or green- or red-striped) insects will hop 1 foot high and 2 feet sideways when disturbed. Hold one hand over the foliage and shake the plant with your other hand, and you might catch one.

Once you've confirmed their presence, suck them up with a handheld vacuum, spray your plants with a dilute solution of garlic and hot pepper (test the spray first on a small area before dousing the entire plant) or use insecticidal soap.

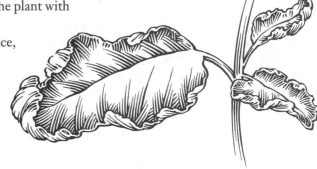

POTATO LEAFHOPPER
AND LEAF DAMAGE

Cucurbit Crashers

Cucumber beetles are the squash and cucumber counterparts to bean leaf beetles. They are free-flying, ¼ inch long, and yellow with three black stripes down their back (the striped cucumber beetle) or 12 black spots (the spotted cucumber beetle). Both feed on several other vegetables, including peas.

Typically, you'll find the striped cucumber beetle inside the flowers of the cucumber and squash. Hold a butterfly net over a dry squash or cucumber flower on a hot day to nab the flying beetles.

If you see large numbers of adult beetles throughout your garden, you may want to dig up a struggling plant and immerse the roots in water to check for beetle larvae. As with bean beetle larvae, beneficial nematodes are an effective remedy.

The spotted cucumber beetle prefers to chew ragged holes in squash and cucumber leaves. On a cool day, spray the plants with water to get the beetles moving, then pick them off by hand. Another tactic against both kinds of beetles is to hide your crop among other vegetables, making it harder for cucumber beetles to find. Beetle numbers in mixed plantings can be ten times lower than in cucurbit-only plantings. Try planting wilt- and mosaic-resistant varieties.

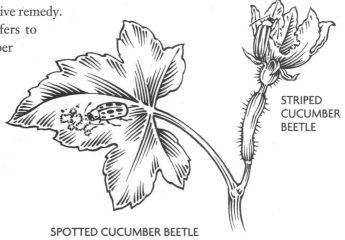

STRIPED
CUCUMBER
BEETLE

SPOTTED CUCUMBER BEETLE

Cover Your Cukes

If you know that cucumber beetles are a persistent pest in your area, you can protect your cucumbers and other squash-family crops, at least while they're young, with floating row covers. Tuck floating row covers over your planting hills before the seedlings even emerge. Leave some slack so the plants have room to enlarge, but weight the edges of the row covers down securely with boards or soil so beetles can sneak underneath. Once the plants start to blossom, you'll have to remove the row covers for pollination, but you'll certainly have prevented damage to the plants when they're young.

Compared to the beetles, the ⅝-inch-long, shield-shaped squash bugs are a piece of cake to control. "Getting rid of the adults early in the season can make a big difference," says Scott Fargo, Ph.D., former associate professor of fruit and vegetable insects at Oklahoma State University. "Hand-pick them early in the morning, when they can't move fast."

Begin your scouting for the pests when your squash and pumpkin plants are still seedlings. Check plants daily, and you'll eventually encounter some squash bug egg clusters. They'll be bronze to brown, laid in neat groups, on either side of the leaves. (Check the main stems of summer-sown cucumber seedlings, too.) "Roll your thumb over the top of the egg mass to crack and dislodge them," advises Fargo.

Or, if you live in a cool climate, lay boards between squash rows. "The bugs seek shelter under the boards at night," explains Fargo. In the morning, lift up the boards, scrape scrape off the bugs, and destroy.

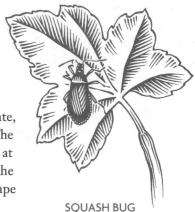

SQUASH BUG

Cabbage Culprits

Like tomatoes, the prime enemies of brassicas (cabbage, broccoli, brussels sprouts, cauliflower, and collards) are moth larvae (caterpillars). Marty Spellman, who scouts cabbage pests in research and farm fields in Delaware, says the prime pests in order are: imported cabbageworm, cabbage looper, and diamondback moth.

Imported cabbageworms lay a single, yellowish, speck-sized egg on the underside of a leaf. The tiny light green, dome-shaped eggs of cabbage loopers are so hard to spot that Spellman doesn't even try to find them. "Besides, at the egg stage both kinds of eggs have a lot of natural predators," he adds.

But when the eggs hatch, the larvae of both cabbage pests demand attention. When you see irregular holes along leaf edges or pebbles of dark green frass, start looking for larvae. Imported cabbageworm larvae are light green with light yellow stripes and up to 1 inch long— look for them along leaf veins, in crevices between leaves, and in plants' curled centers. Cabbage loopers give themselves away by rearing up their little inchworm bodies when disturbed. They have more white stripes than imported cabbageworms and no legs in the midsections of their bodies. To find either pest, Spellman recommends inspecting plants in the brightest part of the day and when the plants are dry.

Imported cabbageworms and cabbage loopers can be found all over the plant, but you're likely to find the ¼-inch-long, greenish yellow larvae of the diamondback moth in the center of a plant. If you see pale meandering trails on the undersides of leaves, you're probably seeing the feeding paths of newly hatched diamondback caterpillars. They rasp off tissue from the undersides of leaves, but they don't eat all the way through the leaf.

For all three caterpillar pests, spray leaf undersides with *Bacillus thuringiensis* var. *kurstaki*, a naturally occurring pathogen that kills only caterpillars. (For more information, see page 103.)

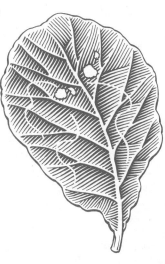

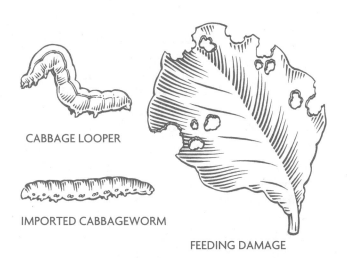

CABBAGE LOOPER

IMPORTED CABBAGEWORM

FEEDING DAMAGE

DIAMONDBACK MOTH LARVA
AND FEEDING DAMAGE

Color Tricks

One interesting tactic for saving cabbage from imported cabbageworms is to try planting red-leaved varieties. Studies indicate that imported cabbageworms don't like them as much as they like green-leaved varieties. (And maybe the gardener can see the pest better and will hand-pick it more often!) It's also true that cabbages that have smoother leaves are attacked less frequently than crinkly leaved varieties.

To protect your precious green cabbage varieties, try an old-fashioned technique of turning the leaves of broccoli, cauliflower, cabbage, and brussels sprouts white by dusting them with white flour while the leaves of the plant are damp. (It sticks best after a rain or on the morning dew.) It's reputed that the caterpillars will eat the flour, the flour will cause the caterpillars to retain water, they'll get bloated, and then they'll die.

Get Beneficials to Protect Your Garden

Invite your neighborhood beneficials to a banquet in your garden! They're insects that help gardeners by killing pest insects, eliminating the need for chemical pesticides. And you won't even need to buy them, because some of the most effective beneficials are already in your garden. The trick is attracting more of them and getting them to hang around. Just like other creatures, beneficial insects need food, water, and shelter. If your garden supplies these, beneficial insects will be glad to patrol your beds for you.

Plant Umbels for Wasps

"Probably the most beneficial insects taht can be attracted into an area are the parasitic wasps," says Robert N. Wiedenmann, Ph.D., biological control expert with the Illinois Natural History Survey at the University of Illinois. Parasitic wasps lay eggs inside a specific pest—usually some type of caterpillar—while the pest is very young. The wasps are so tiny (less than ¼ inch long) you probably won't see them, but as the wasps' eggs develop inside the caterpillars, the pests die.

You can attract parasitic wasps by growing plants from which they can drink nectar, a sugary fluid secreted by flowers. If they are well-fed by such flowers, the adult wasps will live longer and lay more eggs. Because the wasps are so small, they need to visit small flowers so that they can easily reach the nectar. But don't be fooled—some plants that look like they have big flowers actually have some of the smallest. Take dill, for example. When a dill plant gets to be a couple feet high, it forms buds that open into flat, lacy, greenish yellow heads a couple inches across. Each head is actually a cluster of many little flowers. And because the nectar in these tiny flowers is so easy for them to reach, tiny wasps will flock to them.

Dill has lots of relatives with similar flowers, called umbels, because their compound flowers are umbrella shaped. The umbel family includes fennel, caraway, parsley, coriander, carrots, and parsnips. (The last two bloom in their second year, if you don't harvest the roots!) The wildflower Queen Anne's lace (really a wild carrot) attracts beneficials, too.

And while all umbels are good for attracting parasitic wasps, dill seems to be the best. The 'Bouquet' variety of dill is especially good because each plant sends up multiple stalks with lots of flower heads in just 45 days. And if you deadhead it, it continues to bloom.

Another parasitic beneficial is the tachinid fly, which resembles the common housefly. Tachinids are especially good at controlling European corn borers (see table on page 90). You can bring them into your garden by growing members of the mint family—the tiny mint flowers are very attractive to tachinids.

Aim for Constant Bloom

The trick to attracting parasitic wasps into your garden is to always have some of these flowers in bloom. One way to do that is to start seeds of dill and coriander in April and then again in May, for bloom throughout the summer. Plant some again in late July or August for September bloom.

It's also important to have something blooming in your garden as early as possible to attract these helpful wasps. Early flowering sweet alyssum attracts all kinds of hungry beneficials waking up from their long winter's nap. Look for started plants of alyssum already growing at your local nursery. Or, start the seeds indoors yourself extra early so your seedlings will be big enough to transplant outside just before your last spring frost.

If you left any carrots, parsley, or parsnips in your garden over winter, don't pull them up—let them grow and flower! (These biennials wait until their second year to bloom.) Or, if any of these roots have begun to sprout in your refrigerator, don't compost them—try planting them into your garden soil. They just might surprise you by sending up beneficial-attracting blooms.

Plant Daisies for Predators

While parasitic wasps visit those little flowers for nectar, predatory insects also will stop by to eat their pollen. Such insects include lady beetles, lacewings, hover flies, ground beetles, rove beetles, tiger beetles, minute pirate bugs, and beneficial stink bugs.

Most of these predator insects are much larger than those tiny parasitic wasps and so are able to visit larger flowers for food. Many of their favorites are members of the composite (daisy) family. Their flowers are composed of a circle of petals around an easy-to-reach pollen-laden center. Members include chamomile, purple coneflowers, and sunflowers.

The very best strategy may be to plant a mix of all of these flowers that attract beneficials. That way, as each pest appears, you'll be sure to have some type of beneficial parasite or predator in your garden to take care of the problem.

Best Beneficials to Buy

You'll get the best value for your money by ordering insects that will stay in your garden after you release them—those that are wingless or that haven't yet earned their wings.

Lacewing larvae. Control aphids. Suppliers sell as eggs; larvae hang around for about 3 weeks.

Predatory mites. Control spider mites. Release at the first sign of pest mites.

Lady beetles. Control aphids. Release in the evening after rain, or water before you release. Release two beetles for each 3 square feet of garden.

Pediobius foveolatus. Controls Mexican bean beetles. Release when the first generation of Mexican bean beetle larvae are about half grown.

20 Common Garden Pests

Pest	Range	Description	Diet	Symptoms	Controls
Aphids (Aphidae family)	Throughout North America	Less than $\frac{1}{10}$ inch long, pear-shaped and soft-bodied; green, yellow, red, brown, or black; usually wingless.	Tender growth of almost any plant	Aphids suck sap, causing discolored, curled leaves.	Plant virus-resistant cool-season crops as early as possible; use reflective mulch; rinse affected plants with strong spray of water; use insecticidal soap; encourage beneficials.
Cabbage Maggot (*Delia radicum*)	Throughout North America	Adult flies are $\frac{1}{4}$ inch long and ash gray, with black stripes on thorax. White eggs laid at base of plants. Larva is white, $\frac{1}{4}$ inch long, and pointed at front.	Cabbage, cauliflower, broccoli, brussels sprouts, radish, turnip	Larvae tunnel into roots, causing plant to wilt and develop disease.	Row covers; use 6-inch collars around the base of transplants; pull up and destroy infected plants; remove wild mustard weeds, which can harbor the pest.
Cabbageworms (*Pieris* spp.)	Throughout North America	Adults are white cabbage butterflies with dark spots on their wings. Larvae are light green caterpillars.	Brassicas, including cabbage, broccoli, cauliflower, kale, and brussels sprouts	Larvae chew holes in leaves and heads of plants, leaving trails of dark frass.	Plant fast-maturing varieties and harvest by late spring. Also, row covers; *Bacillus thuringiensis;* hand-pick worms; clean up spent plants.
Carrot Rust Fly (*Psila rosae*)	Common in cooler regions of North America	Adult flies are less than $\frac{1}{5}$ inch long, with dark bodies and yellow-orange eyes and legs. They lay tiny eggs on the soil at the base of plants. Larvae are up to $\frac{1}{4}$ inch long and light colored.	Roots of carrots, parsnips, and celery	Larvae make tunnels in lower two-thirds of root. (Tunnels in upper part of carrot roots are caused by another pest, the carrot weevil.)	Delay planting until 2 weeks before last frost date; row covers; garden cleanup; beneficial nematodes.
Colorado Potato Beetle (*Leptinotarsa decemlineata*)	Throughout North America	Beetles are $\frac{3}{8}$ inch long and black and yellow in color. Larvae are plump and red with black head and black spots.	Potatoes, tomatoes, and eggplant	Beetles and larvae chew holes in foliage; can eventually kill plants.	Choose fast-maturing varieties; mulch potatoes 2 to 3 inches deep with straw; hand-pick beetles; apply *Bacillus thuringiensis* var. *tenebriosis* (formerly *san diego*); locate potato planting site away from wooded areas.

Pest	Range	Description	Diet	Symptoms	Controls
Corn Earworm (*Heliothis zea*)	Throughout North America	Light grayish brown moths lay pale yellow eggs on corn silk. Larvae are light green, pink, yellow, or tan striped, 1½-inch-long caterpillars.	Corn, peppers, lettuce, tomatoes, beans	Damage to corn tassels, silk, and tips of ears; deep, watery cavities in tomatoes and peppers; damage to bean leaves, flowers, and pods	Plant susceptible crops early. Spray with *Bacillus thuringiensis*; use a medicine dropper to apply mineral oil or parasitic nematodes to corn silk, 3 to 7 days after silks appear.
Cucumber Beetles (*Acalymma* spp. and *Diabrotica* spp.)	Most of North America	Striped cucumber beetles are ¼ inch long and yellow with three black stripes. Spotted cucumber beetles are slightly larger, yellowish green, and have 12 black spots. Both lay single tiny yellow-orange eggs at the base of plants. Larvae are ½ inch long, have six legs, and are white with brownish ends.	Striped cucumber beetles feed on cucumbers, squash, pumpkins, melons, and other plants. Spotted cucumber beetles feed on cucumbers, squash, pumpkins, melons, corn, peanuts, beans, flowers, and grains.	Chewing on foliage gives leaves a lacelike appearance. Plants can suddenly collapse from bacterial wilt disease spread by striped cucumber beetle.	Row covers; hand-picking; wilt-resistant varieties ('Marketmore' and 'County Fair' cucumber; 'Ambrosia', and 'Athena' muskmelon). Parasitic nematodes control larvae of spotted cucumber beetles on corn (called corn rootworms).
Cutworms (Noctuidae family)	Throughout North America	Adults are brown or gray moths with a 1½-inch wingspan. Larvae are 1½ inches long and gray to dull brown—they curl up at rest or when disturbed.	Vegetable and flower seedlings, especially corn and tomatoes	Tender shoots are severed at ground level, usually at night.	Mix *Bacillus thuringiensis* with bran and molasses and apply to soil before planting; use cardboard or metal collars around transplant stems; remove weeds and debris before planting. Nematodes and tachinid flies parasitize the larvae.
Diamondback Moth (*Plutella xylostella*)	Throughout North America	Adult moth has ¾-inch wingspan; gray wings have white diamond shapes when folded. Eggs are pale green or yellow. Larvae are ⅓ inch long and pale yellowish green and have a distinctive *V* at the rear end. Cocoons are attached to leaves or litter.	Cabbage, kale, broccoli, cauliflower	Larvae chew small holes in leaves and buds.	Row covers; *Bacillus thuringiensis*; resistant varieties ('Mammoth Red Rock' cabbage, 'Southern Giant Curled' mustard, 'Michihli' Chinese cabbage, 'Seven Top' turnips, 'Vates' kale, 'Cherry Belle', 'White Icicle', and 'Champion' radishes). Lacewings will eat moth eggs.

(*continued on page 92*)

20 Common Garden Pests—Continued

Pest	Range	Description	Diet	Symptoms	Controls
European Corn Borer (*Ostrinia nubilalis*)	Northern and central United States and southern Canada	Adult female moth is 1 inch long and creamy, yellowish brown; male moth is slightly smaller and reddish brown. Larvae: light gray, light pink.	Corn, peppers, and beans	Chewed corn leaves and tassels; interior damage to corn whorl leaves, stems and ears; holes in peppers and beans	*Bacillus thuringiensis*; locate entrance hole and remove borers by hand; destroy stalks after harvest. Beneficials: braconid wasp and tachinid flies
Flea Beetle (Chrysomelidae family)	Throughout North America	Beetles are 1/10 inch long and black to blue-black and jump quickly when disturbed. Some have spots or faint markings. Larvae are 3/4-inch, thin white worms.	Eggplant, potatoes, sweet potatoes, tomatoes, and brassicas	Adults chew small, round holes in leaves; heavy feeding can kill seedlings. Larvae feed on roots and leave brown snaky markings on potatoes and sweet potatoes.	Plant susceptible crops 2 weeks later than usual; plant only large transplants; row covers; white, sticky traps; intercropping; good garden sanitation. Beneficials: wasps and nematodes
Grasshopper (Locustidae family)	Throughout North America, but especially the western plains	Adult and young grasshoppers are 3/4 to 2 inches long and pale yellow brown to black, with long rear legs and wings.	Almost all plants	Can defoliate and kill plants	Row covers; *Nosema locustae;* keep vegetation low around plantings, leave lush growth away from the garden to attract hoppers there.
Japanese Beetle (*Popillia japonica*)	The United States west to Mississippi River and Iowa; occasionally in California	Adults are 1/2-inch-long, metallic blue-green beetles with bronze wing covers. Larvae are C-shaped, 3/4-inch-long, off-white grubs with brown heads.	Adults are a serious pest of many flower, fruit, and vegetable crops, skeletonizing foliage and flowers. Larvae feed on grass roots.	Adults chew on flowers and skeletonized leaves. Leaves wilt and drop. Prefer plants in full sun and may completely defoliate them.	Hand-pick beetles, organize community-wide trapping program to reduce adults. Allow lawn to dry out in midsummer. Apply parasitic nematodes to sod.
May/June Beetles (*Phyllophaga* spp.)	Throughout North America	Adults are nearly 1 inch long and shiny reddish brown or black. Ten-lined beetle, found mostly in the West, has stripes. Larvae are 1 1/2-inch-long, C-shaped white grubs, with brownish heads. Larvae can live in soil up to 3 years.	Grubs are a serious pest of lawn grass; also feed on roots of strawberries, corn, and potatoes. Adults feed on leaves of deciduous trees.	Plants become stressed (wilt, turn brown) and can die of root damage.	Apply parasitic nematodes. Encourage beneficial parasitic wasps by growing Queen Anne's lace, dill, or parsley and allowing them to flower.

Pest	Range	Description	Diet	Symptoms	Controls
Mealybug (Pseudoccidae family)	Widespread outdoors, more so indoors	Soft-bodied, oval insects, less than ⅛ inch long, with a white powdery wax. Large colonies. Egg masses: white, cottony	Ornamentals, houseplants, avocados, and fruits	Insects suck sap, causing leaves to droop.	Inspect and quarantine new houseplants. Remove white spots with a cotton swab dipped in rubbing alcohol. Beneficials: lady beetles and green lacewings
Mexican Bean Beetle (*Epilachna varivestis*)	Most of the East, Southwest, and north to Nebraska	Adults are ¼ inch long and coppery brown with 16 small black spots. Eggs are orange-yellow and are found under leaves. Larvae are ⅓ inch long, orange, and spiney.	All kinds of beans	Larvae feed on leaf tissues, leaving lacelike appearance.	Row covers; hand-picking; horticultural oil spray; early maturing varieties. Beneficials: parasitic wasps, some lady beetles, and spined soldier bugs
Spider Mite (Tetranychidae family)	Outdoors in warm, dry West; indoors in greenhouses everywhere	Very tiny members of the spider family; Two-spotted spider mite has two dark spots on its back; overwintering adult is orange.	Beans, grapes, strawberries, almonds, peppers, cucurbits, greenhouse plants, and houseplants	Leaves yellow and drop. Ornamental palm leaves turn dusty gray. Mites also spin fine webs.	Keep plants humid; spray water on undersides of leaves, weekly; insecticidal soap. Predator mites, lacewings, and ladybeetles eat mites.
Squash Bug (*Anasa tristis*)	Throughout North America	Adults grow to ½ inch, are brownish yellow to black, and emit an odor when crushed. Nymphs begin pale green, then turn dark with white powder.	Cucumber, melon, pumpkin, squash, and gourd	As insects feed, leaves droop, darken, and die.	Row covers; hand-picking; clean up garden debris. The tachinid fly can kill up to 90% of the squash bugs in an area; attract them with dill and parsley.
Squash Vine Borer (*Melittia cucurbitae*)	Throughout United States and Canada east of the Rocky Mountains	Adult moth has red body and metallic, olive brown wings. Reddish eggs laid at base of stem. Larvae are 1-inch caterpillars with brown heads.	Squash, gourds, cucumbers, and melons	Larvae bore into vines near base, causing vines to wilt. Telltale piles of frass outside holes of squash vines.	Continually wipe away eggs before they hatch; spray insecticidal soap; clean up garden debris. Inject stems with *Bacillus thuringiensis* or beneficial nematodes.
Whiteflies (Aleyrodidae family)	Common on houseplants and in greenhouses everywhere; outdoors in the South	Adults are ¹⁄₂₀-inch-long, white, mothlike insects covered with white powdery wax. Oval nymphs eventually the size of a pencil point. Adults fly up when disturbed.	Fruits, vegetables, and flowers; especially in greenhouses. Outdoors: potatoes, sweet potatoes, squash, tomatoes	Adults and nymphs suck juices from plants. Diseases or viruses may be transmitted, causing leaves to yellow or look dried.	Insecticidal soap; horticultural oil; vacuum leaves; yellow sticky traps. For sweet potato whitefly, allow garden to be empty for 2 weeks before successive plantings.

Outsmart Bean Beetles

Here's a timing trick from Master Gardener Fran Evans of Hamburg, New York, to reduce Mexican bean beetles. The precise timing will vary by region, but the principle applies everywhere you can grow beans. Plant snap beans as early as possible. Then pick the beans until the crop begins to dwindle. Pull up all of the crop or mow it down and till it into the soil by the third or fourth week in July. "About 90 to 95 percent of the time, weather cooperating, you'll be finished with the beans before the Mexican bean beetles can lay eggs and establish themselves," says Fran.

Use Timed Plantings to Beat Pests

You can prevent many pest problems by timing your plantings carefully. Here are 10 pernicious pests that can be foiled just by changing the planting time of their veggie targets.

Aphids

Aphids suck the life out of many garden plants with their piercing mouth parts and often transmit viruses. Plants that have curled, distorted leaves or that are covered with sticky honeydew are likely aphid infested.

If these tiny, pear-shaped pests have plagued cool-season crops like lettuce and broccoli in the past, start them indoors early so you can set out good-sized transplants 4 to 5 weeks before your last frost date. In other words, start lettuce and other quick-growers indoors 8 weeks before your last frost. Start broccoli, cauliflower, and other slower-growers indoors 12 weeks before your last frost date. Early planting will help to minimize the aphid-caused virus problems. And don't let cool-season crops linger as the weather warms up—pull them up and replace them before they bolt and become an aphid breeding ground.

Here's a fall-planting tip for gardeners in the South: Wait 2 to 4 weeks after most of the cotton is harvested before you plant your fall crops of lettuce and spinach. Aphids love to feed on cotton and they will search for their next meal right after the crop is harvested. By setting out fall transplants after the cotton is harvested, your crops will be less likely to be troubled by hungry aphids.

Cabbage Looper

To prevent these light green caterpillars from chewing up your cabbage and other brassicas, choose quick-to-mature varieties that you can harvest by late spring or early summer—before the first wave of loopers hits. Start the seeds indoors, 12 weeks before the last frost date, then transplant them to the garden when they are 7 to 8 weeks old.

To avoid fall crop damage, start transplants indoors about 18 weeks before your first fall frost so you can put 7- to 8-week-old plants in the garden about 10 weeks before your first fall frost.

Cabbage Maggot

When brassica crops wilt unexplainably, the most likely cause is cabbage maggots. The first wave of these little root and stem feeders in early spring usually is the most destructive. By delaying planting until after yellow rocket (wild mustard) has bloomed, you can avoid these maggots.

If there are no brassicas (such as the yellow rocket) in the garden for the adult flies to lay their eggs around (which eventually hatch into those root-eating maggots), they'll move on. If you're direct-seeding your crops, wait a week after the peak of yellow rocket's bloom to sow. Wait about two weeks if you're putting out transplants.

Corn Earworm

One of the most destructive sweet corn pests in North America, corn earworms chew through the silks and into the tips of the ears, making an unattractive mess. Plant early maturing varieties as early as possible to avoid sharing your sweet corn. Corn planted much after that will probably be silking just as the corn earworm moths are looking to lay their eggs.

Consider starting your corn indoors in peat pots and then trans-planting, pots and all. Corn won't germinate in cool soil, but it grows just fine in it. Or cover your corn bed with clear plastic for a week or two before planting to warm up the soil and speed germination.

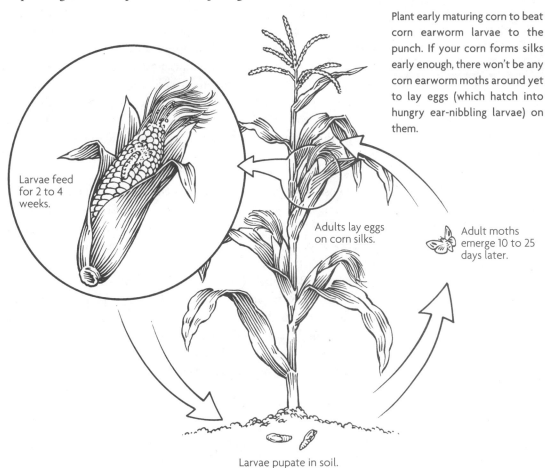

Plant early maturing corn to beat corn earworm larvae to the punch. If your corn forms silks early enough, there won't be any corn earworm moths around yet to lay eggs (which hatch into hungry ear-nibbling larvae) on them.

Larvae feed for 2 to 4 weeks.

Adults lay eggs on corn silks.

Adult moths emerge 10 to 25 days later.

Larvae pupate in soil.

Mix Up
Flea Beetles

Timing planting right helps prevent flea beetle problems, and so can interplanting, says Sally Cunningham, author of *Great Garden Companions*. "One year I planted eggplants all alone in one area, and in another place, I interspersed eggplants with marigolds and basil," Sally says. "Guess what? The solo eggplants were full of holes, but the other ones were camouflaged enough that they squeaked through the season undiscovered! Flea beetles are easily confused."

Colorado Potato Beetle

Simply delay planting your potatoes for 7 to 14 days after the usual planting date in your area and you could defeat this defoliating pest! Adult Colorado potato beetles (CPBs) emerge from the soil in early spring. If they don't find any potato plants, they move on.

Just be sure you plant fast-maturing varieties so the tubers will be a good size when the second generation of beetles comes around in midsummer. A little leaf chewing by the beetles (who only eat the aboveground growth) at that point won't hurt your harvest.

To further protect your late-planted potatoes, build a trench trap when you plant your potatoes. Surround the bed with a 16-inch-deep vertical-sided trench lined with black plastic—the beetles will crawl to get to the potatoes, fall into the trench, and won't be able to escape.

European Corn Borer

Another sweet corn menace that can be outwitted by planting time! This caterpillar is a pest in northern and central United States and southern Canada. Bent tassels or broken, chewed leaves and ears with holes in them are the signs of European corn borer damage.

To combat this corn pest, you must avoid very early and very late corn plantings. For most, that means planting corn about 2 weeks after the last frost date (or as close as possible to the midpoint of your corn-planting season). If your corn usually suffers from both of these pests, choose the timing that will beat your most troublesome pest.

Flea Beetles

These jumpy little black beetles chew small, rounded holes in the leaves of many vegetables (such as brassicas, eggplant, potatoes, and tomatoes). They sometimes kill seedlings. If you've had flea beetle problems in previous years, avoid them by delaying the planting of susceptible crops by a week or two beyond normal planting times for your region.

Because flea beetles overwinter as adults, full-size adult beetles appear in your garden very early in the season. If food isn't there when the adults emerge, they won't lay their eggs in the garden, which means fewer problems later in the season. When you do plant, use transplants rather than direct-seeding your crops whenever possible—transplants can withstand flea beetle damage much better than young sprouts.

Pepper Weevil

Found across the south from California to Florida, these weevils puncture immature peppers with their sharp snouts and lay eggs in the peppers. The eggs hatch and the larvae feed on the peppers, causing them to turn yellow, get misshapen, and/or drop from the plant.

But you won't witness such horrors in your garden if you start your peppers indoors and plant them outside as early as possible (about 2 weeks after the last frost), before the weevil population builds up. At the end of the season, get your peppers out of the garden as fast as possible, too—allowing the plants to linger will invite future weevil problems.

Root Knot Nematodes

These tiny, eel-like creatures feed on the roots of almost all veggies and are especially problematic in the warm, sandy soils of southern and coastal regions. Affected plants look weak and sickly. Their roots are covered with galls (knobby, abnormal growths).

Early spring planting (at least 4 weeks before the last frost) is the key to getting a good harvest of crops like lettuce, broccoli, and cauliflower, because nematodes don't become active until soil temperatures are fairly warm. Start your broccoli and cauliflower indoors about 12 weeks before the last frost and plant them outdoors when they are 7 to 8 weeks old. Lettuce and other greens should be started 8 weeks before the last frost and planted outside when the seedlings are 4 weeks old.

In fall, reverse this timing: Delay lettuce, spinach, and other cool-season plantings until the soil temperature drops below 64°F. Choose nematode-resistant varieties when you can.

Sweet Potato Whitefly

These tiny, sap-sucking insects attack vegetables just about everywhere in North America. When infested plants are disturbed, clouds of adult whiteflies fly into the air. The greatest damage to plants is done by the viruses they transmit.

Allowing 2 weeks between crops is an effective way to control whiteflies. After you harvest one crop, clean up and allow a 2-week fallow period before planting the next. Sweet potato whiteflies will have nothing to feed on during those 2 weeks and will either die off or move on.

In the fall, a simple delay in planting will help. In the South, wait about 2 weeks after the late summer cotton harvest to avoid the masses of whiteflies that were feeding on the cotton.

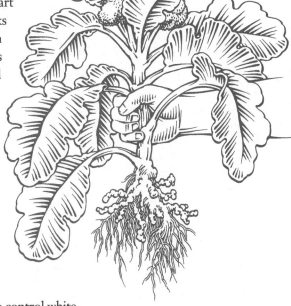

When root knot nematodes invade the roots of vegetable crops like broccoli, knobbly galls form. Root growth is poor, so plants are sickly. Planting early and late can help crops escape nematode damage.

Plant Slug-Defying Plants

There are some plants that slugs usually pass up. Try these plants, which are generally considered slug-resistant: agapanthus, ageratum, alliums, amsonia, anemone, artemisia, arum, asters, astilbes, bee balms (*Monarda* spp.), begonias, bellflowers (*Campanula* spp.), black-eyed Susan (*Rudbeckia hirta*), bleeding heart (*Dicentra* spp.), calendulas, candytuft (*Iberis sempervirens*), columbines (*Aquilegia* spp.), coral bells (*Heuchera* spp.), coreopsis, cosmos, daffodils, daylilies, edging lobelia (*Lobelia erinus*), evening primrose (*Oenothera* spp.), ferns, foxglove, goat's beard (*Aruncus* spp.), hellebores, impatiens, lamb's ears (*Stachys* spp.), lavender, mints, nasturtiums, oregano, penstemons, peonies, pinks (*Dianthus* spp.), poppies, rosemary, sage, santolina, sedums, Solomon's seal (*Polygonatum* spp.), sunflowers, sweet alyssum, thymes, violets, wild ginger (*Asarum* spp.), yarrows, and zonal geraniums (*Pelargonium × hortorum*).

14 Ways to Negate Slugs

The slug may be the most inspiring garden creature of all. What other living thing evokes so much . . . creativity? Here are a few techniques gardeners use to stop slugs (and snails) in their slimy tracks!

1. Stage a slug exposé. Pull back your garden mulch, and expose the slugs hiding therein to light. When you find them, destroy them.

2. Shed more light on the subject. If your slug situation is severe, consider cutting down a tree or two to let in more sunlight. The soil will be drier, as a result, and less hospitable to slugs.

3. Leave 'em high and dry. Raised beds drain quickly after rainstorms, further reducing your garden's attractiveness to slugs.

4. Bag 'em. Go on a search and destroy mission after dusk. Arm yourself with a flashlight and inspect garden foliage. When you uncover a slug, pluck it, and drop it into a bucket of soapy water.

5. Draw a line in the sand. Soft-bodied slugs can't stand the sharpness of crushed eggshells. Spread out a batch of shells, let them dry for 24 hours, crush them up, then encircle the plants you want to protect.

6. Test the chestnut hull theory. If you've ever stepped on a sharp and spiny chestnut hull in your bare feet, you know why this works. When you see the hulls in late summer, collect and save some, then use them the following spring and summer as a barrier or mulch.

7. Enlist a skeleton crew. Diatomaceous earth is made up of fossilized diatom (plantlike creatures) remains. Although it's powdery, it's microscopically sharp. Surrounding your plant with it will deter marauding slugs. The earth will also kill other insect pests such as aphids, beetles, and earwigs. (*Note:* Wear a dust mask when you work with this or any dusty garden product. You may have to reapply after heavy rains.) You can buy diatomaceous earth at garden centers.

8. Pave your paths. Lay wooden planks in your garden pathways. They'll become a favorite hangout for slugs as soon as the sun rises. Simply lift the boards in the morning, scrape them off, and then dispose.

9. Open a sluggy Starbucks! Dump coffee grounds on your beds—slugs seem to be repelled by the stuff we love. The grounds will add nitrogen to the soil as they decompose

10. Give 'em a brew or two. Use the tried and true slug bait— beer! Bury shallow containers (like empty margarine tubs and tuna cans) up to their rims in the soil, then fill them with beer. Slugs will dive in and drown. Refresh the beer every 24 to 48 hours—studies reveal that only fresh beer attracts the slimers.

11. *Edge your beds with copper.* An interesting chemical reaction occurs when slugs come in contact with copper barriers. You can buy copper sheets or use premade products.

12. *Set a trap.* If you lack the time or inclination to make your own slug traps, you can buy them. The Snailer is a green plastic pen that you fill with a barley-and-rice-yeast bait and bury up to its lid near plants you want to protect.

13. *Stop slugs with Slug Stop!* To protect individual prized plants, try Slug Stop, a coconut oil slug-repelling product. Just put two rings of it around seedlings, hostas, or any other plant you want to protect, and you'll create a barrier that slugs won't cross. Slug Stop, manufactured by Concern, is available at many garden centers.

14. *Get ducks.* Ducks are remarkably effective at controlling slugs and grubs. Besides their pest-controlling activities, ducks supply manure daily, are unusual and sometimes affectionate pets, and if you have a female, will lay large fresh eggs. You can put the eggshells in the compost pile or scatter them right on the garden.

> ## Quack Grass Foils Slugs
>
> According to USDA research, quack grass (*Agropyron repens*)—a perennial weed—is toxic to slugs. To protect established perennials from slugs, try surrounding plants with dry, finely chopped quack grass. Use just 2 ounces of dried quack grass per 10 square feet—more than that could inhibit the growth of plants.
>
> To protect tender seedlings, mix dried quack grass with beer and bran, then run the resulting "dough" through a grinder to create pellets. Air dry the pellets, then spread them around the perimeter of seedling beds. Slugs will go for the beer and end up eating the toxic grass. *Note:* Don't plant this weed on your property—instead, harvest it from a nearby field.

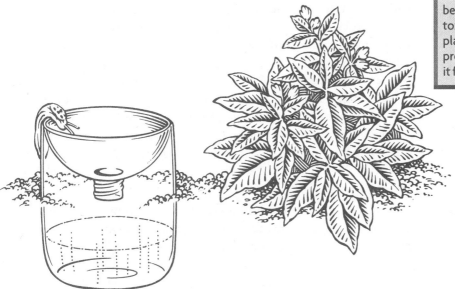

A 1-liter plastic soda bottle makes a cheap, effective slug trap that practically disappears amid your flowers. Pour ½ cup of beer into the trap and watch the slimy pests slide down the funnel to meet their fate.

Curtains for Your Garden

Many gardeners use row covers to protect plants from pests or to coax a few extra weeks from the growing season in spring and fall. But sunlight and handling both take their toll on the fabric, and the material eventually rips and tears. Instead of buying new row covers every year, I simply use curtains— either sheer nylon or polyester-type. They'll last for years in the garden.

If you don't have your own old curtains, you can buy some for pennies at a secondhand store. They come in many lengths (up to 8 feet) and widths. To cover a large area, I just overlap a pair of curtains and clip them together with clothespins. To provide extra warmth, I use a double layer. Yellow, ecru, and white colored sheers have all worked well for me.

Vonnie Kovacic
Gibsons, British Columbia

A Compendium of Organic Pest-Control Techniques

Once you've identified the troublemakers, you can control them with an assortment of organic pest-control products. Here are the major types of products you can buy and how to use them to your best advantage.

Floating Row Covers

This translucent, white, porous polyester fabric acts as an insect barrier, while letting in up to 80 percent of the available light. You can buy either lightweight or heavyweight types—you'll want to use the lighter one for controlling pests in summer, because it will keep out bugs without cooking your plants. The heavier reportedly traps more warmth and so is better for season extending.

The material is sold by the yard, generally in rolls 4 to 8 feet wide. You cut it to the length you need, then drape it over PVC or metal hoops, attach it to wooden supporting frames, wrap it around wire tomato cages, or simply lay it directly on your crops like a blanket. *Important:* You must secure the edges of the row cover with soil, U-shaped pins (either commercial or homemade ones crafted from wire coat hangers), boards, bricks, or rocks.

Use floating row covers as temporary barriers to get plants past critical stages, such as when they are seedlings or while the pest you are deterring is most active. Of course, you could keep the crop covered for its entire life span. Although, this isn't a good option for crops that require insect pollination.

Pests controlled: Row covers are especially useful against mobile pests, including cabbage moths (imported cabbageworms), Colorado potato beetles, most aphids, Mexican bean beetles, flea beetles, squash bugs, and tomato hornworms. Combine row covers with crop rotation if you're dealing with pests that overwinter in the soil.

Pheromone Traps

Many insects produce powerful smells called pheromones that they use to lure the opposite sex. Scientists have duplicated several of these scents and used them to bait special traps for luring the target insect. But because these "sex" traps attract mostly male insects, they aren't very effective controls. They're useful as an early warning that a particular pest is moving into your area. When you find the first pests in your trap, you know it's time to launch your control strategies, such as putting your row covers in position and applying *Bacillus thuringiensis*.

Pests monitored: Pheromone lures are available for diamondback moths and moths that produce armyworms, cabbage loopers, corn earworms, European corn borers, tomato pinworms, and cutworms.

Sticky Traps

These traps—a rigid material of a particular color that's coated with a sticky substance—are used to catch insects that are attracted to that color. To be effective, the traps must be clean and sticky. Also, use at least one trap (hung at plant height and close to the plant) every 3 to 5 feet.

You can buy packaged sticky traps or make them yourself. To make your own, use any rigid material of the right color (for colors, see below) or that you can spray paint. Cut the material to size (4 × 6-inch rectangles are the standard), and if needed, paint it the correct color. Cover the trap with a plastic bag or clingy plastic wrap, then coat it with a sticky substance, such as Tangle-Trap. (The plastic wrap makes cleanup easy—when your trap is covered with bugs, just remove the plastic and rewrap the trap with a new piece of plastic. Then coat it with more sticky stuff.)

For cucumber beetles, use a mobile trap: Wrap clingy plastic food wrap around a white bucket or other large object, then coat the plastic with Tangle-Trap. Carry the bucket along the rows of vines, shaking and brushing the plants as you go. The beetles will fly up and stick to the traps.

Pests controlled: Yellow traps attract whiteflies, fruit flies, male winged scales, leafhoppers, fungus gnats, midges, male winged mealybugs and leafminers, thrips, psyllids, and winged aphids. White traps lure whiteflies, plant bugs, cucumber beetles, and flea beetles. Light blue traps attract flower thrips, and red spheres attract the flies whose eggs hatch into apple maggots.

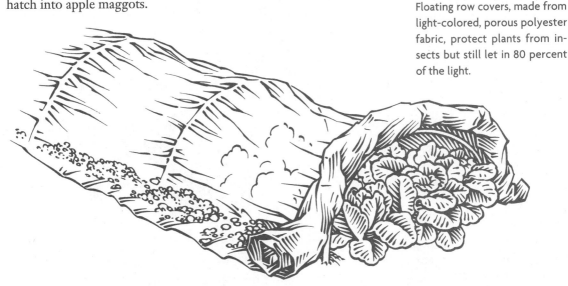

Floating row covers, made from light-colored, porous polyester fabric, protect plants from insects but still let in 80 percent of the light.

Better Maggot Trap

I did an experiment to try to catch apple maggot flies on our apple tree so they wouldn't make worms in our apples. My experiment worked better than a similar type of trap my mom bought.

First, buy an apple from the store. Then coat it with Tangle-Trap (or other sticky insect-trap coating). Attach a string to the apple and hang it in the apple tree. Within days, lots of bugs will be stuck to the apple. Using a real apple attracts twice as many maggot flies as the plastic traps you can buy. And the apple doesn't rot because the coating protects it.

Kurt Fredrickson (age 6)
Sacramento, California

Insecticidal Soap

Insecticidal soap contains unsaturated long-chain fatty acids (derived from animal fats) that dissolve the cuticle (skin) of insects. Insecticidal soap sprays are commercially formulated products sold specifically for insect control. (Don't confuse these products with herbicidal soaps, which kill vegetation instead of insects, or household soaps, which are detergents.)

To be effective, the insecticidal soap must come in contact with the insects while it's still liquid—it has no effect after it dries on the plants. Spray only on pests and try to avoid hitting beneficial insects with the spray. *Caution:* Insecticidal soap can burn some plant leaves. Test each type of plant before spraying the entire plant. Spray a few leaves, then wait 48 hours. If there's no damage, go ahead and spray the entire plant. Don't spray on hot days, and rinse the soap off your plants after a few hours if the plants are receiving a lot of sunshine. If you have hard water, mix the soap with distilled water to help the soap dissolve.

Pests controlled: Insecticidal soap sprays are highly effective against mites, aphids, whiteflies, and other soft-bodied insects as well as the softer nymph stages of some tough-bodied bugs.

Make your own sticky trap, or buy a commercial sticky trap. Then, hang it near your houseplants to attract pesky whiteflies.

Oil Sprays

Oil sprays work by suffocating pests. To be effective, the oil spray must hit the pest directly.

Use "dormant" oils to kill insect pest eggs and disease spores on the bare branches of trees and shrubs during the dormant season. To treat growing plants, use a lighter-weight, more refined horticultural oil (called "summer," "supreme," or "superior" oil). Lighter oils evaporate more quickly than dormant oils and are less likely to damage plants.

To avoid plant damage, don't spray any plants suffering from moisture stress. Also, don't spray on very hot days. Test the spray on just a few leaves before you spray the entire plant. Wait 48 hours to make sure no leaf spotting or discoloration occurs.

To minimize potential harm to beneficial insects, limit your spraying to small areas where you can see pests lurking, and leave a couple of unsprayed "refuges" for any good bugs you can't see. Protect nectar-feeding beneficials by not spraying during peak flowering times and by not spraying blossoms. Spray early in the morning, before bees become active. And if you plan to release beneficials, do it after you apply the oil spray.

Pests controlled: Use horticultural oils to combat aphids, mites, beetles, leaf miners, caterpillars, thrips, leafhoppers, and whiteflies.

Bacillus Thuringiensis

Bacillus thuringiensis (BT) is a naturally occurring bacterium found in the soil. There are many different types, and some can be used to kill a specific insect or class of insects. When a target insect takes a bite of a plant sprayed with the type of BT the insect is sensitive to, the insect gets infected and stops feeding. Inside the insect, the bacterium releases a protein that causes the pest to die within a few days.

Each type of BT is effective only on one specific insect (or group) and only on insects that actually eat it. However, that doesn't mean you can spray it indiscriminately. For example, the type that kills cabbage loopers can also kill the caterpillars of the beautiful butterflies you're trying to attract to your garden. Only spray it when you know you have a pest problem, and only spray the pest-infested plants.

Most formulations of this bacterium are sold as a liquid or wettable powder that you dilute with water and then spray on the plants you want to protect. Some products are sold in the form of dusts or granules that you dust directly on plants.

Because BT usually is effective only against the nonadult stage of pest insects, you must time applications carefully. As soon as you spot the pest larvae, thoroughly coat the affected plants with the spray or

---

GARDENER TO GARDENER

Reusable Cutworm Collars

Tired of creating new cutworm collars for your seedlings every year, only to have birds or wind relocate them elsewhere? Here's my solution: Cut off the top and bottom third from 20-ounce plastic soda bottles (save the top sections to make cloches to protect baby plants). Cut the middle section in half, then press the resulting plastic collars into the soil around your seedlings. Birds don't steal them and the wind won't blow them away. At season's end, collect the collars, hose them off, and store them to use the following year.

Stevie Allen
Columbia,
South Carolina

Nematode Sauna

In Florida, root-knot nematodes are among the worst garden problems, but I've developed a solar strategy to defeat them, without using chemicals. My plan begins with a crop rotation scheme that leaves a few beds completely empty between rotations. On one of the hottest summer days, I thoroughly water the empty beds, then cover them with clear plastic. After a week or so, I roll back the plastic, water again, then replace the plastic. Two weeks later, I roll back the plastic and give the beds a final watering, then allow them to bake and steam in the hot sun for 2 weeks more—until I feel certain that all the nematodes in the soil have been eradicated. At this point, I remove the plastic and add a 2-inch layer of compost to the bed to reintroduce beneficial microorganisms. Since I began using this method, nematode problems have been nonexistent, and my vegetable plants grow strong and lush.

Frank Bareuther
Williston, Florida

dust. (For corn pests, deposit a little of the granular product into the whorl or on the corn silk.) Avoid spraying during the heat of day. BT breaks down a day or two after spraying, so you may need to reapply it if you're up against a severe infestation. As with all sprays or dusts, always wear goggles and a mask to prevent contact with the bacterium when you apply it to your plants (there have been a few reports of allergic reactions in those who have inhaled it).

Pests controlled: The most common strain of the bacterium—BT var. *kurstaki* (sometimes called BT var. *berliner*)—kills hundreds of different kinds of caterpillars, including cabbage loopers, tomato hornworms, cabbageworms, corn earworms, European corn borers, and squash vine borers. BT var. *tenebrionis* (a new name—until recently this one was called BT var. *san diego*) kills Colorado potato beetles.

Parasitic Nematodes

Don't confuse these beneficial nematodes with destructive root-knot nematodes. Once inside a pest, parasitic nematodes release bacteria that kills the insect host within a day or two. Although these good nematodes occur naturally in the soil, there usually aren't enough of them in one place to control pests that have gotten out of hand in your garden. But you can buy them by the billions for use as a living—and organic, safe, and nontoxic—form of pest control.

The dormant nematodes are shipped in a moist medium, which you mix with water when you're ready to apply. When you receive a shipment, put the sealed container in your refrigerator until you are ready to use it (the nematodes will keep there for about 4 months). Try to use them as soon as possible, though; their effectiveness declines the longer you store them. Once the nematodes are mixed with water for application, they are only viable for a very short time. Use all of the mix within a few hours—don't try to save any of it.

Apply the nematodes to moist soil that has reached a temperature of at least 60°F, either in the evening or when it's overcast, at a rate of about 23 million nematodes per 1,000 square feet. Thoroughly cover the area with the nematodes, then water them in. *Exception:* If your pest is in the plant (the squash vine borer or corn earworm), mix up a small batch of nematodes and use a garden syringe or eyedropper to apply them just inside the tip of the ear of corn, or into the squash vine entrance holes.

Pests controlled: Nematodes attack and invade armyworms, corn earworms, squash vine borers, soil-dwelling grubs (including Japanese beetle larvae), weevils, root maggots, and cutworms (in their soil-dwelling stages).

GARDENER TO GARDENER

Support Your Local Spiders

Here's a simple way to encourage spiders to help keep insect pests from getting out of hand. After reading that farmers in the Far East build straw "huts" for spiders, I began doing the same in my garden to encourage spiders to overwinter there. (Spiders typically spend the winter in dead leaves, tufts of dormant grass, or other insulated spots.)

You can make your own winter spider shelters from unchopped corn stalks, straw, and/or leaves. In late summer, pile up the materials in a sunny spot away from foot traffic. Then, whenever you see a spider, transfer it to the pile. I also capture house spiders and let them go into the pile; you can do this all winter—just use a pitchfork to create an entryway through the snow and into the pile. In the spring, young spiders will naturally colonize the pile as well. Now that I provide housing for my spiders, I have many more of them patrolling pests in my garden.

Eileen McHenry
Brighton, Michigan

Brassica-Allium Alliance

I had almost given up growing members of the brassica family (such as broccoli, cauliflower, cabbage, and brussels sprouts). The cabbage loopers and cabbageworms were so bad that I seemed to spend all my spare time dusting the crops with Bacillus thuringiensis. No more, thanks to intercropping. I planted double rows of onions along both sides of my cauliflower, in effect surrounding the cauliflower with onions. Normally, I'd find at least four loopers or worms per plant. This year I had only four worms total on 20 plants.

Jeff Davis
Charlotte, North Carolina

Stinger Trap

Whenever we venture outdoors with food or drink during the summer, we're plagued by hordes of yellow jackets. So I designed an inexpensive trap to intercept these stinging pests on their way to our picnic:

Cut 1½ inches off the top of a large plastic soda bottle. Then cut a hole into the bottom of a similar bottle, just large enough to push the top section from the first bottle through it. Fill the trap with a small amount of sugar water or soda. Yellow jackets crawl inside, but can't get out. To hang the trap (outside, but away from family activity), attach string or wire to the top of the trap.

Dave Hunt
Philadelphia, Pennsylvania

Mastering Cutworm Collars

The easiest way to prevent cutworm attacks is to use the cardboard cylinders from rolls of toilet paper. Cut each tube in half and slip the resulting collars over transplants, pushing the tubes about an inch into the soil.

If the transplant's leaves are too large to slip through the collar, you can use popsicle sticks instead: Place the stick at the base of the plant, right up against the stem. Cutworms must completely encircle a stem to eat it, and the stick keeps them from doing this. Toothpicks work too, but I prefer popsicle sticks because you can label them with the plant variety name.

Joan Richards
Falls Church, Virginia

GARDENER TO GARDENER

Melons Rinds to the Rescue

Normally, our annual outbreak of boxelder bugs is merely a nuisance and not a garden problem. But during droughts, these bugs become voracious spoilers of ripening fruits and vegetables, including cucumbers, strawberries, summer squash, tomatoes, and peppers. Last year, my fruits were literally covered with them, no matter how often I hand-picked them or applied soap sprays.

What finally saved my garden were melon and cuke rinds. Because the bugs were piercing and sucking the contents of ripening fruits, I reasoned that they sought moisture more than anything else. By spreading the juicy rinds around my most vulnerable plants, I was able to lure away many of the bugs. Once or twice a day I carried a pail of soapy water with me to the garden and quickly dunked the bug-covered rinds into the pail; then I replaced the rinds in the garden to lure more bugs.

Susan Beasley
Reno, Nevada

Doggone Slugs

I believe that the slugs in my garden are the biggest anywhere. But I found a way to beat them. After giving our dog Shaggy his summer haircut, I left little piles of puppy hair on the ground, intending to compost them later. The next morning my daughter noticed something shiny all over the hair—slug slime! That gave me an idea. I decided to surround some of my slug-damaged seedlings with a bit of the hair. The next morning, the hair was covered with slime, but the seedlings were uneaten.

Birgit Ramsey
Hodges, South Carolina

Ode to a Slug

Oh, you slippery slimy fellow,
Gray or brown or spotted yellow,
Lounging in my lettuce bowers,
Skulking underneath my flowers,
You leave a telltale silvery scrawl
Wherever you crawl on walk and wall.
I don't begrudge your right to live
But even so I can't forgive
The wounds you leave on hapless plants
As you pursue your sustenance.
So mark you well these words I say
and be on guard both night and day:
Approach with caution and great fear
Each alluring plate of beer
And extra caution will serve you well
When you are near N-a-C-l;
For if your mischief you won't halt,
I'll slay you with my lethal salt!

Char Apgood
Organic Gardening reader

Chigger Cure

I've found that potato water (the liquid left in the pot after boiling potatoes) helps relieve the itch of chigger and mosquito bites. Of course, it isn't very convenient to stop and boil potatoes every time you get an itch, so I save the water whenever I make potatoes for dinner. I pour some into an ice cube tray, freeze it, then after the cubes are frozen solid, I put them in a labeled, 1-quart freezer bag. Rubbing one of those cubes onto the problem area really helps!

Mary Beth Burger
Durant, Oklahoma

GARDENER TO GARDENER

. . . Rinds, the Sequel

In the past we used watermelon and muskmelon rinds to lure "picnic" beetles (also known as sap beetles—small, black, hard-shelled pests that are attracted to ripening fruit) away from our raspberries. Besides making picnics miserable, picnic beetles can ruin a raspberry crop if you let them.

This year we improved our beetle traps by putting the melon rinds inside plastic bottles. I cut 2-inch slots near the bottoms of 2-gallon plastic bottles (lids still on) and then put several pieces of rind, a little water, and some liquid soap inside the slots. Two days after placing the bottles near the raspberry patch, the bottoms were covered with dead beetles. I tried both yellow and white jugs, and the white seemed more effective. Also, melon rinds made a better lure than either vinegar or beer. Note: Set the jugs a short distance away from the raspberries so the beetles will be lured to the rinds and not the berries.

Stan Durin
Steward, Illinois

Foil Slugs and Cutworms

I tried various methods for controlling slugs without success until I began making plant collars from aluminum foil. The foil thwarts both slugs and cutworms, providing excellent protection for my cabbage, pepper, and tomato seedlings. To make a foil plant collar, crumple a 6-inch square of foil until it feels slightly rough. Then make a single tear from the middle of one side of the foil to the center. Slip the stem of a plant through this slit, and then pinch the edges of the foil together to seal it around the plant stem, making sure that the edge of the foil near the stem flares away from the plant. That way, slugs can't reach it.

Anita Nielsen
Saugatuck, Michigan

Planting Cans

Years ago, a friend gave me some institutional size (#10) food cans. I made good use of them in my garden—they're perfect for protecting tomatoes and other plants from birds and cutworms. I removed the tops and bottoms of the cans, leaving only cylinders. When I set out plants into the garden, I push a can into the soil around each plant, angling the can to the south so the plants get more exposure to the sun. Since I started "planting cans," I haven't lost any plants to birds or cutworms. The cans also protect the young plants from the spring gales that are common here. Once the plants are off to a strong start, I remove the cans and store them until next year.

Jeannine Tucker
Danville, Illinois

Vacuum Away Pests

My best weapon against insect invaders is my Wet/Dry Shop-Vac. It works especially well for controlling aphids. Just lower the nozzle over the stem and the aphids vanish, leaving even the most delicate buds and foliage unharmed. It also works great for sucking up pill bugs that hide beneath pots. My chickens follow me around eagerly because they know what comes next: I empty the Shop-Vac in the chicken coop and they get a delicious dinner.

Jim Longacre
Freestone, California

GARDENER TO GARDENER

Multipurpose Molasses

When I moved to Colorado, I was faced with a grasshopper problem. I'd read about trapping them with a mixture of molasses and water. So I put ½ inch of molasses in the bottom of some old jars, then added water to make the jars about three-quarters full. After thoroughly mixing the molasses and water, I set the jars around my garden.

Well, I didn't catch any grasshoppers, but I did catch hundreds of earwigs. Last year I decided to try the traps again. This time I caught plenty of slugs as well as the earwigs. I didn't even bother to sink the jars into the soil—the earwigs and slugs crawled up the sides of the jars and dove right in. (Anyone have any good ideas for grasshoppers?)

Karen Norback
Lafayette, Colorado

Repel Root Maggots with Vinegar

For many years, I had trouble growing turnips. Usually the roots were small and badly damaged by maggots, even when I covered them with a floating row cover. Last year, I tried something new and finally succeeded.

As before, I sowed the seeds in a raised bed and covered the bed with a row cover. When the turnip seedlings had their second pair of true leaves, I sprinkled dolomitic lime lightly down each side of the plants. But this year, when the turnip roots looked like they were about 1½ inches in diameter, I put 1 tablespoon of white wine vinegar on the soil around each plant—being careful not to get the vinegar on the leaves. For the first time ever, I harvested 5 and 6 pound 'Marion Swede' turnips—absolutely free from maggot damage.

R. A. Meeks
Parksville,
British Columbia

Wireworm Collector

Wireworms were a big problem in our garden. We had so many that we often turned up more than 60 of them after just 15 minutes of digging. One day, while working on another project, we inadvertently found a solution.

We laid down a 3 × 3-foot piece of plywood for a painting project, and left the plywood on the ground for several days. When we finally lifted the wood, the side facing the grass was covered with click beetles (the adult form of the wireworms). So we drowned them all in a jar of soapy water, then moved the plywood to another area of the garden. When we checked it a couple of hours later, there were lots more beetles. Our best trapping to date yielded 64 beetles. We move this piece of plywood all over the yard, but it seems to work best in the sunshine—like us!

Deb & Ken Brodie
Richmond,
British Columbia

Chapter 7

July

High Summer:
Tending the Garden

Heavy is the green of fields,
heavy the trees with foliage hang,
drowsy the hum of bees.
In the thund'rous air: the crowded scents lie low.
Thro' tangle of weeds the river runneth slow.

—R. Bridges, "July," *The Remembering Garden*

W hy do you garden? Is it because you love to watch plants subtly change as they grow? Of course, you look forward to the beautiful color and sweet fragrance of a bed in full bloom and to the satisfaction of harvesting a basketful of delicious, tender vegetables—all grown without harmful chemicals. You're also undoubtedly eager to taste and savor your healthy summer harvest.

But there's much more to gardening than just the end result. There's also the pure pleasure of caring for your plants and your garden's soil—day by day. And that's what makes July so special. Yes, there are flowers to enjoy and veggies to harvest this month. But July is mostly about the simple act of taking care of your garden: watering, trimming dead blossoms, mulching, staking plants, tending your compost, pulling weeds, feeding plants, checking for pests—things that sometimes seem like chores but are actually much of the fun of gardening. After all, isn't any excuse to be in the garden a good one?

Gardener's To-Do List—July

**If you don't know what USDA hardiness zone you live in,
check the map on page 246 to find out.**

Zone 3

- [ ] Hill soil around potatoes and carrots to prevent green shoulders.
- [ ] Continue to stake and tie up tall plants, such as raspberries, roses, dahlias, and peas.
- [ ] Brighten your home with bunches of cut flowers.
- [ ] *Don't* cut grass lower than 2½ inches tall.
- [ ] Water lawns, trees, and shrubs in dry weather.
- [ ] Water annuals at least three times a week during periods of intense heat with no rain.
- [ ] Continue to add organic matter to the soil to retain moisture.
- [ ] If collecting seeds from mature plants, harvest only from the most healthy plants; label storage containers.

Zone 4

- [ ] Sow a second planting of green beans and summer squash.
- [ ] Use *Bacillus thuringiensis* on cabbageworms and other caterpillars.
- [ ] Divide crowded iris and daylily clumps.
- [ ] Spread mulch and irrigate to keep soil moist in dry weather.
- [ ] Set out transplants for fall crops of broccoli, cabbage, and cauliflower.
- [ ] Sow seeds of kale and Chinese cabbage for fall harvest.
- [ ] Add new perennials to flowerbeds.
- [ ] Remember that you can still plant potted or balled trees and shrubs, but water them well.

Zone 5

- [ ] Reseed dill and cilantro every few weeks for continuous harvest and/or to attract beneficials with blooms.
- [ ] Sow autumn peas; presoak seeds for a faster start.
- [ ] Harvest summer squash and cukes while they're still young and tender.
- [ ] Start seeds of Shasta daisies in a coldframe, where they'll overwinter until large enough to plant next spring.
- [ ] Harvest vegetables and flowers in the cool of the morning.
- [ ] Shear back tired-looking impatiens and petunias by half, then boost their regrowth by feeding with fish emulsion.

Zone 6

- [ ] Keep harvesting veggies and annual flowers regularly to keep plants producing.
- [ ] Plant last runs of bush beans and summer squash.
- [ ] For fall harvest, sow carrots, kale, beets, and chard for fall crops; also set out transplants of cabbage, cauliflower, and broccoli.
- [ ] Prune out old, woody raspberry and blackberry canes.
- [ ] Presprout and then sow, snap, shelling, or snow peas.

Zone 7

- [ ] Savor the last summer berries, then prune out old, dying canes.

- [ ] For fall-bearing berries, lightly feed newer canes with fish emulsion or compost tea, then mulch with straw.
- [ ] Harvest potatoes when leaves begin to die back.
- [ ] At month's end, sow seeds of collards, carrots, and rutabagas.
- [ ] To keep carrot seedbed moist, cover it with cloth or a board until seeds sprout.
- [ ] Stay on top of weeds.
- [ ] For bloom next year, start seeds of biennials, such as foxglove, hollyhock, evening primrose (*Oenothera* spp.), and lunaria.

Zone 8

- [ ] Set out fall tomatoes, peppers, and eggplants late this month.
- [ ] Sow Halloween pumpkins.
- [ ] Clean up the garden, then mulch the bare soil to conserve moisture.
- [ ] Mulch perennials and new trees with a layer of compost topped with bark mulch.
- [ ] Don't overstimulate dormant plants with unnecessary water or feeding; they'll resume growth when the weather cools.
- [ ] Tend the compost pile so it will be ready to work into the soil in preparation for fall planting.
- [ ] Set out ageratums, balsam (*Impatiens balsamina*), cockscomb, croton, feverfew, marigolds, petunias, wild blue phlox (*Phlox divaricata*), pinks (*Dianthus* spp.), portulaca and vinca (*Catharanthus roseus*).
- [ ] Add 2 to 3 inches of mulch to retain water.

Zone 9

- [ ] If foliage of midsummer-blooming roses begins to yellow, check soil pH—add peat or sulfur if it tests much above 7.

- [ ] Keep roses well watered to promote bloom into late fall.
- [ ] Early in the month, cover fruit trees with nets to protect fruit from birds.
- [ ] Spread compost on areas where you plan to grow fall veggies and flowers.
- [ ] For fall harvest, plant lettuce, carrots, beets, turnips, early beans, brassicas, and summer squash.
- [ ] Protect peppers, tomatoes, eggplants, and lettuce from sun scald by providing partial shade.
- [ ] Remember that you can still sow fast-blooming portulaca and sunflowers.
- [ ] Prune back chrysanthemums for bushier plants in fall.

Zone 10

- [ ] To grow roses here, be sure they're grafted onto '*Rosa × fortuniana*' rootstock, which is nematode- and disease-resistant.
- [ ] Feed roses with compost, fish emulsion, and seaweed spray.
- [ ] For late summer planting, start seeds of collards, okra, eggplant, southern peas, and heat-resistant tomatoes.
- [ ] Pay attention to gardenias, walking iris (*Neomarica caerulea*), and monstera (*Monstera deliciosa*)—all are susceptible to iron deficiencies and may need supplemental feedings.
- [ ] Harvest full-size monstera fruit, bring it indoors, and put it in a paper bag with an apple slice to finish ripening.
- [ ] Turfgrass is growing fast—mow high and never remove more than one-third at a time.
- [ ] When working outdoors in heat, take frequent breaks and drink plenty of water.

How and When to Water

Gardeners can't depend on Mother Nature to do all the watering, all the time. That's why watering your garden wisely (and conserving moisture once it gets in the soil) is a fundamental skill that your crops will thank you for cultivating.

What Type Is Your Soil?

How well your garden soil retains the water it receives depends on what type of soil you have. To keep things simple, we'll classify soils into three general types: sand, loam, and clay.

Sandy soils have lots of air spaces between the particles. This allows for good drainage—sometimes too good. Water moves through sandy soil fast, and the soil tends to dry out rapidly.

Clay soils are just the opposite. They have almost no air spaces between particles and drain very poorly. Clay absorbs water slowly but once wet, holds lots of water (often too much).

Loam is the middle ground between sand and clay. It absorbs water well and dries out at a nice moderate rate.

But no matter what type of soil you have, the key to keeping water in your garden is compost, compost, compost. Compost helps improve any soil by acting like a moisture-retaining wick. Every shovelful of that rich organic matter you add to the garden boosts your soil's ability to hold water.

Keep in mind that you'll have to apply more—not less—water to a garden high in organic matter to wet the soil to the depth you want. But because the soil holds more water, your garden may be able to go longer between waterings.

How to Watch for Water Stress

When plants are chronically underwatered, they experience water stress—a more serious situation than simply wilting a bit during the heat of the day. A plant that gets a little too hot usually recovers when the day cools off, but plants still drooping in the morning or late evening need water fast! (Some waxy-leaved plants like cabbage, onions, and garlic don't show water stress as readily as plants like peas, lettuce, and spinach do, so water them very carefully for signs of water stress.)

Water-stressed plants can have leaves that are smaller than normal. The edges of those leaves may turn brown, and the flowers and fruits will be delayed or drop from the plant. Water stress also reduces the quality of the produce—for example, your cucumbers may be small and misshapen; tomatoes may develop blossom-end rot; and salad crops and celery may have tough fibers. (*Note:* Water-logged soil causes plants to exhibit many of the same symptoms.)

When Water Is Critical

Moist soil is essential for seed germination and seedling growth. Try to set your young transplants in the garden on cloudy days or in the evening. And always water your seedlings when you set them out.

Once plants pass the seedling stage, essential watering times vary from crop to crop. Sweet corn needs an abundant supply when the silks and tassels are forming. Tomatoes, cucumbers, and squash are especially thirsty when they're flowering and when their fruit starts developing.

On the other hand, there are times when it's necessary to cut back on watering. Most muskmelons will taste better and have better quality if you start to cut back on water 7 to 10 days before harvest. And onions cure faster and store better if you hold off the water after they reach maximum bulb size and about half the leaves have fallen over. For pumpkins and winter squash, you want to dry the vine up before harvesting.

One thing to remember if you have to ration water: Certain plants can take drought better than others. Deeply rooted melons are somewhat tolerant to such stress, as are asparagus and beets. Tomatoes and brassicas are semitolerant. But don't deny a drink to sensitive celery, strawberries, lettuce (especially head lettuce), cucumbers, squash, and peppers.

To deliver water right to plant roots, set up a soda bottle watering reservoir (*left*) or stick a length of perforated PVC pipe (*right*) next to the rootball of a young tree.

When to Water

Water in the morning or in the evening, but never during the heat of the day, during which time you waste the water because it evaporates quickly.

Water in the morning if you garden in a humid climate or are watering plants that are prone to foliage diseases. If you water in the evening, the soil and the plants will stay wet most of the night, promoting disease and fungal growth. This is especially important if you use overhead watering (like a sprinkler), which sprays water right on the plant.

Water at night if (1) you have no disease problems in the garden; (2) you live in an arid climate; or (3) you use a drip-irrigation system that waters the soil, not the plant leaves.

Holes poked in bottle cap allow water through

How Often and How Much

The best guideline is to water your garden when about half the available water in the soil is depleted. (Don't wait until a lot less is available; big fluctuations between wet and dry harm plants.) To figure out when that is, dig down 4 to 12 inches and feel the soil. Squeeze a handful of soil into a ball and see what happens.

If you have sandy soil, your sample should stick together slightly or form a weak ball under pressure. If it doesn't, you need to water.

For loamy soils, your sample should form a loose ball under pressure. If the soil looks dry and won't form a ball, it's time to water.

Clay soil should form a ball easily and ribbon out between your thumb and forefinger when you squeeze it. If you have to apply even a little pressure to form a ball, your garden needs some water.

But how much water should you apply? Always wet the soil at least 1 foot deep. Otherwise, plant roots will stay in the top 4 inches of soil, causing plants to be more vulnerable to water stress. Deep watering encourages deep roots, which allow plants to better withstand drought.

You often see the general recommendation that a garden should get 1 inch of water a week (either from rainfall or watering or a combination of both). But that doesn't take into account what you're growing or your soil type. For a better idea of your garden's unique needs, see the graph on the opposite page. Remember, you'll need to increase the amount of water slightly if your soil contains lots of organic matter. (See "How Long to Leave Your Hose On" on this page for useful tips on how to convert the amount of water needed from inches to gallons and how to figure out how long you need to leave the water running.)

One last factor: How should you apply water? Drip irrigation? A sprinkler? Your choice affects how much water you need to put on the garden. Drip irrigation is more efficient—about 85 percent of the water goes directly to the plants' root zone; overhead watering is about 70 percent efficient. Be sure to add more water to compensate for these inefficiencies. And no matter how you apply the water, remember to water slowly to minimize runoff.

Other Water-Wise Tips

Conserving water can be just as important as adding water to your garden especially during dry spells. Here are some hints to help ensure your garden loses as little water as possible.

Mulch, mulch, and mulch some more. Mulching can save almost one-third of the water you put on your garden, according to researchers. Mulch will also help keep soil cooler and protect tender roots. And it will keep down your biggest competitor for garden moisture—weeds.

Apply up to 3 inches of compost, wood chips, grass clippings, or any other organic mulch. (If you mulch on top of a drip-irrigation system, you may have to cut back on the amount of water you apply because mulch makes drip irrigation superefficient.) Just don't use plastic mulch with overhead sprinklers—the water won't get through to the soil.

Plan ahead to conserve water. First, try to do as much of your planting as early as possible in the spring and late in the fall. In these cooler times of year, a minimal amount of water is needed to get plants going strong (and strong plants are better able to tolerate droughts later on). Be aware, however, that cool-season crops generally have shallow root systems and require more frequent watering.

Garden in raised beds. The deeply loosened soil in a raised bed absorbs water better than the soil in a standard garden will.

Space plants closely. Reducing spaces between plants in beds and between rows will make mature plants into a living mulch—much of the soil will be shaded by their leaves.

Group crops that have similar water needs. Plant your heavy water users, such as beets and broccoli at one end of the garden, light users like beans and squash at the other. Then water the two areas separately.

Cut down on cultivation. Working your soil quickly dries out the upper few inches. Instead of hoeing to keep down weeds, smother them with moisture-conserving mulch.

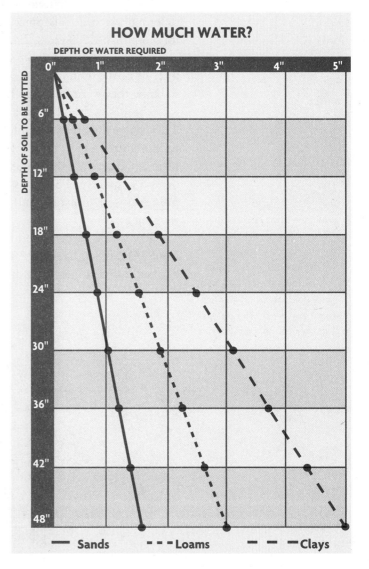

HOW MUCH WATER?

DEPTH OF WATER REQUIRED

DEPTH OF SOIL TO BE WETTED

— Sands   - - - Loams   — — Clays

A little water can go a long way if you have sandy soil—1 inch of water can wet the soil up to 30 inches deep. But if you have clay soil, you might need to apply about 3 inches of water to have a similar effect.

Waffle Gardens for Arid Climates

When Todd Price and his wife began gardening in Landing, Utah (6,700 feet in elevation and 8 to 12 inches of annual rainfall), they followed the example of others and planted in irrigated rows. But after 2 years of exceeding their water supply and watching their plants become sandblasted, they decided to try something else.

As an archaeologist, Todd knew that prehistoric gardeners in the Southwest overcame similar limitations by planting in "waffle gardens"—a gridwork of raised beds with soil mounded up around the sides to form protective walls. Since this technique has been used successfully for more than 1,000 years, Todd and his wife decided to try it.

They formed 3 × 4-foot mounds, and then pulled the soil from the interior of the mounds to the edges to form a basin in the center. By the time they were finished, their garden looked like a giant waffle.

The Prices found many advantages to the waffle-garden method: They water the crops much less often than they did before. And watering is easy—they simply fill the basin beds once a week. As the plants mature, they shade the surrounding soil so the ground doesn't dry out as quickly. The thin straw mulch spread over the mounds also preserves soil moisture and keeps any recently sown seeds from washing away.

The waffle garden also protects young plants from strong spring winds. And the walls act like tiny solar panels, warming up early in the day and radiating heat back onto the plants at night.

If you live in an arid climate, waffle gardening may be your ticket to a successful harvest. Instead of forming raised garden beds, form basins of soil with mounded edges. Water the waffles once a week. Their edges will shelter your plants and help conserve soil moisture.

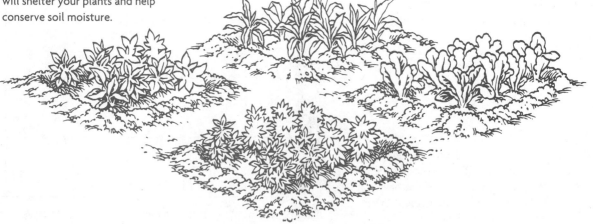

An Organic Gardener's Guide to Mulch

You probably already know that mulching is one of the best things you can do for your garden. Covering your soil with a thick layer of organic matter can block weed growth, keep the soil cool and moist, and—as the mulch decays—feed both the soil and the plants growing in it. But you also need to know which mulch to use in a given situation, so here's a guide to the benefits of the many different kinds of easily available organic mulches.

Grass Clippings

Freshly cut grass clippings are rich in nitrogen and other nutrients that will feed your plants as the clippings decompose. If your lawn can't supply enough grass clippings for your garden, check with a local lawn care service or a neighbor and see if you can get clips that (1) don't contain any grass or weeds that have gone to seed (the seeds will germinate in your garden); (2) don't come from an herbicide-treated lawn (if you aren't sure, don't use them); and (3) aren't from a freshly cut Bermuda grass or zoysia lawn—the clippings could take over your garden simply by rooting in moist soil! (Let such clips dry out completely before you use them as mulch.)

In the North, warm-loving crops like tomatoes and eggplant do well with grass clippings as long as they're applied after the soil is warm. Don't use grass to mulch growing plants in the South, though. Where blazing sun heats up the soil, you want a mulch that will help keep plants cool.

Compost

Mulching plants with compost inhibits plant diseases because the microbes in that "black gold" suppress bacteria that cause diseases. An inch of compost applied to the surface of the soil will prevent plant diseases.

But can compost control weeds? In USDA research, compost suppressed weeds almost as well as leaves and straw. If you have a lot of compost, use it everywhere! But if your supply is limited, reserve it for mulching your most disease-susceptible plants, such as tomatoes and roses.

Leaves

To put leaves to work in your garden, mulch your veggie patch with a layer of leaves in fall, when you have lots of them. Then turn the leaves into the soil in spring before you plant. Research indicates that tomato and pepper yields will increase.

You can also save some leaves and apply them in spring as mulch around cole crops, such as broccoli and cabbage, or beans. But avoid

---

Weird Mulches

Lots of great but unusual mulch materials are hidden away waiting for you in your house and yard. See if you're overlooking any of these handy resources.

Carpet. If you just tore out some cotton or wool (but *not* synthetic) carpeting, lay strips of it between rows in your veggie garden for a long-lasting weedproof mulch.

Herbs. Herbs like mint, perilla, and artemisia can be fast-spreading and even invasive. But if you already have a patch in your yard, put it to good use. Cut back the plants with hedge shears and use the stems and leaves as a mulch. It will smell wonderful, and it may even help repel insects.

Weeds. Weeds make good mulch if you're selective about what you use. For a low-maintenance living mulch, leave noninvasive weeds like chickweed in your garden if they spring up between vegetables or around trees and shrubs.

Straw Mulch Stifles Beetles

A layer of straw mulch in your potato patch can help control Colorado potato beetles. Two entomologists (G. W. Zehnder at the Eastern Shore Agricultural Experiment Station in Painter, Virginia, and J. Hough-Goldstein at the University of Delaware) found that the number of potato beetle adults, larvae, and eggs was significantly lower in plots mulched with 3 to 5 inches of straw than in unmulched plots. The mulched plots also produced nearly 40 percent more potatoes.

using leaf mulch around crops that thrive in warm soils (like tomatoes, eggplants, and peppers), until the soil has warmed up. Applying leaves to these crops in spring will cool the soil and decrease productivity.

Flowerbeds benefit from leaf mulch, too. By acting as an insulator, leaf mulch applied to flowerbeds in the fall—after the soil freezes—prevents perennials and bulbs from heaving up out of the ground during winter warm spells.

One caution about leaf mulch: Slugs love to hide in the stuff. If you garden in slug country, you can still use a leaf mulch during the growing season—just be sure to use one or more strategies for controlling slugs, such as beer traps and copper barriers.

Newspaper and Other Paper

Remove and recycle the slick-papered color supplements from your Sunday paper and what you have left is a garden worth of safe weed-suppressing mulch—and yes, it's safe to use, too! "There's nothing in black and white or color newsprint that will damage your plants or harm the soil," says Rufus Chaney, Ph.D., a scientist who works in the USDA-ARS environmental research laboratory in Beltsville, Maryland.

That's good news because newspaper is exceptionally effective at suppressing weeds. Norman Pellett, Ph.D., a professor of plant and soil science at the University of Vermont, showed that a 6-inch layer of shredded newspaper applied at the beginning of the summer allowed no more than eight weeds per square yard to grow that summer and the following one. That's right—without renewing the layer of newspaper, it controlled weeds for two summers!

Kraft paper (the brown paper used to make grocery bags) and cardboard are even more effective at preventing weeds. Just a sheet or two of kraft paper or a single piece of cardboard will block light and provide a physical barrier to keep weeds from sprouting.

You can use paper instead of black plastic to warm up cool spring soil. In fact gardening tests in Virginia showed paper warms soil 3° more than black plastic.

If your garden has acid soil, newspaper may not be the best mulch because newspaper can make acid soil even more acidic.

Pine Needles

Maybe you've avoided using pine needles as mulch in your garden because you've heard that they'll acidify your soil. That's not necessarily true. Some research studies show nearly no change in pH over time in soils mulched with pine needles. As long as you don't use pine needles excessively, you don't need to worry about an acidifying effect.

The pine needles were also great mulch. Eggplants mulched with pine needles produced 20 percent more than eggplants grown with no mulch. Spruce, fir, and pine boughs make fine winter mulch in flower gardens—particularly for fall-planted pansies that you want to rebloom in spring.

Straw

Straw mulch has proved to be a boon to tomatoes, preventing diseases like anthracnose, leaf spot, and early blight. It acts as a physical barrier between the fruit and the soil-borne diseases. Mulches also help prevent blossom-end rot, a condition caused by uneven levels of soil moisture.

Straw also works very well as an insulator, protecting crops like carrots, parsnips, and potatoes kept in the ground during the cold months. And by keeping the ground loose, the mulch also makes it easier to harvest the roots.

Fall-planted garlic bulbs thrive under straw mulch, too. In a 2-year study, garlic planted in October and mulched with straw in December survived winter more reliably and had 30 percent fewer weeds the following season than unmulched control plots.

Wood Chips

Whether you make them with a chipper/shredder or buy them, chips of hardwood branches make a durable mulch that keeps the soil moderately cool and does a fair job of suppressing weeds. Wood chips scored top marks in tests designed to measure how different mulches remain in place after heavy rains and high winds hit test plots.

If you're buying chips, take a careful look at them. Some merchants take old pieces of pressure-treated wood, chemical-soaked pallets, and other undesirable wood and chip it up to sell as mulch—you definitely DO NOT want such wood chips at any price. You DO want chips made from tree trimmings; many power companies offer free chips from branches they've trimmed around power lines.

Don't put chips around plants if they smell sour or like vinegar, though. That sour-smell usually comes from acetic acid and other compounds produced when the chips decompose without enough oxygen, and it can kill your plants. Instead, spread out the chips in a single layer and let them air out for a couple days. Once the smell is gone, it's safe to use the chips for mulch.

Wood chips are best used as mulch in your perennial beds and on your garden paths; they're durable and work best where soil isn't often tilled or turned. Don't turn them into your garden soil—they'll tie up nitrogen in the soil as they decompose (unless you try tactics like those used by the gardener who grew "Better Peas with Mulch"—see this page.)

GARDENER TO GARDENER

Better Peas with Mulch

I love growing peas, but they don't appreciate my unpredictable spring weather. Last year I found a way to moderate the spring soil temps—much to the benefit of my peas.

After planting peas in early April as usual, I began mulching them with small wood chips as soon as the seedlings were a few inches tall. To prevent the mulch from tying up soil nitrogen as the chips decomposed, I sprinkled nitrogen-rich bloodmeal over it. As the peas grew, I added more chips until the mulch was 2 inches deep. The chips kept the soil cool, and the spring crop was so successful that I planted another run of peas in late July. I was picking delicious sugar snap peas in November.

Bessie Balog
Hillsboro, Ohio

Burn Baby Burn

My new garden was overrun by chickweed and lamb's-quarters. I tried to control them by pulling them by hand, but the weeds grew back faster than I could pull.

Then my husband bought me a flame weeder. I hilled up soil along the planted rows to protect my good plants from the flames and began burning. It worked so well that I now burn off all the weeds before I start my spring planting. After I sow seeds, I continue using the flame weeder until my crops appear. After the plants are up, I flame-weed as needed, aiming the nozzle away from the crops and toward the pathway.

The improvement has been amazing. Now I only hand-pull a small amount weeds. I think I've finally won the war of the chickweeds.

Juanita Benefield
North Pole, Alaska

Bark

You may find this hard to believe, but tree bark lasts longer than wood chips—because bark doesn't hold water; it sheds. Just how durable is bark? In a study at North Carolina State University, only 30 percent of the pine bark mulch was lost to decay over a 2-year period—far less than other kinds of organic mulch.

Bark also keeps soil cool: In a Florida study, soil beneath pine bark was cooler during July and August than beneath any of the other mulches tested, including leaves.

But as with chips, take time to thoroughly check out what you're getting before you buy bark mulch. Some unscrupulous merchants spray shredded wood scraps—even arsenic-filled treated wood—with chemicals that make light-colored wood look like dark bark. Break a few pieces of the mulch in half to be sure that they're dark all the way through before you pay.

Bark is very attractive and durable—so use it in your most prized flower beds or other spots where you want to make a good impression. But don't use bark mulch, particularly softwood bark like spruce, in your tomato patch. Bark can release substances that can harm tomato plants. Instead, use that bark for mulching around your blueberry bushes. In a study conducted by the USDA-ARS Small Fruit Research Station in Poplarsville, Mississippi, yields of Southern highbush blueberries mulched with pine bark surpassed that of those mulched with black plastic or woven mulches.

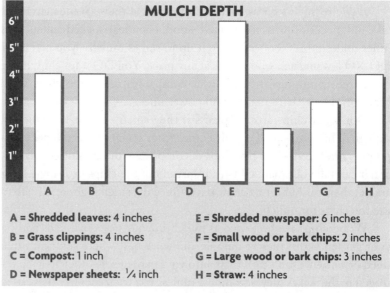

MULCH DEPTH

A = **Shredded leaves:** 4 inches

B = **Grass clippings:** 4 inches

C = **Compost:** 1 inch

D = **Newspaper sheets:** ¼ inch

E = **Shredded newspaper:** 6 inches

F = **Small wood or bark chips:** 2 inches

G = **Large wood or bark chips:** 3 inches

H = **Straw:** 4 inches

Use this graph to determine how deeply to apply different types of mulch.

Weeding with Fire

Many gardeners are discovering a very effective tool that's tough on weeds and easy on your back: fire. With specially designed propane torches called "flame weeders," you can kill weeds quickly and permanently. Here are some tips for using a flame weeder with maximum success and minimal risk.

Flame weeding works best on young, broadleaved annual weeds, like pigweed and lamb's quarters. The older the weed, the deeper its root system, and the less effective flame weeding will be. A flame weeder will kill the aboveground growth of perennial weeds, but big, old tough weeds will probably grow back from their roots.

Weeds growing in sidewalk cracks and garden paths are perfect targets for flame weeding. For vegetable gardens and flowerbeds, be sure to clear away dried leaves and potentially flammable mulches before flame weeding. (And keep a shovel loaded with dirt nearby at all times so you can throw some smothering soil on anything that ignites.)

Dos and Don'ts

Don't flame-weed when it's dry and/or windy. Flame weeding should be done only during the green time of year—you can even flame-weed in a rainstorm. (Check with your local fire officials to be sure conditions are safe in your area.)

Don't ignite the weeds—just boil their insides. The flame will heat the sap inside the plant's cells, which will expand and rupture the cells' walls.

Do keep the flame 3 to 6 inches above the weed until leaves show discoloration—with young weeds, that's usually just a few seconds. The weed will begin to wilt almost immediately, but may not look completely dead for another 24 to 48 hours.

Do rake out the wilted weeds, then toss them into your compost pile.

Don't flame-weed poison ivy, poison oak, or poison sumac. Heating could release their oils into the air.

Do be extra careful. Protect your skin by wearing boots, a long sleeve shirt and pants, gloves, and safety goggles.

Remember that a propane-fueled flame has a nearly invisible "cone" of intense heat around the visible part of the flame. Keep everyone away while you're using this tool so you can focus your attention on the nozzle at all times.

GARDENER TO GARDENER

Soak-Free Soaker Hose

I use a soaker/sprinkler hose to water the shrubs and bulbs along the front of my house. Because of the location of my faucet, the hose must cross the walkway that leads to my front door. To keep from watering my guests, I cover that section of the hose with foam pipe insulation (sold to keep water pipes from freezing).

The insulation comes in 3-foot lengths and is already split down one side, so it slips nicely over my hose. I position it with the split side up and set a small rock under one end so the water flows down into the flowerbed instead of forming a puddle on the walk.

When it's time to store the hose, the insulation can be easily removed and used again—perhaps even for its intended purpose in the off-season.

Lila Ralston
Athens, Georgia

Dandy Vinegar

Vinegar keeps my yard dandelion-free. In the spring, as the dandelions pop up, I fill my sprayer with undiluted vinegar, then walk around my yard, spraying the center of each dandelion plant. I get down at ground level so I can spray the plants directly, but I try to keep the vinegar away from the surrounding grass. I also try to spray on a sunny day, when clear weather is predicted for at least the next few days so rain won't wash away the spray. The dandelions quickly die after they're sprayed and don't grow back. Spraying once a week for 2 to 4 weeks keeps my yard dandelion-free all season. (Vinegar also works great for getting rid of unwanted grass in sidewalks and driveways.)

Pamela Miksch
Leawood, Kansas

Edge Naturally with Driftwood

Blocking grass from creeping into my flowerbeds has been a constant challenge. Edgings have proven to be the best solution, but I don't like the look of the commercial plastic and metal ones, so I use natural-looking driftwood instead. (We live near a bay, where long narrow pieces of driftwood are plentiful.)

Putting in the edging is easy. I just dig a 2-inch-deep trench between my lawn and flowerbeds, lay in the driftwood end to end, then pack the pieces in with soil to hold them in place. Each piece rises 3 to 4 inches above the ground all around the border. I like to use taller pieces in the corners for visual accent—and to keep lawn mowers and wheelbarrows from rolling into the beds. Long narrow pieces also make terrific "props" for unruly flowers like gladiolas, delphiniums, and poppies.

Sue De Kelver
Marinette, Wisconsin

Hello, Hose There?

Here's how to recycle an old garden hose for your children's amusement. Drain out the water and insert a clean funnel into each end so they can use the funnels as "telephones." Or let them borrow your good garden hose when you aren't using it.

June Lewis
Milton, Pennsylvania

GARDENER TO GARDENER

Two-Gloved Approach

When I settle down for a serious session of hand-weeding, I protect my hands with an unmatched pair of gloves. I wear a regular cotton glove on one hand and a sturdy leather glove on the other. The cotton is more flexible and allows me the dexterity I need to pick out small weeds and seedlings. The leather glove is for pulling tenacious weeds with stickers like nettles and blackberries. This two-handed approach makes this tedious chore a little less painful.

Carolyn Battle
McCalla, Alabama

Smile! Your Hands are Clean

I'm a hands-on, down-in-the-dirt gardener, and I love the feel of earth between my fingers and under my fingernails. But I don't like taking soil to the dinner table. I tried hand creams, gloves, and nail brushes before I finally found something that works: denture cleaning tablets.

Simply wet your hands and rub a tablet over the dirt. The tablet is mildly abrasive so you can even scrub your skin with it. It also foams, and the foam seems to get into all the previously unreachable crevices. When you're finished, your hands will be smooth and clean and may even smell mildly of peppermint. If you still have a bit of tablet left, toss it into the toilet bowl, and your toilet will be cleaner, too.

Barbara Beukema
Victoria, British Columbia

Smother Purslane

Purslane's succulent leaves can store water for weeks—allowing the weed to reroot at its leisure. But I've discovered that this weed does have a weak spot: Those fleshy leaves rot easily. So if you encounter purslane while weeding, simply place it under a pile of mulch or other weeds that you've pulled, or even under a dense planting of vegetables. Just about any damp, dark place spells certain death for persistent purslane.

Sydney Penner
Berwick, Nova Scotia

Pull Poison Ivy Safely

Here's a trick for removing poison ivy sprouts without becoming itchy. During the spring and summer I always tuck a few plastic newspaper or grocery bags into my gardening basket. Then, whenever I see a shoot of poison ivy, I simply pick up a pair of bags, put one inside the other and slip my hand inside the bags. Thus "gloved," I can reach down and pull up the ivy, making sure to get the entire root, then pull the doubled bag back down over my hand. The poison ivy never touches my skin, and the sprig is safely encased in the plastic bag, which I then carefully knot and toss in the trash.

Susan Caughlan
East Norriton,
Pennsylvania

Weeding Al Dente

Treat your weeds like spaghetti and prevent an aching back! Take an old kitchen fork and affix it to a broom handle with duct tape. Place the fork in the middle of young weeds, give the handle a twist, and presto!—the weed is out!

Yvonne Murphy
Colorado Springs, Colorado

GARDENER TO GARDENER

Rain Barrels Refined

I made a simple system to collect rainwater from our roof and run-off from our air conditioner so that we don't have to use precious well water on our garden during periods of low rainfall.

The system consists of four rain barrels, which together hold 200 gallons of water (a single storm can fill the barrels in a matter of minutes). A frame, made from 2 × 10s and 3-inch diameter PVC pipe, supports the barrels. The left two barrels are set lower than the right, so water fills them up first. Each barrel has its own spigot, so the water doesn't stagnate. When the first two barrels are full, the barrels on the right fill up. When all the barrels are completely full, the water runs out an overflow pipe between our raised beds.

David Beam
Mount Airy, Maryland

Clean Hand Solution

Ever wonder what to do with all those little bits of soap that litter the sink and shower? We save these leftover odds and ends until we have a handful or so, then knot them into one leg of an old pair of pantyhose. We then tie it to our outdoor faucet nearest the garden. This soap-filled stocking offers great no-slip cleaning for dirty gardening hands.

Betsy Race
Euclid, Ohio

Weed-Free Raspberries

We've been growing organic raspberries for market for many years. Here's our simple method for keeping our plantings free from weeds: In early spring, we lay sheets of cardboard between the rows, then top the cardboard with wood chips obtained from a local tree-cutting service. The chips hold down the cardboard, and together they block out the weeds.

We also mulch directly around the plants with pine needles collected from the nearby woods. The needles help keep weeds at bay and keep the soil around the plants cool, as the raspberries prefer. On top of the pine needles we scatter composted horse manure to provide needed nutrients.

Edward and Margaret Wanserski
Rosholt, Wisconsin

Get a Grip on Weeding

Channel-type pliers are invaluable for weeding—especially for tough weeds like blackberry brambles and poison ivy seedlings. The long handles of the pliers allow me to get a good grip and yank out even stubborn weeds like catbrier, without having to touch the plant with my hands.

Jan Osborn
Rome, Georgia

Budge-Proof Kneepads

None of the garden kneepads I've purchased have ever stayed in place when I've used them—so now I make my own. My homemade pads stay right where they belong because they're "attached" to me. I sew large patch pockets onto the knees of my gardening pants, then slip a piece of foam into each pocket. The pads always stay in place, even while I'm bending and working in the garden. And the foam is easy to remove when the pants need to be laundered.

Leota Cornett
Roanoke, Virginia

Chapter 8

August

The Perpetual Garden: Saving Seeds, Dividing Plants

August. The opposing of peach and sugar, and the sun inside the afternoon like the stone in the fruit.

—*Federico Garcia Lorca*

Although this month's sultry days feel as though the growing season will never end, August nights usually begin to hint that the end of this year's season soon will be here for most regions. There are at least a couple of ways you can keep your garden growing, however. One way is to extend the season for this year's crops, as we'll tell you about in Chapter 10. Another is to propagate your plants—take "offspring" (such as seeds, divisions, cuttings) from already established ornamentals and edibles to replant now or to prepare for the next season.

Although plant propagation might sound complex or mysterious, it isn't necessarily difficult. And it's definitely fun! You don't need a laboratory or special equipment—but depending on the method you use, you might benefit from a bit of patience.

There are several ways you can propagate your plants, and we'll cover a couple of the easiest methods in the next few pages—most of them simple. When you're feeling more adventurous, be sure to try your hand at other techniques, such as taking hardwood or leaf cuttings, layering, air rooting, or breeding your own new variety.

Gardener's To-Do List—August

**If you don't know what USDA hardiness zone you live in,
check the map on page 246 to find out.**

Zone 3

- [ ] Harvest time! If you're saving seeds, save only healthy ones, and make sure they have thoroughly dried. Clearly label seed storage containers.
- [ ] Pick zucchini when fruit are 4 to 8 inches long—you'll get twice as many.
- [ ] Spray water on the top and undersides of zucchini foliage, early in the mornings, to control spider mites and aphids.
- [ ] After midmonth, pinch off any new tomato flowers to direct energy to ripening fruit.
- [ ] Slowly reduce watering of perennials, trees, and shrubs to allow them to harden-off for the winter.
- [ ] Be prepared to protect plants from early frost.
- [ ] At month's end, take cuttings of geraniums, fuchsias, and begonias. Root them in damp perlite.

Zone 4

- [ ] Fall will soon be here: Plant lettuce and other fast-growing crops to replace those harvested.
- [ ] Order spring-blooming flower bulbs and garlic to plant next month.
- [ ] Thin strawberry runners.
- [ ] Save seed from favorite open-pollinated tomatoes and peppers to develop the best regional variations of those varieties.
- [ ] At month's end, sow spinach in a coldframe for spring harvest.

- [ ] Clean up spent early crops and replace with cover crops, such as clover, oats, or barley.

Zone 5

- [ ] Indoors, start seeds of quick-maturing lettuce and brassicas for fall harvest.
- [ ] Cut back berry canes that have finished fruiting.
- [ ] Weed strawberries, then mulch them with compost.
- [ ] Transplant extra strawberry plants to a new bed.
- [ ] If you garden in a semiarid climate, give plants a deep soaking of 1 to 1½ inches of water weekly.
- [ ] Re-seed carrots, beets, turnips, and radishes.
- [ ] Remove rose leaves infected with black spot.
- [ ] Take photos and make notes for next year's landscape.
- [ ] Gather globe amaranth, celosia, and golden-rod for air drying.

Zone 6

- [ ] Water the garden weekly if it isn't getting enough rain.
- [ ] For fall salads, plant leafy greens like lettuce and spinach.
- [ ] Start pansy seeds in flats to transplant in fall for early spring bloom.
- [ ] Sow seeds of poppies, bachelor's buttons (*Centaurea cyanus*), and sweet William (*Dianthus barbatus*) where you want their blooms next spring.

☐ Gather and dry herbs and flowers at their peak.

☐ Send off your order for spring bulbs and garlic for fall planting—ASAP.

Zone 7

☐ If the weather's dry, water your vegetable garden gently but deeply every 5 to 7 days.

☐ Before midmonth, sow cool-weather crops like Chinese cabbage, beets, Swiss chard, and mustard.

☐ Cover seedbeds with shadecloth and mist the soil often to induce sprouting.

☐ Late this month, set out transplants of broccoli, brussels sprouts, cauliflower, and collards.

☐ Stop watering potted amaryllis bulbs; store them in a dark, dry spot for several weeks, then bring them out again to initiate winter bloom.

Zone 8

☐ Prune berries.

☐ Gather and dry herbs.

☐ In empty beds, plant a cover crop of red clover to build soil and reduce erosion.

☐ Start seeds of broccoli, cabbage, and cauliflower to transplant later.

☐ Work compost into the garden now so it can mellow before planting.

☐ Continue to set out tomato and pepper transplants.

☐ Direct-seed limas, corn, cucumbers, squash, dill, and basil.

Zone 9

☐ Prune back tomatoes and peppers to stimulate new growth and continued production.

☐ Shade lettuce, chard, tomatoes, peppers, melons, and eggplants from intense sun.

☐ For prize-winning winter squash and pumpkins, pinch off any female flowers and young fruit that develop from now on.

☐ Fertilize heavy feeders—such as corn, cukes, lettuce, squash, and onions—using a dilute solution of fish fertilizer, once a week.

☐ Harvest annual statice, strawflowers, and ageratum, and then dry them in a cool, airy place.

☐ Plant annual candytuft (*Iberis umbellata*) and marigolds for fall color.

☐ Plant calendulas, stocks (*Matthiola incana*), bachelor's buttons (*Centaurea cyanus*), and forget-me-nots (*Myosotis sylvatica*) for early spring color.

Zone 10

☐ Repot indoor plants in fresh soil.

☐ Plan the fall and winter food garden and assemble seed orders.

☐ Start tomatoes, eggplants, peppers, and watermelons in pots—make sure they get enough afternoon shade.

☐ Protect the compost pile from full sun—coconut palm fronds or shade cloths will do the job, but leave air space between them and the top of the pile.

☐ Keep veggies growing strong with a top-dressing of compost.

☐ Continue to solarize empty beds to kill weed seeds and disease pathogens: Water the soil thoroughly, then seal it with clear plastic for 6 to 8 weeks.

Tie a Yellow Ribbon

"Once you've chosen a plant you want to save seed from," states Nancy Bubel, the author of *The New Seed-Starters Handbook*, "you'll want to identify it in some way." She suggests tying on a brightly colored ribbon or a tag. You can find weather-resistant ribbon, such as fluorescent surveyor's ribbon, at your local hardware store. Marking the plant reminds you and other family members to treat it with care. Most important, it will remind you not to eat the plant's fruit for dinner or cut it for your table centerpiece!

Don't depend on just a single tagged fruit or plant for your entire seed harvest. Tag several in case one gets damaged.

Saving Seeds for Next Season

Things are getting round and ripe in your garden. That means it's time to think about saving some seeds from your best tomatoes, peppers, squash, cucumbers, and melons.

If left to themselves, these fleshy fruits would naturally fall to the earth, where some of their seeds would sprout when spring arrives again. Saving seeds from these plants mimics Nature's way—and it's not at all difficult to do.

But remember, only seeds from open-pollinated, not hybrid, plants will produce the same crop next year. (The packet that the seeds came from will tell you whether the variety is open-pollinated or hybrid.) And, except for tomatoes, the plants shouldn't be cross-pollinated by insects (which would happen if several varieties grew in the same area). Such saved seeds might grow into something that resembles the parent, or something tough and tasteless.

Tomatoes are self-pollinating. So if you avoid hybrid varieties, you'll be able to grow the same tomato next year from seeds you save this year—even if different varieties were grown close together. That's not the case with peppers and eggplants. Their flowers can be cross-pollinated by insects, so different varieties of these must be separated by 500 feet for the seeds to be pure.

Cucurbits—such as squash, cucumbers, gourds, and melons—need even more personal space. All of these garden favorites must be pollinated by insects. So unless close relatives (of the same species) are separated by a half-mile or more, you'll get a surprise if you grow the seeds.

For example, a zucchini and an acorn squash (both *Cucurbita pepo*) in the same garden will cross, thanks to pollinating insects. And the seeds probably won't produce a replica of either parent plant. But if you're growing zucchini and a butternut squash (*C. moschata*) in the same garden, you can save the seeds from each and expect to have your plants come up true to type when you plant them next year, since they are different species.

Easy to Save Seeds

The seeds of tomatoes, peppers, melons, and winter squash are ready for saving when the fruits are ripe and ready to eat.

Peppers. Peppers are the easiest. The seeds are mature after the peppers have changed color, indicating final ripeness. Cut the peppers open, scrape out the seeds onto a plate (eat the pepper), and let the seeds dry in a nonhumid, shaded place, testing them occasionally until they break rather than bend. What could be simpler?

(*Note:* Dry all wet seeds on a glass or ceramic plate. Spread the seeds evenly over the surface of the plate and stir twice daily to ensure even drying and to keep them from clumping together. Don't dry seeds on paper plates or paper towels—they'll stick like glue. A food dehydrator set at 85°F works well, but don't dry them in a warm oven or any place the temperature exceeds 95°F.)

Tomatoes. Saving tomato seeds takes a little more time, but it's just as easy. Harvest ripe tomatoes from several different vines of the same variety, cut each across the middle and gently squeeze the juice and seeds into a bowl. You'll see that each tomato seed is encased in a gelatinous coating. (This prevents the seed from sprouting inside the tomato). Remove this coating by fermenting it. This mimics the natural rotting of the fruit and has the added bonus of killing any seedborne tomato diseases that might affect next year's crop.

To ferment the seeds, add about half as much water as there are tomato seeds and juice in the bowl and stir the mixture twice a day for about three days. Keep a close eye on the mixture—especially if it's a warm area—fermentation happens more quickly at high temperatures. As the mixture ferments, its surface will become covered with white or gray mold. (Don't keep the bowl in the kitchen, anywhere it can be tipped over by animals or children, or where you'd be able to smell it— it will get pretty rank.)

When bubbles begin to rise to the top of the mass, or when a thick coat of mold has formed, stop the fermentation by adding enough water to double the mixture, and stir vigorously. The clean, good seeds will settle to the bottom of the bowl. Gently pour off mold, debris and any seeds that float (they're hollow). Add more water and repeat the process until only clean seeds remain.

Capture the seeds to be saved by pouring the liquid through a strainer, wipe the strainer bottom with a towel to remove as much moisture as possible, then dump the seeds onto a glass or ceramic plate to dry. Stir twice a day to ensure even drying and to prevent the seeds from clumping together. *Warning:* Tomato seeds will germinate unless you dry them quickly. To speed drying, you can use a fan, but don't put the seeds in sunlight or an oven.

Melons and squash. Muskmelons, watermelons, and winter squash? Super easy. Cut muskmelons open, scoop the seeds into a strainer, rinse, and set out to dry. Watermelons are almost as easy. Put the seeds in a strainer and add a dash of dishwashing liquid to remove any sugar left on the seeds. Rinse and dry.

Saving Tomato Seeds

Tomato seeds are easy to save, if you follow this simple three-step process.

1. Cut fully ripe tomatoes in half to expose seed cavities; then squeeze seeds into a container.

2. Add water. Keep the container at room temperature for about 3 days until fermentation occurs and mold forms on the surface.

3. Add water, stir, then gently scrape mold and debris off the top. Repeat until only clean seeds remain. Strain and rinse.

The Unsmushable Seed

How can you tell when your seed is dry enough? "I use the smush-mush technique," says Suzanne Ashworth, the author of *Seed to Seed*. If you can't bite into it or smush it, or if you hit it with a hammer and it shatters, the seed is dry enough to store. Smaller seeds are harder to judge, but they usually aren't as much of a problem as larger seeds, which you need to dry thoroughly before storing. When the seeds are unsmushable, store them in an airtight container as soon as possible so they won't reabsorb moisture.

Winter squashes need to be carefully cut to expose the seed cavity. Don't cut straight through the center of the squash—you'll cut through some seeds, too. Just stick the knife in as far as necessary to cut through the flesh and move it around the circumference. (Be careful—some squashes will fight back!) Pull the seeds from the fibers, rinse, and dry. And don't cut a squash before you're ready to eat it—seeds can be saved from most winter squashes many months after harvest (although a few of the long-storage varieties may have sprouted seeds inside after 6 months or so).

Seeds That Need More Time

Eggplants, cucumbers, and summer squash must ripen beyond the normal, ready-to-eat stage to allow viable seeds to develop inside.

Eggplants. To save the seeds of your eggplants, you'll need to wait until the fruits are far past the stage when you'd pick them for eating. Any seeds saved from table-ready eggplants will be immature and won't be viable. If left on the plant, purple eggplant varieties will ripen to a dull brownish color, green varieties to a yellowish green, and white varieties to golden. Eggplants ready for seed saving will be dull, off-colored, hard, and sometimes shriveled.

Cut the ripe eggplants in half and pull the flesh away from the seeded areas. If you want to save more than a few seeds, use a food processor or blender to mash the flesh and expose the seeds. Process (without peeling), and put the pulp in a bowl. Add water, let the good seeds settle, then pour off the water and debris. Repeat until only clean seeds remain. Add a bit more water and pour the mix through a strainer with a mesh fine enough to catch the tiny seeds. Dry the bottom of the strainer with a towel to absorb excess moisture and dump the seeds out onto a plate to dry.

Cucumbers. After cucumbers ripen, they change color and become soft. (Remember, if you stop picking cucumbers, their vines will stop producing new fruit, so pick your fruit for seed saving toward the end of the season.)

Cut the ripe cucumber in half and scrape the seeds into a bowl. To remove the seeds' coating, rub them gently around the inside of a sieve while washing them or soak them in water for 2 days. Rinse and dry. (*Note:* Make sure the cucumbers you use for seed are disease-free; some diseases can be carried on seed and could affect your future crop.)

Summer squash. You'll need to let summer squash ripen past the tender stage, too. When you can't dent the squash with a fingernail, the fruit is at the right stage for seed saving. Pick it, cut it open, scrape the seeds into a bowl, wash, drain, and dry.

The Fine Art of Hand Pollination

All members of the cucurbit family (squash, gourds, melons, cucumbers, and so on) produce both male and female flowers on the same plant. Insects pick up pollen from male flowers and deposit it on female flowers. Cucurbits can be pollinated by almost any variety within their same species. The plants that grow from seed produced by random pollination usually bear little resemblance to the parent plants. So to successfully save seeds, you'll need to keep insects away from some of the flowers and pollinate these flowers yourself.

You'll need to know the difference between male and female flowers. Female blossoms are attached to tiny, immature fruit (a bulge in the stem right behind the flower). Male blossoms have straight stems.

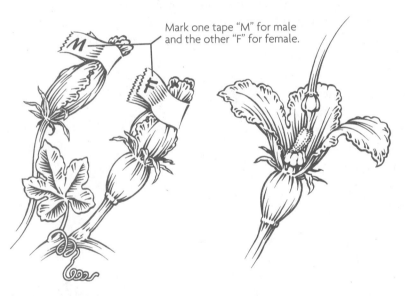

Mark one tape "M" for male and the other "F" for female.

In the evening, select blossoms that look like they're ready to open the next morning (beginning to show color and petals beginning to flare outward). Select a male flower from one plant to pollinate a female flower on a different plant of the same variety—this will result in greater genetic diversity and healthier seed stock. Use masking tape to gently hold the blossoms closed.

Early the next day, remove the tape from the male flower, pick it, and carefully tear off the petals, exposing the pollen-covered anthers. Gently remove the tape from the female flower. The flower should slowly open. Take the male flower and gently rub its pollen onto the stigma sections of the female flower. Repeat with several male flowers for best results.

Retape the female flower and mark the stem, using string, yarn, or any bright and durable material. (That's your cue to leave the developing fruit to mature fully.) Be sure you mark the fruit when you harvest it, too, so you'll know it's the one from which you want to save the seeds.

Dividing Perennials

Many perennials need to be divided every three to five years to stay healthy and vigorous. And by doing so, you'll be rewarded with even more perennials for your garden—or for sharing with friends.

The best time to divide most perennials is early spring, when the plants are just coming out of dormancy. But spring-blooming plants— like iris, astilbe, and primroses—should be divided immediately after they finish flowering. That way, you'll get bloom this year and the new divisions will have a whole year to get established before they bloom again. Perennials also can be divided when they go dormant in fall in the Deep South and other mild-winter areas.

Before dividing, water the plant well for a few days. To further ensure success, don't divide during the hottest, sunniest part of the day— either pick a cool, cloudy day or wait until late in the day.

To prepare a perennial for dividing, push a garden fork down into the dirt as far as it will go along the edge of the clump you want to divide. Then, push down on the handle to begin prying up the plant. Repeat the pushing and prying process all the way around the plant until the clump is loose. Now lift the clump out with the fork, trying to keep as many roots intact as possible.

Thrust two forks back to back right through the center of the clump, then push the handles together or pull them apart. This will result in two divisions, which can be can split up further by using your hands, a knife, or the forks (whatever is easiest). Divide the "mother plant" into as many babies as you can, keeping each baby clump to a minimum size of about 4 inches across.

The technique you'll use for dividing the clump depends on whether the plant is fibrous rooted (forming a tight clump of roots) or loose crowned and whether the plant sends out runners. The three different techniques are shown in the illustrations on this page.

After you've finished taking divisions, replant the new clumps at the same soil depth as when they were part of the "mother clump." Water your newly divided plants frequently during their first season.

Shake off most of the soil from the roots and pull the clump apart by hand to separate the divisions. Be sure each division has a few good-looking roots and shoots.

Cut the miniplants away from the parent and replant several of them together, forming a good-sized (about 4 inches across) clump in each replanting site.

Perennials to Divide

FIBROUS ROOTED

Asters

Astilbes

Bee balms (*Monarda* spp.)

Black-eyed Susans (*Rudbeckia* spp.)

Daylilies (*Hemerocallis* spp.)

Garden phlox (*Phlox paniculata*)

Hostas

Lily-of-the-valley (*Convallaria majalis*)

Lilyturf (*Liriope* spp.)

Miscanthus

Purple coneflower (*Echinacea purpurea*)

Yarrows (*Achillea* spp.)

LOOSE CROWNED

Blanket flowers (*Gaillardia* spp.)

Gayfeathers (*Liatris* spp.)

Hardy geraniums (*Geranium* spp.)

Heucheras

Pincushion flower (*Scabiosa caucasica*)

Sweet woodruff (*Galium odoratum*)

RUNNER PRODUCERS

Chrysanthemums

Coreopsis

Mountain bluets (*Centaurea montana*)

Pachysandra

Sedums

Speedwells (*Veronica* spp.)

GARDENER TO GARDENER

Tomato Suckers to Plants

When I find large suckers on my tomato plants, I cut them off and put them in water. After they've rooted, I stick the rooted cuttings in the bare spots of my garden—places where spring crops have finished their season. These tomatoes often go on to produce even better than the parent plant.

James C. Dalton, Sr.
Fredonia, Kentucky

Regenerated Cabbage Heads

Being a seed saver with a small garden, it used to pain me to allow a perfect head of cabbage to set seed instead of harvesting it to enjoy at my dinner table. At last I've found a way to save the seed and eat my cabbage too.

When the cabbage is ready to harvest, I simply cut the head as high up on the stalk as is possible, and allow the remainder of the plant to continue to grow. The plant usually recovers and eventually goes to seed. If I need to reclaim the garden space it occupies in the meantime, I carefully dig up the plant and transplant it to my "seed only" area, an out-of-the-way section of my garden.

Sue LeMontre
San Diego, California

Low-Cost Lemongrass

Lemongrass (Cymbopogon citratus) plants root readily from cut stalks, which you can buy at a farmer's market, Asian specialty market, or supermarket (some will order it for you). To start a supply of this lemony herb, purchase a bundle of six to eight stalks.

Trim off the bottom of the stalks, leaving about 8 to 10 inches. Remove the outer sheath if it's dry or beginning to brown. Place the stalks in a cup with about an inch of water—you should see roots form in a few days. (Stalks that don't root in a couple of weeks probably never will, so trim them again and use for cooking.)

Plant the rooted stalks in the garden or a large container, where they'll grow into 3- to 4-foot plants with long slender blue-green leaves. Lemongrass is only winter hardy in Zones 9 and 10, so you may need to trim back the leaves, pot up their plants, and bring them indoors for the winter. (Dry and store the trimmings for winter cooking.) Use lemongrass leaves in tea or in marinades for vegetables and meat. The tender inside of the new shoots are delicious, especially when cooked together with celery, onion, and chicken stock in rice dishes.

Joey Elizabeth Burke
Versailles, Kentucky

Bad Onions Make Good

Don't throw out storage onions when they start to sprout—pot them up instead and eat spicy greens all winter long!

When my husband was about to carry some sprouting onions out to the compost pile, I suggested we plant them indoors in some potting soil, instead. About a week later, we had tasty leaves for eating. The greens are so deliciously crisp and mild that my children even sprinkle them on their pizza. They also make a great houseplant during chilly winters.

Vicki Delph
Jefferson, Oregon

GARDENER TO GARDENER

Impatiens for More

Here's how I turned a single impatiens seedling into more than 100 bedding plants for my garden. Last spring a friend gave me some impatiens seedlings, and somehow one of them didn't get planted. So I stuck it in water until I could get to it.

Three to four weeks later, the seedling was still in the water on my kitchen counter. But it was growing like crazy. I decided to experiment: For the next couple of months, I regularly changed the water and fertilized my flower. By fall the plant was about a foot tall with four large stems and many sideshoots. I took a dozen cuttings from the stems, and put all of them in water, where they developed roots in just three weeks! I repeated the process several times over the fall, and by spring, I had more than 100 new plants ready for the garden.

Jackie Souliers
St. John's, Newfoundland

Sedum from Cuttings

Two years ago I put some sedum 'Autumn Joy' along with other fall flowers into a vase for an indoor display. When I noticed small green leaves forming at the junctions of the sedum leaves and the stem, I figured I might be able to start some new plants over the winter for planting next spring.

I removed the flowers, changed the water in the vase, and set the vase on a shady windowsill. I changed the water weekly, and before long, the stems grew new leaves and roots. When the roots were well developed, I carefully removed the tiny sedums from the main stem and planted them into small pots filled with soil. Eventually, the plants grew large enough to plant into the garden, where they now are the size of bushel baskets.

George Seifrit
Sinking Spring, Pennsylvania

New Sweet Potato Plants from Vines

We've stumbled upon an easy way to reproduce sweet potato plants, and it works better than the usual "slip" method (taking cuttings from a sprouting sweet potato and rooting them).

A couple of years ago, another gardener gave us some heirloom sweet potatoes. The variety performed beautifully in our mountain soil, but when we tried to start new plants from "slips," we were only able to get one or two of them to root.

Then we noticed how the sprawling vines had rooted in various places along the stem. So when we dug up our sweet potatoes in the fall, we also dug up some of the rooted vines. We planted the "starts" in pots, then grew them indoors over the winter. By spring, the vines were ready to plant in the garden. This method gave us enough starts to triple the size of our patch, so we no longer worry about losing this wonderful heirloom variety.

Nancy Owen
Hatfield, Arkansas

GARDENER TO GARDENER

Recycler's Mini-Greenhouse

I've found that the large, rectangular 2½-gallon water jugs make great mini-greenhouses into which you can put small pots for starting cuttings and seeds. And you can transform the jugs in just three easy steps. Here's how:

Use a knife or scissors to cut the bottle to the desired height—an 8-inch height works well.

To create a roof, cut the hook off of a coat hanger, straighten the remaining wire, then bend the ends to form a U-type ridge. Using duct tape, secure the ends of the wire to the sides of the container.

Wrap the container with a clear plastic.

Because I use high-intensity grow lights in my unheated basement, the temperature there drops dramatically when the lights go off. To keep the cuttings warm, I set the pots on a brick inside each greenhouse. The brick absorbs heat while the lights are on, then keeps the plants cozy when the lights are off.

Steve Harding
Indianapolis, Indiana

Use Fish Tanks for Cuttings

When we moved into our new home, I wanted to create shrub and perennial flower borders everywhere. To get enough new perennials for my borders and beds, I decided to propagate them myself from cuttings, using a homemade propagation unit.

For the units, my husband collected some old fish tanks at garage sales. Although some have minor cracks, they still make excellent plant nurseries because they provide the high-humidity cuttings need to root and grow. Right before I take the cuttings, I lay damp sheets of newspaper on the bottom of the tanks to provide humidity. Then, after I take the cuttings, I stick them into 4-inch pots filled with a moist, sandy potting soil. I set several of these pots into each tank and cover the tanks with plastic. The tanks remain in a semishaded place until the cuttings root.

I open the tanks daily to stimulate air circulation and mist with a hand sprayer to keep the air humid. After a few weeks, I have lots of new plants to add to my beds or to trade with friends.

Nancy Whitehead
Hebo, Oregon

Multipurpose Strainer

I've discovered many great garden uses for the fine-mesh nylon paint strainers that you can buy at paint supply stores for about $3 each. These durable pouch-shaped strainers come with a bound elasticized rim that normally would stretch over the top of a 5-gallon paint can.

One of my favorite uses for these strainers is for saving seeds of pumpkin, squash, and cucumber. All you do is put your cleaned seeds into one of the strainers, close the opening with a twist-tie or rubber band, and then dry the seeds by spreading the bag out flat or hanging it up. Shake the bag every now and then to redistribute the seed so any hidden damp spots can dry. Be sure to label each bag with the name of the variety.

Rick Frey
Kendallville, Indiana

Chapter 9

September

Stocking Up: Preserving the Garden's Bounty

When apple seeds, all white before
Begin to darken to the core,
I know that summer scarcely here,
Is gone until another year.

—Edna St. Vincent Millay

In most places, the garden puts on its grand finale this month. Vegetables and fruits are producing at their peak and late summer asters, roses, and chrysanthemums are in full color.

Usually weeds come on strong this month too, and beds begin to look a little, well, tired.

When the garden winds down, gardeners do what they can to preserve its bounty through the winter. September is for stocking up—filling your home with preserved vegetables, fruits, and herbs and arrangements made from the season's last blooms.

As you begin peeling your 2nd bushel basket of tomatoes, preparing your 5th batch of pesto, freezing your 8th quart of green beans, and canning your 20th jar of applesauce, you're likely to wonder why you planted so much this year. The answer, of course, is that you always do. But the solution is not to *plant* less—just spend less time in the kitchen putting up your harvest, as we'll explain in the next few pages.

Gardener's To-Do List—September

If you don't know what USDA hardiness zone you live in,
check the map on page 246 to find out.

Zone 3

☐ Plant new fall bulbs so they develop roots before the ground freezes.

☐ Harvest corn, potatoes, apples, cucumbers, tomatoes, squash, and strawberries before a killing frost.

☐ If tomato vines are covered with green fruit, pull up whole plants and hang them in a basement or garage until fruits ripen.

☐ After onion tops have fallen over, dig the bulbs and let them cure on the soil surface for about a week before you store them.

☐ After harvesting, spread compost over the soil surface.

☐ Rake leaves and clean up plant debris, then add them to the compost pile.

Zone 4

☐ On the first of the month, plant spinach for overwintering.

☐ Use up any remaining compost in your bins to make room for the leaves you'll soon add.

☐ Dig up and store tender bulbs and tubers, such as cannas and dahlias.

☐ Pick the seedpods and heads of any open-pollinated flowers you want to grow again next year; store the seeds in a cool, dry spot.

☐ Set out pansies, mums, and kale for later fall color.

☐ Plant bulbs and garlic in midmonth.

☐ Get ready to protect tender plants from early frost with row covers and blankets.

☐ Look for dry pods on bean plants; save the seed for planting next season.

Zone 5

☐ Sow seed of next year's biennial flowers, such as forget-me-nots (*Myosotis sylvatica*), sweet William (*Dianthus barbatus*), and foxglove.

☐ Plant spring-flowering bulbs.

☐ Dig up tender dahlias, cannas, caladium, and gladiolus before frost hits; store tubers and bulbs in a cool, dry spot.

☐ Start spinach and kale under row covers or in a coldframe for tasty winter salads.

☐ Still time to patch bare spots in the lawn—cover grass seed lightly with compost.

☐ Plant perennials to take advantage of cool weather and rainfall.

Zone 6

☐ Get fall compost cooking with the last of your grass clippings, spent plants, and leaves.

☐ As garden beds empty, sow quick-growing cover crops like winter rye.

☐ Sow spinach midmonth for spring harvest.

☐ Work spring-flowering bulbs into perennial beds.

☐ Plant garlic by month's end for harvest next June.

☐ Dig up, divide, and replant clumps of overgrown perennials.

Zone 7

☐ Early this month, sow seeds of a mixed greens for fall and winter salads.

☐ Harvest young lettuce planted in August.

☐ Snip off long stems of parsley and freeze them in a bag or jar for winter use.

☐ Trim evergreen hedges (such as holly and privet) on the first cool day.

☐ Set out pansies in a spot that will receive full sun all winter.

☐ Harvest peanuts as soon as shells become hard.

Zone 8

☐ Plant transplants of broccoli, cauliflower, cabbage, and kale; surround them with a thick mulch to cool the soil.

☐ Direct seed spinach, lettuce, beets, carrots, parsley, turnips, and kohlrabi.

☐ Plant pansies, stocks (*Matthiola incana*), snapdragons, sweet alyssum (*Lobularia maritima*), Johnny-jump-ups (*Viola tricolor*), and pinks (*Dianthus* spp.).

☐ Apply a ½-inch layer of compost to areas of the lawn that are susceptible to brown patch; apply organic fertilizer to the entire lawn at the end of the month.

Zone 9

☐ Plant winter lettuce, peas, carrots, cole crops, and Asian greens.

☐ Harvest winter squash and pumpkins before frost, when their skin is hard enough to resist pressure from your thumbnail.

☐ Set out transplants of calendula, primroses, larkspur (*Consolida ambigua*), snapdragons, bachelor's buttons (*Centaurea cyanus*), stocks (*Matthiola incana*), and pansies.

☐ Refrigerate spring bulbs for 6 weeks to plant later this fall.

☐ Pick 'Bartlett' pears for ripening indoors, but allow Asian pears and 'Seckel' pears to ripen on the tree.

☐ Protect grapes from birds and wasps by covering the ripening clusters with brown paper lunch bags.

Zone 10

☐ Prune poinsettias for holiday bloom.

☐ As grasshopper numbers die down, plant tuberoses (*Polianthes tuberosa*), gloriosa lilies, amaryllis, and other subtropical bulbs and rhizomes.

☐ Plant okra. It's your last chance of the season.

☐ Seed cucurbits and herbs, and set out transplants of tomatoes, peppers, and onions.

☐ Repair or replace drip irrigation lines.

☐ Work in soil amendments, including compost, bonemeal, and greensand.

Preserving the Tastes of Summer

Sure, you want to put up some of your harvest so you can enjoy it all winter long. But you don't want to spend the last of the summer indoors, laboring in the kitchen. The solution? Freeze and dry your bounty. Both methods are easier (and cooler) than canning. Here's the scoop, crop by crop.

Tomatoes

Before freezing, remove the tomato skins. Immerse your fresh tomatoes in boiling water until the skins crack, then plunge the fruits into very cold water for another minute. Take them out, peel off the skin, and pack them whole or quartered in plastic freezer containers.

A faster method is to freeze whole, unpeeled tomatoes. When you're ready to use them, put the frozen bag under hot water briefly, until you can remove the tomatoes. Then stick the tomatoes under the hot water for a few more seconds to loosen the skin, which will easily peel off.

Dehydration removes all that messy water and leaves you with pure tomato flavor. And almost any kind of tomato—even cherry types—dry into a sweet, chewy chip. Some people say that meaty paste tomatoes work best for drying, but others prefer to dry the big, sweet beefsteak types.

Cut slices about ½ inch thick (cut cherry tomatoes in half) and set the slices on the dehydrator trays. Don't let the pieces touch. Most machines will dry them in about 4 hours, but many people let them go overnight (they're done when the pieces are leathery and flat). You can store them in tightly lidded jars or put them in bags in the freezer. After drying, a bushel of tomatoes takes up very little space. (To keep the dehydrator from heating up your house, run it outdoors in a sheltered area.)

Corn

To get a taste of summer sweetness in the middle of winter, freeze some of your corn. First, blanch the ears by boiling them for 3 to 4 minutes. Plunge the blanched ears into cold water. After the ears have cooled, scrape the kernels off the cob. Put meal-size portions of the cut kernels into plastic freezer bags. You can eat the corn lightly steamed, right out of the freezer (don't defrost it before cooking it). If you prefer your winter corn on the cob, blanch the fresh ears for 6 minutes, then freeze the whole ears. When you're ready to serve them, just steam the frozen ears for another 6 minutes.

Peppers

Peppers (both hot and sweet) freeze beautifully without blanching. Just chop or slice them, freeze the pieces on a cookie sheet until they're solid, then transfer the pieces to plastic freezer bags. When you're cooking, just scoop out what you need.

Thin-fleshed peppers will dry outside, hung on a string or set on a screen lined with brown paper in an airy, shady spot, as long as your weather is still hot and dry. (Cover the peppers with cheesecloth to keep off insects.) Thick-fleshed peppers require a food dehydrator. Small, hot peppers will dry just fine whole, but cut larger, thicker peppers into ½-inch slices. They're dry when the skin becomes papery or crackly when you touch it. Store them in jars with tight lids. Mix your dried peppers into winter chili, stir-fries, and other dishes in need of a little punch. Or grind some of the dried peppers (hot or sweet) in a blender or food processor. Use the flakes as a shake-on seasoning.

Beans

Prompt freezing will well preserve your homegrown beans' vitamin content. The key to successful bean freezing is carefully timed blanching. First, bring your water to a rolling boil. Then add no more beans than the water will take and still remain boiling. After 3 minutes (not a moment more or they'll be limp when they come out of the freezer), remove the beans and immerse them in ice water. When they're cool, blot them dry, and pack into meal-size portions in plastic freezer bags.

Peas

Like beans, freeze your peas quickly after harvesting. Blanch shelled peas for 1½ minutes and sugar snaps and snow peas for 2½ minutes—not any longer or they'll be mushy when you cook them later. Cool them in ice water, blot them dry, then store them in freezer bags. Don't defrost them before cooking.

Shelled peas are easy to dry. Use dried peas in soups and stews. Forget about drying the edible-podded ones; they'll lose their crispness and become chewy and pulpy.

Cucumbers

Freeze a few cukes at the end of the season to use later in chilled soups or for a cool summer drink. Peel the cukes, chop them into chunks, drop them into plastic bags and put the bags in the freezer. For a thick off-season slushie, puree the frozen cucumber chunks along with a splash of fruit juice, a few chunks of frozen melon, some honey, and a pinch of pineapple sage.

GARDENER TO GARDENER

Basil All Winter

Garden-grown basil is a family favorite, so I grow and preserve as much of it as possible. At the end of the summer, I simply pull up the plants and hang them on a clothesline in the basement to dry. When the leaves are dry, I crumble them together to create a dried basil mix for winter cooking.

For making pesto (the traditional Italian sauce of chopped basil, olive oil, pine nuts, and cheese), the fresh, crinkled leaves of the large-leaved basils work best. You don't have to work as hard to get the massive amounts you need, and the big leaves are easier to chop.

I find the purple basils perfect for making ruby red, basil-flavored vinegars. And the complex, clove flavor of the Thai basils (including 'Siam Queen') complement both fiery and delicate dishes—including Thai, Indian, and other southeast Asian cuisine.

Andrea Ray Chandler
Olathe, Kansas

Stocking Up Simplified

Try these tips for saving time and space when you preserve the harvest:

Faster tomato sauce. Simmer pureed tomatoes slowly in a heavy pot, but don't stir. Water will separate from the tomatoes and rise to the top. Skim off this thin liquid, run it through a sieve, then return any pulp to the pot to continue cooking. (Save the clear liquid for soup.) You'll have thick sauce in no time.

Easy-peel tomatoes and peaches. Place fruit in a strainer or colander, plunge it all into boiling water for 30 to 60 seconds, then remove. Immediately submerge all into ice water.

Easier apple butter. Instead of standing over a hot stove to make apple butter, use a Crock-Pot. Set the cooker on high for 10 hours, with the lid off. Stir occasionally.

Excess zucchini. Puree a few zukes with some herbs and onion. Freeze in pint containers for a thick, flavorful base for winter soups.

Space-saving casseroles. Prepare the casserole and freeze it until solid. Then, remove the frozen contents from the dish. Wrap the ready-to-cook meal in freezer wrap and pop it back into the freezer until you are ready to serve it.

No-blanch freezing. Too hot to boil water for blanching? Sauté root vegetables (carrots, beets, turnips) in a little oil until they begin to soften, then freeze. Later, thaw and roast the veggies in a 350°F oven.

Fast-freeze peaches. Freeze peaches and nectarines whole (without peeling and slicing first). Later, put frozen fruits in a colander and pour boiling water over them until the skins crack. Peel, pit, and slice.

Longer-keeping potatoes. When storing potatoes, add a few dried sprigs of rosemary, sage, or lavender. Researchers have found that oils in the herbs suppress potato sprouting and inhibit rot.

Carrots

If your region has mild winters, the best way to keep your carrots is to leave them in the garden under mulch until you're ready to use them. In colder regions, pull up your carrots before a hard frost sets in and freeze them (sliced or diced) after 2 minutes of blanching. Besides using the carrots as a cooked vegetable, you can use them in muffins and cakes. For these baking uses, first grate the carrots, then give them a quick dip in boiling water. Freeze the grated carrots in recipe-size portions.

You can dry sliced carrots into chips. You can either eat the chips or grind them into flakes. The flakes add sweetness to stews and soups.

Onions

Firm, pungent storage onions will keep for months in a cool, dry basement, and even longer in a root cellar. But Vidalias and other sweet, mild onions don't store well. To preserve their goodness, just chop them up and freeze them in plastic containers.

You can also dry ½-inch-thick onion slices in a dehydrator, then grind the dried slices into flakes or powder to use as a seasoning.

Broccoli

Freezing preserves broccoli's taste, texture, and nutrients. Cut up the heads into small florets so the pieces blanch uniformly. Blanch cut-up florets and little side shoots only for a minute before freezing. Cool the blanched broccoli, then pack it into plastic bags and freeze.

Pumpkins

Many pumpkins will store until spring in an ordinary cool basement. You can also cook the pumpkins, then freeze the cooked flesh in plastic freezer bags. Cooking pumpkin is simple: Just cut it in half, remove the seeds, put the halves cut side down on a cookie sheet, then bake at 350°F for 20 to 40 minutes (it's done when the skin begins to turn brown and you can easily push a fork through it).

Scoop the flesh out of the skin and either puree it or just mash it up with a fork. You can spice some of it with cinnamon, allspice, and apple juice concentrate before freezing. Then it will be ready to make into a pie later.) Pack the cooked pumpkin in plastic freezer bags in 1 or 2 cup quantities—that makes it easy to use in recipes later.

Summer Squash and Zucchini

Tender summer squash and zucchini get mushy in the freezer. So puree yellow and green summer squash in your blender or food processor, then freeze the puree to use in cakes, breads, and soups.

Dried zucchini chips are great with sandwiches or dips. Before drying, slice them into ¼-inch-thick rounds and quick-blanch them (just a few seconds in boiling water). Then dry the rounds overnight in the dehydrator. They're ready when they snap in half when bent.

Eggplant

Coat slices of fresh cut eggplant with an egg-and-bread-crumb mixture, bake until almost tender, let them cool, and then freeze them in plastic bags. You can use these breaded slices as a kind of crust for pizza—top them with dried tomatoes, roasted peppers, and cheese and then bake until the eggplant is crisp and the cheese is melted.

Strawberries

Strawberries are highly perishable, so preserve them quickly when they're at their peak. Let the berries freeze solid on a cookie sheet, then move them into plastic bags. You can also crush, puree, and freeze them. Thaw, then pour this supersweet treat into punch or over desserts.

For chocolate-covered strawberries, slice a big batch of fresh strawberries, roll the slices in a powdered instant hot chocolate mix, then dry them overnight. Delicious!

To blanch vegetables, set the veggies into boiling water for the required time.

Then plunge them into ice water until cool.

Roll dry with a paper towel and freeze in plastic freezer bags.

Watermelon and Cantaloupe

Freeze chunks of watermelon or cantaloupe. For a thirst-quenching slushie, simply puree the frozen chunks. (If you're using cantaloupe, you may want to add lemon juice or honey.) Or puree fresh watermelon, then freeze the puree in ice cube trays to add to cool drinks later on.

Better yet, cut the melon flesh into long, thin slivers and dry them. With the water evaporated, you get a fruit-leather-like sticky, chewy candy. But don't cut the slivers any thinner than ½ inch or so, or you won't get them unstuck from the dehydrator trays.

Raspberries

Ripe berries don't last long, so put any excess into long-term storage when they're fresh from the garden. Freeze unwashed berries on a cookie sheet. When they're firm, pack them into freezer containers to use later in desserts. Or, simply fill the blender with perfect berries, puree, then freeze the puree in plastic containers. For a very special cake, add a pint of puree to chocolate cake batter.

Raspberries also dry very well. Just a few hours in the dehydrator and they're ready to put into tightly sealed jars or in a bag in the freezer.

To freeze fresh herbs, put enough for several meals in each freezer bag; label with type and date.

Blueberries

Blueberries are a snap to freeze. Pick out any bruised or not quite ripe berries, remove the stems, and rinse gently with water. Put the best berries into a freezer container. They're great on cereal, thawed or frozen, and excellent on ice cream.

Peaches and Nectarines

Sliced or halved peaches and nectarines are a snap to freeze. Remove the skin, dip the slices in ascorbic acid solution or citrus juice to preserve their color, then freeze them in sweet syrup. The sugar acts as a preservative and helps them hold their texture. (But you can eliminate the sugar solution, if you'd prefer.)

Both fruits also dry well in the dehydrator. Just be sure to dip the cut pieces in citrus juice or honey first to preserve their color. Or, puree either fruit with honey or pineapple, then dry the puree into a fruit leather using a special insert available for your dehydrator tray. Kids love it!

Storage Requirements of Vegetables and Fruits

COLD AND VERY MOIST (32°–40°F; 90–95% RELATIVE HUMIDITY)	COOL AND MOIST (40°–50°F; 85–90% RELATIVE HUMIDITY)	COLD AND MOIST (32°–40°F; 80–90% RELATIVE HUMIDITY)	COOL AND DRY (35°–40°F; 60–70% RELATIVE HUMIDITY)	MODERATELY WARM AND DRY (50°–60°F; 60–70% RELATIVE HUMIDITY)

Beets
Broccoli (short term)
Brussels sprouts
   (short term)
Carrots
Celery
Chinese cabbage
Collards
Leeks
Parsnips
Rutabagas
Turnips
	Cucumbers
	Eggplants (50°–60°F)
	Muskmelons
	   (cantaloupes)
	Peppers, sweet
	   (45°–55°F)
	Tomatoes, ripe
	Watermelons
		Apples
		Cabbage
		Cauliflower
		   (short term)
		Grapefruit
		Grapes (40°F)
		Oranges
		Pears
		Potatoes
		Quinces
			Garlic
			Onions
			Soybeans, green, in the
			   pod (short term)
				Peppers, hot (dried)
				Pumpkins
				Squash, winter
				Sweet potatoes
				Tomatoes, green
				   (tolerate up to 70°F)

Pantry Records

ITEM	HOW MUCH	STOCKING-UP METHOD	NOTES

GARDENER TO GARDENER

Easiest Tomato Sauce

Because I always plant more tomatoes than our family can eat fresh, I cook up and can a lot of tomato sauce and paste. One year we had so many tomatoes that I couldn't keep up with the canning—I worried that some fruit would go to waste.

So I chopped a bunch of fresh tomatoes into large chunks, tossed them into gallon-size plastic zipper bags and stored the bags in the freezer. When I was ready to make sauce, I thawed out the bags, poured off the liquid (to use in soups), then slipped the skins off the chunks. I put the chunks into a crank-style juicer/strainer, which separated out the seeds and produced a delicious, thick pulp.

Because I had already poured off the excess water, the pulp required half as much cooking time as usual—saving me hours in a hot kitchen. I also found that the frozen tomatoes could be thawed slightly and cut up to use "fresh" in recipes and salads.

Lisa and Brett Long
St. Helens, Oregon

No-Cook Tomato Paste

Here's my no-cook method for making great tomato paste. First, I juice raw tomatoes using the juice attachment on my mixer (similar to a Squeezo strainer).

Then I line a large colander with fine-mesh nylon fabric (such as for curtains), place the lined colander over a large bowl, and carefully pour the juice into the colander. (The first juice to drain out is pink, but the rest is almost clear.) After a couple of hours, only a thick tomato paste remains in the colander. I spoon the paste into 1-cup containers and freeze them.

A heaping 2-gallon pail of cut tomatoes makes about 23 cups of juice, which yields (after straining) about 5 cups of thick tomato paste.

Susan Setzler
Dublin, Virginia

Savory Radish Pods

If you allow a few radishes to go to seed, delicious pods will form along the seed stalk. These edible pods taste great in soups, salads, and stir-fries—or just "as is," for snacking. You can pick pods from the same plant for as long as two months, if you pick the pods every three or four days and water the plants when the weather is dry. When the pods start to get woody, pull out the plant and start some new ones.

The pods will keep in the refrigerator for up to 3 weeks. (They'll keep best if you don't wash them before you refrigerate them; wait until just before you use them). They also freeze well and can be used later in cooked dishes. Bonus: The bees seem to enjoy the radish flowers in the garden. (Note: Some heirloom radishes, such as 'Rat's Tail' and 'Madras', are grown specifically for their delicious edible pods—but any variety will do.)

Cynthia Putt
Cloverdale, Oregon

GARDENER TO GARDENER

Easy Pea Shelling

If you like to freeze peas but find shelling a chore, try my method: First blanch them in boiling water for a couple of minutes right in the pod, then remove them from the pot and plunge them into cold water to stop the cooking process. When you're ready to shell them, just squeeze the end of the stem like a tube of toothpaste, and the peas will slip right out.

Sharon Relford
North Myrtle Beach,
South Carolina

Freeze Onions for Easy Cooking

I'd had a lot of success growing Southern ("short-day") onions, but not much luck storing them—until I tried freezing. Now, after harvesting my onions, I dice them up (that way I get all my crying over with at one time), then freeze the cut pieces on cookie sheets. When the pieces have frozen, I pack them in freezer containers and store them in the freezer until I need them for cooking. They taste great this way and are very easy to use.

Al Spoden
Cold Spring, Minnesota

Burdock: An Italian Treat

Our family has a long tradition of gathering and eating burdock (Arctium lappa), passed on to us from our grandfather who has been eating these nutritious wild plants since his boyhood in Italy. Every year toward the end of May, my grandfather and I go digging up burdocks, roots and all. May is when the plants are best for eating—not too tough and the burrs have not yet developed.

We use the stalks to create several different dishes. First we cut away the large leaves and roots, leaving us with celery-like stalks. We cut the stalks into bite-size pieces, rinse them well, and then boil them in salted water until they are soft. Before serving, we drain off the water, but we don't throw it away—grandfather drinks this nutritious spring tonic.

We also leave some of the stems whole, then dip the pieces in a beaten egg and roll them in flour seasoned with salt and pepper. We sauté the battered chunks in olive oil until golden brown.

But maybe our favorite burdock dish is frittata. We sauté chopped burdock stems with a clove of garlic and some chopped onion in olive oil, then pour over it a mixture of eggs and milk seasoned with breadcrumbs, salt, pepper, and grated Romano cheese. When the egg mixture is firm on the bottom, we flip it over and cook the other side. The finished frittata is sliced into wedges just like a pie. It's delicious.

Maria Ligget
Erie, Pennsylvania

Pepper Power

Ever plant more peppers than you can eat? Or have room for in the freezer? Do what I do, and make your own pepper flakes. It's easy and saves plenty of storage space. Pick your peppers, cut them open, remove the seeds, then lay the cut pieces on a screen in a dry, airy location (or dry them in a food dehydrator). After the peppers dry, grind them up and jar them. Bell peppers make a great sweet shake; hot peppers make a spicy one! (Remember to wear rubber gloves when handling hot peppers.)

James J. Kelly
Clairton, Pennsylvania

GARDENER TO GARDENER

Sweet Potato Storage Tips

After we harvested more than a bushel of nutritious sweet potatoes last September, we had to figure out how to store the windfall. Here's what we did:

First, we separated the perfect sweet potatoes from the ones that were blemished (we ate or gave away the blemished ones). Then we "cured" the best potatoes by storing them in a bushel basket inside a cool shed for a couple of weeks. For storage, we just transferred them to a large box, folded over the flaps of the box, then set the whole thing in a cool corner of our basement. After several months, our sweet potatoes still looked and tasted fresh.

George Seifrit
Sinking Spring,
Pennsylvania

Timely Storage Advice

Here are a couple of timesaving food preservation tips, to give you more time to spend in the garden. To store herbs, hang them up in loose bundles until they dry thoroughly, then crumble the dried whole herbs into a food mill. Give the mill a spin—it will separate the twigs from the useable parts, which you can then store in jars.

When canning or freezing tomatoes, avoid the messy job of blanching and peeling to remove skins. Instead, cut ripe tomatoes in half and rub them (cut side down) on the largest holes of a grater, set inside a bowl. The pulp goes through the holes into the bowl, while the skin stays behind.

Jil McIntosh
Oshawa, Ontario

Multipurpose Sunchokes

Sunchokes, also called Jerusalem artichokes, a perennial vegetable plant with beautiful flowers, are an essential part of my garden. I harvest half of the delicious tubers in the spring and the rest in the fall, storing the chokes in my root cellar where they stay fresh all winter.

Because every tuber left in the ground sprouts a new stalk (resulting in overcrowding and smaller chokes), I make sure to dig out all the chokes when I harvest. Then I replant only the biggest tubers—4 inches deep and 8 inches apart. That assures me tall plants for shade the following summer and a big crop of tasty tubers for year-round eating.

John E. Gannon
Dexter, Michigan

Overwintered Onions

A few small onions left in the ground in fall can provide a tasty treat the following spring—long before any other crops are ready. We discovered this last year, when we inadvertently left a few small onions in the ground at harvest, then covered them with mulch in the fall. In mid-March we were delighted to find green shoots breaking through the leafy cover! The small onions weathered our harsh cold winter beautifully.

When the weather began to warm, our stored onions were starting to soften and sprout. Not wanting to waste them, we planted them in the garden. By early summer we were harvesting wonderful green onions again.

Bob Uptagrafft
Clarkston, Washington

Chapter 10

October

Stretching the Season:
Coldframes and Greenhouses

Something told the wild geese
It was time to fly.
Summer sun was on their wings, Winter in their cry.

—*From "Something Told the Wild Geese," by Rachel Field*

Denying it is impossible: For most of us, the true growing season comes to an end this month. Leaves change color and fall from trees, days grow short, nights cold—sure signs that winter is dead ahead.

But just because nature is getting ready to take a break doesn't mean you must give up the garden entirely. You can extend your growing season beyond its natural limits with the help of some simple devices. Depending on your level of determination and how much time and money you want to invest, you can use blankets, row covers, coldframes, hoop houses, or a full-scale greenhouse to stretch your season. The reward: crispy lettuce, red ripe tomatoes, and fresh parsley in December. Pretty good incentive, isn't it?

Of course gardeners in the warmest areas (USDA Zones 9 and 10) are just beginning to gear up for their main growing season—summer there is simply too hot to grow most temperate crops. Even so, tender seedlings are still subject to damage when the temperature drops. So gardeners north and south must use ingenuity (and sometimes more) to protect their crops this month.

Gardener's To-Do List—October

**If you don't know what USDA hardiness zone you live in,
check the map on page 246 to find out.**

Zone 3

- [ ] After a light frost, begin harvesting sweetened turnips, parsnips, and other late veggies left in the ground.
- [ ] Collect and store flower bulbs—such as gladiola, freesia, calla, and cannas—after their tops have frozen.
- [ ] Water trees, shrubs, perennials, roses, and lawns before the ground freezes hard.
- [ ] Cut back tender roses to 10 to 12 inches, and remove all foliage so insects and diseases can't winter over.
- [ ] Cover tender, hybrid roses with leaves or straw to protect against winter temperature changes.
- [ ] Harvest late apples before the end of the month.
- [ ] Clean up garden debris before the first snowfall.

Zone 4

- [ ] Harvest or heavily mulch the last carrots, beets, and other root crops; store them in a cool place that won't freeze.
- [ ] Plant garlic and shallots.
- [ ] Sow a cover crop of winter rye in vacant beds.
- [ ] Plant spring-blooming bulbs.
- [ ] Remember that it's still time to plant potted trees and shrubs.
- [ ] Dig up and store gladiolius and other tender corms and tubers.
- [ ] Cover tender roses and grapes.

Zone 5

- [ ] Thin out one-third of the oldest branches of forsythia, lilac, spirea, and potentilla for better bloom and shape next spring.
- [ ] Dig up tender tubers and corms of dahlias, cannas, caladium, and gladiolius.
- [ ] *Don't* cut back ornamental grasses, sunflowers, and wildflowers—leave them for winter interest and for wildlife.
- [ ] Collect leaves to shred (with a shredder or mower) and compost.
- [ ] Clean up all fallen fruits to reduce disease and pest problems.
- [ ] Work well-rotted manure or compost into asparagus beds.
- [ ] Dig up geraniums, and bring them indoors for the winter.
- [ ] Pot up some paperwhite bulbs for holiday forcing.

Zone 6

- [ ] Squeeze in a few last sowings of spinach and other cold-hardy greens, beneath row covers or coldframes.
- [ ] Have frost protectors handy to extend the harvest of tender veggies.
- [ ] Begin cleaning up the garden.
- [ ] Compost all spent plants, shredded leaves, and the last grass clippings.
- [ ] Continue planting spring-blooming bulbs, trees, and shrubs.

Zone 7

- [ ] Bring zonal geraniums and vacationing houseplants indoors before the first frost.
- [ ] Thin the radishes, carrots, and turnips you sowed last month; then sprinkle the bed with 1 inch of compost.
- [ ] Dig up sweet potatoes before winter rains cause them to split and rot.
- [ ] Set out garlic cloves and continue to plant onions.
- [ ] Sow late spinach to overwinter; it will resume growing in spring.
- [ ] Clean up the blueberry patch: Prune broken or diseased limbs, and thicken the mulch with a layer of pine needles or shredded oak leaves.

Zone 8

- [ ] Plant more lettuce, Chinese cabbage, spinach, carrots, beets, peas, radishes, onions, turnips, garlic, shallots, and cress.
- [ ] Set out strawberry plants.
- [ ] Sow a cover crop of winter rye (*Secale cereale*), purple vetch (*Vicia benghalensis*), Austrian winter peas (*Pisum arvense*), or 'Elbon' rye (*Secale cereale* 'Elbon') in vacant beds.
- [ ] Use rye clippings to add nitrogen to compost, speeding the breakdown of fall leaves.
- [ ] In flowerbeds, plant anemones, oxalis, and ranunculus for spring bloom.
- [ ] Also, seed annual candytuft (*Iberis umbellata*) in bare spots of flowerbeds for spring bloom.
- [ ] Broadcast wildflower seeds to establish a meadow.
- [ ] Plant trees and shrubs: Warm fall temps will help them get established before winter.

Zone 9

- [ ] For spring bloom, broadcast wildflower seeds over soil that has been lightly cultivated.
- [ ] Plant fast-growing, frost-resistant veggies: radishes, mustard, spinach, 'Tokyo Market' turnips, and corn salad.
- [ ] Divide and transplant bearded irises, daylilies, phlox, cannas, and Shasta daisies.
- [ ] Harvest sweet potatoes after tops wither, but before the first hard frost.
- [ ] Harvest winter squash, pumpkins, and peanuts before frost.
- [ ] Clean up fallen fruit in the orchard.
- [ ] Build a hot compost pile to kill pathogens lurking in garden debris: Use a high-nitrogen material, such as grass clippings or seafood shells.

Zone 10

- [ ] Set out transplants of tomatoes, peppers, and eggplants.
- [ ] Mulch and water well—dry spells this month can last a week or longer.
- [ ] Finish pruning fruit trees so new sprouts can harden before cold arrives.
- [ ] Plant colorful bloomers, such as sweet alyssum, begonias, petunias, and pansies.
- [ ] Prepare beds for planting roses; plant them late this month.
- [ ] Fertilize plants that flower in winter.
- [ ] Plant strawberries and brassicas (except brussels sprouts—it's too warm) early in the month.
- [ ] In midmonth, direct seed root crops and beans.
- [ ] Near the end of the month, sow lettuce, spinach, and other greens.

Simple Season Extenders

Protecting plants from an early frost will extend your season a few weeks, and it doesn't have to take more than a few minutes of your time. The quickest method is to cover the plants with sheets, blankets, or plastic on nights when frost threatens. It's primitive, but it works. Keep the lightweight covers from blowing away by anchoring loose corners with rocks or bricks, or by resting dead branches over the tops. Avoid crushing especially delicate plants by placing a tomato cage over them before throwing on the cloth or plastic. Use clothespins to clip the cover to the framework.

Make Your Own Coldframes

A coldframe—simply an enclosed area with a clear top to let in sunlight—is one of the easiest ways to extend your growing and harvest season. All you need are a few basic supplies and your imagination. (Imagine: crunchy fresh lettuce for the holidays!) Here's what to do.

Start at the Top

The only essential for the frame's cover is that light gets through. Almost any transparent material will work: glass, fiberglass, polyethylene, or flexible greenhouse coverings—the differences between them are insignificant.

Many people use old window sashes. Be aware, however, that some old frames may be covered with lead-based paint. If in doubt, pass on them, and keep looking until you find windows that the owner can assure you are lead-free. Also, make sure the wood isn't rotting and the glass is secured firmly inside the frame. Be careful when handling the glass, and keep small children away from it.

In extreme northern areas, glass isn't always the best option. "Here in Alaska, glass coldframes break under the weight of our heavy winter snow," explains Jeff Lowenfels, gardening columnist, "so we tend to rely on thick sheets of Lucite or other window-strength plastic instead.

If you're buying material to cover your coldframe, consider Lexan, an improvement over Lucite. Lexan stands up well to the elements (like rain, sleet, ice, or snow). And it insulates especially well.

Other gardeners prefer the corrugated fiberglass (4 × 8-foot panels) sold for greenhouse walls. Although it costs a little more than other plastics, it lets in a lot of light and doesn't turn yellow with prolonged exposure to sunlight.

Frame It Up

The simplest frame uses hay bales: Just arrange four bales of hay or straw into a square shape to make the sides of your coldframe. Put your glass or plastic cover on top of the bales. (Use the straw for mulch next spring, after you disassemble the frame.)

If you can't get bales of hay or straw where you live, you can use other materials for your side walls. Cinder blocks are a good alternative; just be sure to turn them on their sides so the holes point up and down. Otherwise, air will pass through. Cover the top holes to keep the structure warmer.

To make a more permanent and easily vented structure, build the sides from wood and attach your top to it with hinges. Cedar, cypress, and redwood are naturally rot-resistant, but you can use almost any kind of wood—as long as it isn't pressure treated (CCA, Wolmanized, and so on). Pressure-treated wood contains highly toxic substances, including arsenic. Secure the pieces of wood with elbow braces at each corner, glued and then screwed in with two 1- or 1½-inch galvanized screws.

If you garden in an extremely cold area, you'll need a more permanent and better insulated coldframe. Jan Scheefer, a high-altitude gardener in Gunnison, Colorado, made her coldframe walls out of 6-inch-thick poured concrete, which she painted black to absorb solar heat. She capped the frame with corrugated fiberglass framed with pine 2 × 4s.

Stone and mortar walls are another option. Building stone walls requires more labor and know-how than pouring concrete, but they can be much less expensive if you happen to have stone on your property.

Insulate—or Not

By digging a pit beneath your coldframe, you can plant 6 to 8 inches below the surrounding soil level—so the soil will insulate your plants. But digging a pit requires moving a lot of soil, and it makes your coldframe more permanent than you may want.

If you do dig, be aware that rain can run off the frozen ground and into the unfrozen frame bed, causing flooding problems. To prevent this from happening, put a layer of gravel at the bottom of the pit, beneath the layer of soil.

There are other ways to insulate your plants that don't require a pit. You can pile soil, leaves, or wood chips around the outside of an aboveground frame to hold heat. Or consider adding heat more directly. "Many Alaskans warm their coldframes by putting fresh manure or jugs of water inside," says Lowenfels. If you go the manure route (creating a hotbed), don't plant directly in the manure—your plants will burn. Instead, cover the manure with 6 to 8 inches of soil before planting.

Make a simple straw bale coldframe. Use straw as the frame base, and set old window sashes over the tops of the bales for a super insulated garden enclosure.

What's in for Coldframes?

What can you grow in your coldframe? Anything you grow in your garden: In many areas, you can still sow seeds of spinach, lettuce, kale, choys, and other salad greens to enjoy in winter. Or, transplant heads of lettuce, cabbage, and cauliflower inside the frame. Consider transplanting a short pepper plant or two for extended production through another month or two.

In areas with an extra-short growing season, a coldframe may be the only way to grow warm-weather crops. High altitude gardeners and Alaskans use coldframes through summer to raise tomatoes, green beans, and cucumbers.

Set Your Site

If possible, orient your coldframe to the south, with the top angled about 25 to 30 percent from front to back. If that isn't possible, at least make sure your coldframe is in a sunny spot. And angle the top enough for rain to run off.

If you garden in an area with severe northern exposure (such as in Alaska), you'll need to angle your coldframe a bit more steeply because of the sharp angle of the sun during spring and fall at those longitudes.

Don't Forget to Vent

Proper ventilation is probably the most important part of growing inside a coldframe! On warm or cool sunny days, heat can build up inside the sealed frame, so you'll need to open the lid. Leave it closed and you risk cooking your crops *before* you harvest them.

The most basic venting tool is a sturdy stick or dowel that you use to prop open the top, late in the morning of any sunny day when outside temperature is expected to rise above 40°F. (On a sunny 50°F day, the temperature inside your coldframe can quickly soar to 80°F.) Make notches in the stick so you can prop open the top at different heights, depending on the outside temperature. And always close the lid or vent by late afternoon so some of the insulating heat of the day is trapped inside to help protect against the night's chill.

The most reliable solution, though, is to include an automatic vent in your frame design (unless you live in a very snowy region; the vents usually aren't strong enough to lift the load). Such vents automatically open and shut your coldframe when specific temperatures are reached.

So what's the real secret to successful coldframe use? Paying attention to the conditions and your plants—just like you do with everything else in gardening.

If you want a more permanent coldframe, make it out of cinder blocks and top it with old windows. Be sure the holes in the blocks face up and down.

GARDENER TO GARDENER

Maximum Coldframes

Want to get more from your coldframe? Take it out of the garden and attach it to a basement window of your house! This setup lets me harden-off my seedlings 3 to 4 weeks earlier than before!

First, select a basement window. Then take an existing coldframe (or create one especially for this use, designed to fit your window) and cut an opening that matches the dimensions of your window in its rear wall. Next, take some scrap lumber and make an open-ended box (the same dimensions as the opening in the coldframe). Wedge the box snugly inside the window, creating a tunnel between the inside of the coldframe and the basement window. By keeping the basement window open, warm air will rise into the coldframe, preventing temperatures inside the frame from falling below freezing on cold spring nights.

My coldframe measures 5 feet long and 3 feet deep (but yours can be any size you want). Nuts and bolts hold it together, so disassembly is easy.

Ed Mellina
Dalkeith, Ontario

Water Is Greenhouse Climate Control

The best thing I've found for moderating the temperature in my small greenhouse is water. During the fall, I save milk jugs, water jugs, and 2- or 3-liter soda bottles and fill them with water. I set them in the greenhouse—on the floor, in stacked milk crates and on shelves. I even hang them. The water absorbs the heat of the sun during the day and releases it during the night.

Now I don't get the sudden drops or increases in temperature that I used to. The bottles around the trays of seedlings create a mini-environment within the greenhouse. I still use a portable heater, but a lot less than I used to. To make space on the shelves for seedlings, I empty some of the containers (mostly into the seedlings, thus saving me the trouble of hauling out water).

Irene Brown
Garfield, New Jersey

Outdoor Greenhouse Heater

Many greenhouse growers use dark-colored barrels filled with water to absorb and release solar heat inside their greenhouse. But I didn't want to give up all that growing space for the barrels. So I found a way to use the barrels as both space heaters and containers for growing.

I line up 55-gallon barrels along the north wall of my $15 \times 8 \times 8$-foot molded fiberglass greenhouse, fill the barrels with soil, and then water the soil well. The barrels of wet soil make good solar collectors, and I can plant directly in them so space isn't wasted. I use shorter barrels to grow plants in front of the south wall. That allows more light to reach the other plants.

Steve Henderson
Shelton, Washington

GARDENER TO GARDENER

Figs in New England

I grow subtropical fig trees in Connecticut and enjoy an abundance of honey flavored fruit each fall—without bringing the plants indoors for the winter. How? I bundle them up in a winter coat.

Each fall, after frost has blackened the figs' leaves (usually mid-November), I bundle up the trees and tuck them in for the winter, using 6 feet of chicken wire fence, six metal posts (6 feet long), a roll of roofing paper, a roll of 3 mil plastic, some burlap (3 feet wide), a ball of twine, a leaf rake, a big bucket, and some hay or straw. Here's what I do:

1. I bind the main trunks of the fig trees together with twine so they resemble a folded umbrella, but not so tightly that it damages the sensitive bark of the tree.

2. Using a sledgehammer, I drive three metal posts into the ground around each tree, 2 to 3 feet from the center of the bunched up trunks, and pound them in firmly to withstand winter winds.

3. For the first layer of insulation, I bind handfuls of straw or hay to the trunks with twine.

4. Next, I cut off a section of chicken wire fence (8 to 10 feet long), wrap it around the metal posts and tie the ends together with twine.

5. I then dump fallen leaves from my yard into the chicken wire enclosure, and tamp them down with the flat end of an iron rake.

6. When the leaves reach the top of the enclosure, I cap the tip of the trees with a plastic pail lined with straw, and then drape the whole thing with plastic and secure it with twine.

7. Finally, I wrap a layer of roofing paper around the outside base of the structure, and secure it with more twine. And I wrap the entire structure with burlap, again tying it down with twine. (The burlap adds some insulation and looks better than the plastic and roofing paper.)

8. In mid-May, when danger of frost has passed, I remove the protective layers and expose the trees. After several days, the trunks return to their normal position, and I fertilize and water the trees. By July, small tender green figs are forming, and by mid-September we are enjoying the delicious ripe fruits.

Aldo P. Biagiotti
Ridgefield, Connecticut

Compost Warms Sweet Potatoes

Here in western Maine, where the growing season is very short, I manage to grow warm weather–loving sweet potatoes—with the help of my compost pile.

In spring, I add a bit of fresh horse manure to the bottom of a fairly mature compost pile to heat it up. Just before our last frost date, I cover the pile with black plastic to hold in the warmth. Then I plant purchased slips of 'Centennial' variety sweet potatoes into the top of the pile through slits cut into the plastic. To protect the plants from a possible late frost, I cover them with a floating row cover until summer arrives.

When temperatures drop and frost threatens again in fall, I replace the row cover—stretching the growing season as long as I possibly can. Finally, just before the first fall freeze, I harvest my potatoes.

Last year I harvested 2 bushels of beautiful, red sweet potatoes using this method. And when I've finished harvesting, I have a nice pile of mature compost to spread over the garden.

Gladys Hicks
Stratton, Maine

Chapter 11

November

Clean Up: Putting the Garden to Bed

Autumn the bringer of fruit, has poured out her riches, and soon sluggish winter returns.

—*Horace (65–8 B.C.)*

Let's be honest. You probably don't consider fall cleanup to be one of your favorite garden activities. In fact, cleaning up the yard is one of those things that's very easy to "let slide."

Maybe that's because the benefits aren't as obvious or as immediate as, say, planting or even pulling weeds. But believe it or not, cleaning up your garden can be just as valuable as planning or maintaining it.

By spending a few weekends this month putting your garden to bed, you'll actually be making a big investment in *next* year's garden. After all, we all want next year's garden to be better than this year's!

Right now, your property has a wealth of compostables—leaves, grass clippings, and spent plants are yours for the raking. Shredded leaves also make an excellent winter mulch. You can use these abundant, though messy, resources to your advantage.

What's more, removing spent plants and fallen fruit from the garden does much more than make your property look tidy—it goes a long way toward preventing disease and insect problems next year. In this chapter, we'll explain how you can invest in a healthy garden.

Gardener's To-Do List—November

**If you don't know what USDA hardiness zone you live in,
check the map on page 246 to find out.**

Zone 3

☐ If rainfall has been light, deeply water trees and shrubs before the ground freezes.

☐ To successfully overwinter half-hardy plants (such as azaleas, rhododendrons, and butterfly bushes), surround them with a wire cage and cover them with a thick layer of dry leaves.

☐ Force a few bulbs for indoor winter color; plant half now and half in 2 weeks for a longer show.

☐ Check stored tubers, bulbs, potatoes, onions, and garlic for spoilage and softness.

☐ Winterize all power tools before storing.

☐ Sharpen, clean, and repair hand tools before storing them.

☐ Clean and fill bird feeders.

Zone 4

☐ Rid the garden of plant debris that might allow diseases and pests to survive the winter.

☐ Wrap the trunks of young trees to protect their tender bark from winter injury.

☐ *Don't* remove snow and ice from evergreens—rescue efforts may do more harm than good.

☐ Clean up all dropped fruit and other debris from beneath fruit trees.

☐ Cut lawn grass short now—tall grasses can become moldy beneath snow cover.

☐ After the ground freezes, cover perennials with mulch to keep frost-thaw cycles from heaving them out of the ground.

☐ Turn the compost pile and add water if it feels dry.

Zone 5

☐ Plant garlic cloves and shallots 2 inches deep and 4 inches apart; mulch with 6 inches of straw or shredded leaves.

☐ Dig up remaining root crops.

☐ Still time to haul in a pot of parsley: Pot it, water well, and set in a bright window.

☐ *Don't* remove chrysanthemum foliage—leave it to protect the crown.

☐ Cut back other perennials (except spring bloomers, roses, and grasses) to a few inches above soil level.

☐ Prune tea roses back to 8 to 12 inches high, mound compost around the bud union, then cover with a rose cone.

☐ Dig the hole for planting live Christmas trees now—before the soil freezes.

Zone 6

☐ Finish cleanup—gather leaves for the compost pile or for winter mulch on beds.

☐ *Don't* miss your last chance to plant spring-blooming bulbs, such as daffodils and tulips.

☐ Continue to thin lettuce and spinach.

☐ Mulch crops you want to overwinter with a thick layer of straw.

☐ Harvest frost-sweetened brussels sprouts, carrots, parsnips, cabbage, and kale.

☐ *Don't* cut back ornamental grasses; they add beauty to the landscape and provide shelter for overwintering beneficials and wildlife.

☐ Cut back other perennials (except spring bloomers, roses, and mums) to a few inches above soil level.

Zone 7

☐ Cover lettuce, chard, spinach, sorrel, chives, and parsley with with floating row covers, before the first hard freeze.

☐ Continue to plant trees and shrubs.

☐ Set out new strawberries or move rooted runners early this month.

☐ Sow poppy seeds now for flowers next May.

☐ Gather leaves to add to the compost pile or to shred and use as winter mulch.

☐ Pot up a clump of mint, let it freeze one time, then bring it indoors for snipping throughout the winter.

☐ Feed leeks, then hill up soil around them to begin the blanching process.

Zone 8

☐ Fruit trees will arrive at nurseries for fall planting; shop early for the best selection.

☐ Harvest cold-sensitive veggies—such as tomatoes, eggplant, and peppers—that you planted in July.

☐ Under row covers, plant cool-loving crops, such as brussels sprouts, cabbage, Chinese cabbage, broccoli, peas, carrots, kale, radishes, mustard, turnips, beets, and spinach.

☐ Plant more cilantro, parsley, and fennel.

☐ Plant strawberries ('Chandler', 'Sweet Charlie', and 'Sequoia') so plants will be established by spring.

☐ Sow seeds of poppies, larkspur, and delphiniums for early spring color.

Zone 9

☐ Pull up tomato plants, roots and all, to hang in a protected place; pick fruits as they ripen.

☐ Plant prechilled spring-flowering bulbs early this month.

☐ Plant garlic, shallots, fava beans, onion sets, and leeks.

☐ Harvest brussels sprouts, cabbage, broccoli, carrots, turnips, collards, and kale after frost sweetens their flavor.

☐ Cover spinach and lettuce with floating row covers to protect them from frost.

☐ Broadcast wildflower seed, then lightly rake it in, for a bright spring show.

☐ Spread compost or composted manure around citrus trees to encourage spring growth and blossoming.

Zone 10

☐ See that the garden receives at least an inch of water a week (from either rainfall or you).

☐ If a freeze is predicted, soak the ground (not the plants), then cover everything with straw, row covers, or protective material.

☐ Plant successive runs of tender, fast-growing greens, such as cilantro and chervil.

☐ Harvest beans, peas, lettuce, squashes, carrots, cucumbers, early melons, and kale.

☐ Continue to harvest ripening fruit; clean up unusable fruits that fall to prevent disease.

☐ Continue to start tomatoes, peppers, and eggplant, but be prepared to protect tender seedlings from cold.

☐ Cut back raspberries.

☐ Feed roses some low-nitrogen, organic fertilizer.

☐ Plant callas, gladiolus, and dahlias for spring and summer bloom.

When It's Hot, They're Not

Hot compost that reaches 130°F will kill many plant diseases, including:

- Botrytis fungi (gray mold on fruits and flowers)
- Rhizoctonia fungi (damping-off of tomato and potato)
- Phytophthora fungi (late blight on tomato and potato)
- Various sclerotinia fungi (white rot on lettuce and onion)
- Stem rot of tomato
- Bacterial blight of chrysanthemum
- Cyst nematodes on potato

Note: At least two well-known disease organisms—fusarium fungi and tobacco mosaic virus—can survive higher temperatures than home compost piles are likely to reach. Throw plants affected with these diseases in the trash or burn them, if local law allows it.

Clean Up for an Early Green Up!

As much as you'd like to keep your garden going through the winter, some plants simply won't make it. So how can you put those "spent" plants to best use?

Turn In for Winter

Organic matter is key to healthy soil, and both plants that are living and plants that have recently died are rich sources of that organic matter. To increase your soil's organic content, you can turn under most of your spent plants right into the beds they've been growing in. Thin-leaved plants—such as lettuce, spinach, and other greens—and beans, peas, and squash break down fast, so you don't need to do anything before turning them in. Tougher plants, such as corn, need to be cut up into smaller pieces before you till or hoe them in.

Two kinds of plant matter that you *shouldn't* turn in are (1) those that won't decompose completely by spring (cabbage cores, for instance) and (2) those that are diseased or insect-infested.

Plant matter that doesn't break down over the winter usually harbors fungal spores that come to life as soon as the temperature rises. And many common fungal diseases overwinter on dead plant parts. So play it safe by composting slow-rotting plants and sickly looking ones in a hot bin or pile away from the garden. Ditto for plants that have suffered from insect pests, Many insects overwinter on the roots of their hosts. And tilling the plants into the soil would only make the area a breeding ground for next year's problems.

Get Compost Cooking

Just how hot must compost get in order to kill diseases? A University of California researcher found that many pathogens—the microorganisms that cause diseases—are killed when compost reaches 130°F. (See "When It's Hot, They're Not" on this page for likely casualties). And while a hot compost pile is killing these pathogens, it's also inviting more beneficial microorganisms. A compost thermometer (sold at garden centers and through garden-supply catalogs) will tell you just how hot your compost is.

If you have trouble getting your pile to reach that temperature in winter, jump-start the cooking process in spring by adding high-nitrogen materials, such as the season's first grass clippings, fresh manure, or shellfish waste. Turn the pile every few days, moving the cooler material on the outside to the hot center so that it all cooks.

Don't Leave the Leaves

Leaves that flutter to the forest floor nourish the soil around trees and naturally suppress plants that might otherwise invade the trees' space. The trouble is, those leaves can harbor disease. For instance, when apple scab—one of the most widespread apple diseases—overwinters in fallen leaves, the fungi burst out with the first warm spring rains and continue the disease cycle.

So compost your leaves instead, making sure that the pile heats up to 130°F for at least a week. Shred or mow the leaves first so they break down faster. To keep the raked leaves from blowing around, wet them, then surround the pile with chicken wire.

Aged leaf compost (the stuff you made *last* fall) is perfect for mulching beds *this* fall, in preparation for winter. Spread the mulch on your beds to limit soil compaction caused by heavy rain, stop erosion, and create a habitat for many beneficial soil organisms.

In winter or summer, leaf mulch lowers soil temperature by as much as 10°F. Because temperatures in the top few inches of unmulched soil can fluctuate almost as much as daily air temperatures, mulch can make a big difference in preventing freezing and thawing during the winter. Wet soil expands as it freezes, which in turn causes it to heave.

Heaving can damage dormant perennials, bulbs, and other plants with shallow roots, so gardeners in cold climates should wait until after the soil freezes to mulch. That way, the mulch will help keep soil frozen through occasional spells of mild winter weather.

In regions where soil freezes only occasionally, leaf mulch can protect soil and plants and look good to boot. To make your mulch look extra neat in a front-yard bed, surround the bed with inexpensive plastic or wire edging, barely anchored into the ground. Remove the edging after several weeks, when the leaves will have settled into place.

Mulching in the winter can protect small fruits in areas where they're only marginally hardy (such as muscadine grapes in the upper South or blackberries in Canada). After muscadines lose their leaves, move the vines down onto the ground. Cover them with a sheet of clear plastic, then mulch over the plastic with 6 inches of straw. Uncover and retrellis the vines in spring when the last hard freeze has passed.

Just a Trim, Please

Most woody plants are best pruned in late winter, but a few need a trim right now. Here's a quick guide to the kindest cuts you can make to your plants in late fall.

Fruit trees. Trim off diseased twigs and broken branches at least 4 inches past the damaged section. Make cuts just outside the raised collar of bark where the branch joins a larger limb.

Flowering shrubs. For types that bloom after midsummer, such as butterfly bush (*Buddleia* spp.) crape myrtle (*Lagerstroemia* spp.), hydrangea, rose of Sharon (*Hibiscus syriacus*), and summersweet (*Clethra* spp.), thin up to one-third of crowded branches or just enough to keep the plants shapely. Come spring, you may need to trim some more branches.

Use a Light Mulch

More of a good thing isn't necessarily better—even mulch. Around small fruits like grapes and berries, you should gather up all old mulch and replace it with a fresh supply of weed-free straw, leaves, or pine needles. Otherwise, unwanted spores of fungal diseases such as anthracnose and black rot may overwinter in the old mulch and greet you first thing in spring.

Very thick mulches may not be your best bet where mice and other rodents are desperate for homes. Thick mulch is perfect for rodent tunnels and nests. If mice are a big problem where you live, avoid hay or straw mulch completely. Instead, wrap the bases of trees with hardware cloth or foil (to prevent the rodents from gnawing on and potentially killing the trees), and put down just enough mulch to keep soil microorganisms happy.

Plant Cover Crops

A gorgeous green cover crop is one of the best ways to add more organic matter to your soil during winter. In areas where cover cropping can continue until mid-November, several exceptional cover-cropped plants deserve special attention.

If you live in the West or Northwest, consider small-seeded fava beans (*Vicia faba*). They can produce twice as much soil nitrogen as most clovers when turned under before they flower. In the maritime Northwest, some varieties are hardy enough to grow through winter and can then either be turned under or allowed to bear in spring.

In Austin, Texas, John Dromgoole highly recommends 'Elbon' rye (*Secale cereale* 'Elbon') as a winter cover crop. This cereal grain produces lots of organic matter (it grows waist high) and helps control harmful nematodes.

Protect Your Perennials

Your perennial shrubs and flowers need a little end-of-the-season attention, too. Give them a trim, both to make them look good and to eliminate potential homes for pests that overwinter in dead stems. Follow up with a top-dressing of compost to get a head start on preventing next year's diseases.

In areas where snow, ice, or dry, desiccating winds are hallmarks of winter, most perennial flowers will also appreciate a lacy roof over their heads, either in the form of a light straw mulch or a featherweight covering of evergreen boughs. Arch the branches over young plants or those of questionable winter hardiness.

Hand Tool Care and Repair

No matter how careful you are, sooner or later a garden tool will lose its edge, become hard to operate, or suffer a broken blade or handle. But that doesn't mean it's time to go out and spend big bucks on a new tool. With just a few simple techniques and the proper replacement parts, you'll have the equivalent of a new tool again.

Of course, proper maintenance will prevent the need for making frequent repairs. So here's how to care for your hand tools and what to do when they finally do break.

Digging Tool Maintenance

Never leave your hard-working shovels and hoes out in the rain. Clean mud and dirt off digging and weeding tools after each use. Pay particular attention to cleaning out the hollow backs of shovels and spades; this will prevent trapped moisture from corroding the metal and rotting the handle.

Simply hose off the dirt and let the tool dry in the sun, or keep a bucketful of sand near your tool storage area and plunge the tool in the bucket a few times to scour the metal clean. Some gardeners even use dried corncobs as their preferred abrasive. (When the cobs start to break apart, just throw them into the compost pile.)

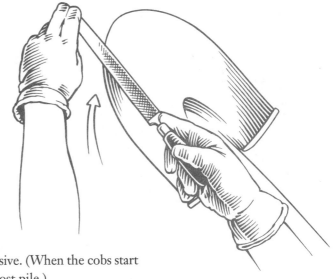

A spade or shovel can become dull when you use it to dig in rocks or gravel. Sharpen it by filing at a steep angle along the tip of the shovel's edge.

After cleaning, spray the working end of the tool with vegetable oil. This prevents rusting and makes dirt less likely to stick to the metal. While you're at it, tighten any nails, nuts, or bolts where the handle meets the socket. (Loose rivets can be tightened with a few gentle raps of a ball-peen hammer.)

Keep those wooden handles clean as well, and sand down any rough spots with a fine grade of sandpaper. A thorough rubbing with linseed or tung oil will protect the wood from moisture. Some gardeners prefer to paint their tool handles with bright colors so they don't misplace them in the garden.

If you get blisters when using your tools, try wrapping their handles with foam pipe insulation covered with electrical tape—it isn't pretty, but it works great and costs less than buying foam-padded tools.

Look Sharp!

Digging and weeding tools, particularly hoes, work a whole lot better with a sharp edge. Sharpen weed-slicing tools at a shallow angle and hone digging tools at a steeper angle to produce a longer-lasting and more effective edge.

Use a flat bastard file (the kind with a checkered pattern on it) with a clamp or vise to hold the tool in position. Hold the file at both ends (always wear gloves) and apply pressure to the file only on the forward stroke. Lift up the file for the return stroke. Keep filing until you can feel a slight burr on the blade's opposite edge.

Do this kind of thorough tool sharpening at least once a year, but also take a few swipes at your tools with a file from time to time during the growing season.

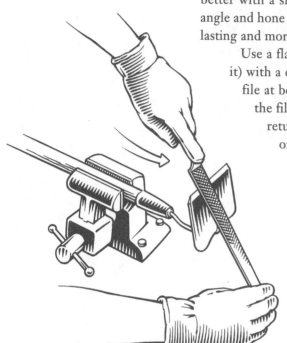

To sharpen a dull hoe blade, secure the blade with a vise; hold the file firmly in place at a shallow angle. With both hands, push away from the blade of the hoe along the entire length of the blade.

Replacement Parts

Shovel handles undergo a lot of stress and will eventually split or break in two. Most hardware stores and home centers that sell hand tools also stock (or can at least special order) replacement handles for most common brands.

Remove the old handle by taking out the rivet or screw holding it to the tool's socket, taking care not to deform the socket's shape. (Driving the old handle out with a short dowel or length of pipe might help.)

Brace the shovel blade against a firm surface, insert the new handle into the blade socket, and tap it all the way into place. If the socket is curved, soaking the handle in hot water or applying a little oil or soap to the socket end will make the job easier.

Once the handle is in place, drill into the socket hole and through the new weed handle and install a nut and bolt to hold everything tight. Then, treat the metal blade to a scrubbing and a quick spritz of vegetable oil. Congratulations—you have a new shovel!

Use the same procedure for hoes, hedge shears, and other wooden-handled tools. For high-quality tools, replacement blades, anvils, and handles usually are available directly from the manufacturer at prices much less than the original price of the tool (less than $5 for most parts). Some companies even provide replacement washers, bolts, and rivets free of charge.

Cutting Tool Maintenance

Everytime you use your loppers, hedge shears, or pruners, wash the blades afterward in warm, soapy water to remove any sap residue. Stubborn sap yields to a little dab of turpentine. Keep all pivot points lubricated with light household oil—don't use motor oil or you'll gum up the works. Newer cutting tools with nonstick coatings keep sap buildup to a minimum, but when the coating does eventually thin along the blade edge, you need to clean more often.

Once a blade gets nicked from misuse—like when you try to cut wire with a pruning shears—it will be much more difficult to use. So reach for the wire cutters when you have to cut a piece of wire, and use your pruning shears to cut what they're supposed to cut! But if the damage is done and the nick in your shears is small (or if the blade is just plain dull), sharpen it with a small, flat single-cut file parallel to the cutting edge. If the nick is deep or if the blade is really gouged, replace it.

Well-made pruners and loppers usually have adjustable anvils to compensate for blade wear. Check often to make sure that the adjustable nut and/or bolt is tight, or you may lose the anvil altogether.

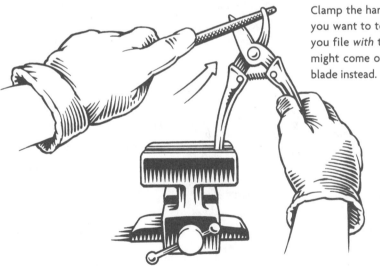

Clamp the handle of your pruners in a vise when you want to touch up the blade edge. Make sure you file *with* the angle of the blades. Large nicks might come out, but if they're deep, replace the blade instead.

GARDENER TO GARDENER

Rx: Lotsa Leaf Compost

After my neighbors have raked up all their tree leaves in the fall, I go around and collect as many bags as I can get my hands on—usually 200 to 300 bags! I need them to make compost for the many beds around my nearly 1-acre property. I also use uncomposted leaves as mulch and as a soil amendment in new beds.

But instead of making one huge compost pile, I make several right where I need the finished product, using about 25 bags of leaves per pile. I start each pile with a 6-inch layer of leaves, then top that with a layer of horse manure-rich bedding, which I get by the truckload from a local stable. I continue layering in this fashion, wetting each layer after I add it, until the pile is about 15 feet long, 10 feet wide, and 3 to 4 feet high. Then I cover the pile with a 10 × 20-foot sheet of plastic. Three weeks later I turn the pile and wet it again, making sure that all the leaves are moist, then cover it again with the plastic.

These piles heat to 125° to 150°F—even when the air is at subzero temps—and I end up with about $1/2$ ton of finished compost from 25 bags of leaves and 1 ton of stable bedding (at $8 per ton). With all of the night crawlers in my beds (from the leaf compost), I could start a worm farm!

Henry Newberry
Gary, Indiana

Leafy Lawn Food

When fall comes around, I never bother to rake the leaves off my lawn. Instead, I get out my mulching lawnmower and use it to chop the fallen leaves until they're unnoticeable. After I've turned all of my own leaves into mulch, I scout the neighborhood and pick up other people's bags of leaves. Some of those leaves are also ground up on my lawn; the rest end up in my compost pile. Come spring, the only lawn food I need to apply is a sprinkling of soybean meal. My soil is full of earthworms and the grass grows great!

Charles R. Burg
Jenison, Michigan

Snow Fence Me In

I used to follow the conventional advice for protecting tender trees and shrubs from winter winds: Each year I drove 4-foot stakes into the ground around each shrub, then I painstakingly wrapped them with burlap and twine. Come spring I had a mess of sagging, torn burlap around each shrub. After a few years of this fruitless procedure, I finally discovered that standard snow fencing works much better.

Snow fence—wooden slats connected with heavy gauge wire, with small spaces between the wire and the slats—is much heavier than burlap, thus infinitely more durable. I attach it to supporting stakes, just as I used to do with the burlap, and fasten it with a sturdy, flexible wire. It does a great job of filtering winter winds and harsh sunlight, while looking neat and lasting practically forever.

Barbara Dege
Hackensack, New Jersey

GARDENER TO GARDENER

Poolin' Resources

Locally, we're known as "the people with the LEAVES." Because we have so many leaves to rake up (and then spread on our garden) in fall, we had to figure out an effective and economical way to contain and transport them. Cheap plastic bags always ripped before we could completely fill them, and expensive plastic bags were, well, expensive— even when we recycled them.

Then we found a $10 solution to our leafy situation at the local discount department store—a plastic kiddie pool, which we now use both to haul and store leaves. (Sometimes you can even get one for free, just by cruising your neighborhood on trash night.)

At leaf-gathering time, my son and daughter help me fill the pool with leaves. Then my son helps me drag the pool across the lawn to the flowerbed where we use the leaves as mulch. The plastic pool slides easily across grass, twigs, and even the sidewalk. Now I don't have to spend any more time packing and emptying bags; I haul bushels of leaves at a time—in a container weighing only a few pounds. A quick rinse with the hose is all the cleanup required.

Carol Schaefer
Carlinville, Illinois

Keep Hand Tools Within Reach

I like to keep my garden tools handy in a 5-gallon bucket that I carry with me as I work in the garden. And because my bucket has a lid, it also doubles as a handy stool when I want to sit down to work. Canvas tool pouches—available (sometimes for free) at hardware stores—are also great for keeping tools within reach. I use mine to carry frequently needed items (such as pruners, clippers, and string), which always seem to fall to the bottom of the bucket. It's also perfect for carrying seed packets at planting time. The packets remain dry and organized while I work.

Lois Minosky
Zanesville, Ohio

New Life for Old Rakes

The lightweight bamboo rakes I use in the fall only last a year or two before the tines break. I hate to throw them away, so in spring I transform them into trellises. I stick the end of the handle into the soil deep enough to solidly anchor it and then plant scarlet runner beans, morning glories, or moon-flowers at the base. The vines wrap around the handle and cover the head of the rake in greenery, making interesting shapes in my garden.

Deborah Burdick
Mount Vernon, Indiana

Easy-on-Your-Hands Tools

My husband was getting tired of wearing out his hands and gloves on an old rake handle. So he grabbed a big bar of paraffin and waxed the living daylights out of that rough wooden tool. The paraffin smoothed the handle so well that he now waxes all of our tool handles and our wheelbarrow handles. Before, we had to buy jersey work gloves by the dozen. Now, a single pair of gloves lasts for ages.

Debi Larson
Mountain View, Missouri

GARDENER TO GARDENER

Complete Garden Toolkit

When working in my garden, I always have whatever I need within my reach because I keep a plastic bucket filled with my garden tools by my side. My bucket holds all the usual hand tools, such as a dandelion digger, pruners, and trowels. Plus, it holds some less common items, including scissors to cut twine for staking, a 1-inch putty knife for weeding close to plants, a serrated paring knife for the same purpose, a wire cutting tool for cutting baling wire from around straw bales, a large handkerchief, a pencil, a journal, and a portable timer—for when I have only a limited amount of time to work.

Even filled with all of my tools, the bucket is lightweight and easy to carry. I don't think I could garden anymore without it!

> *Edith Lang*
> *Carpenter, Wyoming*

Get a Grip

If you suffer from arthritis and find that you often have trouble holding onto your garden tools, here's a simple solution: Buy foam insulation tubes (the kind sold to insulate water pipes) and cut them into shorter lengths to fit around your shovel, rake, or hoe. You can even use them on the handle of your lawnmower. The foam makes the handles easier to grasp and "insulates" your hands from painful vibrations. The insulation is sold in 4-foot lengths, so a single piece provides enough padding for several tools at a cost of about $1.

> *Esther Brown*
> *Danville, Kentucky*

Garden Cart Retrofit

My garden cart works fine for most of my garden chores, but when it comes to transporting leaves in fall, its 16-inch-high sides fall short. To raise the height of the sides another 16 to 24 inches (so that I can haul really big piles of leaves), I slide old window screens between the leaves and the sides of the cart. Each trip with the cart now has double the leaf capacity or more, meaning fewer trips and better use of my time and energy.

> *Elliott Berenson*
> *Chesterland, Ohio*

Tarp and Toss

To transport light debris to your compost bin easily, first spread out a plastic or canvas tarp. Then pile or rake your materials—weeds, cuttings, leaves, and so on—onto the tarp. When it's full, grab two of the corners and drag it to your compost bin. If you haven't overfilled the tarp, you can then gather up the four corners, pick up the tarp, and pour the contents into the bin all at once. (If you did overfill it, two people can handle a larger load.) This method is the best way I've found for moving leaves in the fall; it saves steps and prevents a lot of the bending and forking you have to do with a wheelbarrow.

> *Brad Berry*
> *Decatur, Illinois*

Chapter 12

December

Wildlife in the Garden:
Both Sides of the Fence

I wonder if the sap is stirring yet,
If wintry birds are dreaming of a mate,
If frozen snowdrops feel as yet the sun
And crocus fires are kindling one by one:
Sing, robin, sing;
I still am sore in doubt concerning Spring.

—Christina Rossetti

A garden is much more than a place you designate for growing plants. Look closely and you'll see that your garden is home to all sorts of living creatures—ranging from barely visible insects to larger animals, such as toads, rabbits, and groundhogs.

Observing the wildlife in our garden can be entertaining, educational, and exasperating. Some critters simply don't understand the meaning of the word *garden*. For rabbits, squirrels, groundhogs, and deer, *your* garden is just another potential source of food. With natural habitats rapidly vanishing, thanks to human sprawl, many wild animals are forced to forage for food in our gardens.

How can you learn to live with and even enjoy the wildlife in and around your garden? By observing their behavior. Understanding the habits of animals may help you to manage them. And, when all else fails, a sturdy fence usually does the trick.

Gardener's To-Do List—December

**If you don't know what USDA hardiness zone you live in,
check the map on page 246 to find out.**

Zone 3

- ☐ Restock bird feeders.
- ☐ Twist and coil long stems of Virginia creeper into a Christmas wreath base.
- ☐ Check stored vegetables, tubers, and bulbs; remove any spoiled ones immediately.
- ☐ Try to keep roses and other half-hardy perennials covered with snow—it's the perfect insulator against cold.
- ☐ Start seeds of zonal geraniums (*Pelargonium* spp.).
- ☐ Review your notes from the last growing season.
- ☐ Begin planning next year's garden.
- ☐ Browse through new seed catalogs and order early to avoid disappointment.

Zone 4

- ☐ On a warm day, trim back and mulch perennials.
- ☐ Collect the seeds from pods and seedheads gathered earlier—wrap up some to give as holiday gifts.
- ☐ Check stored veggies—discard any with signs of spoilage.
- ☐ Continue harvesting greens from the hoop house or cold frame.
- ☐ Try growing salad greens and herbs in pots in a south-facing window.
- ☐ Take photos of your property to decide what needs changing before snow cover obscures your view.

Zone 5

- ☐ Cover spinach and other overwintering crops with a row cover, and then top with 8 inches of straw.
- ☐ Make holiday decorations from holly and evergreen prunings.
- ☐ Wrap trees to protect them from deer and rabbits.
- ☐ Force some paperwhite narcissus bulbs: Put them in a bowl with pebbles and water, set the bowl in a bright cool window, then enjoy the show.
- ☐ Don't keep a live Christmas tree indoors for more than a week or two—plant it in the hole you dug last month.
- ☐ Inspect houseplants for insect pests; treat with insecticidal soap spray, if necessary.
- ☐ Use cut Christmas tree limbs to protect tender perennial beds.

Zone 6

- ☐ As weather permits, continue to harvest leeks and kale.
- ☐ Keep straw snuggled around any crops still in the garden.
- ☐ If using a coldframe to grow greens through winter, rig a plastic tunnel over the frame for extra warmth.
- ☐ After the holidays, remove the branches from your cut Christmas tree and lay them over perennials and fall-planted pansies.
- ☐ Divide overgrown Boston ferns: Cut the rootball in half with a sharp knife, then repot.

☐ Cut back asparagus fronds.

☐ Refill bird feeders as needed.

Zone 7

☐ Remember it's your last chance to gather leaves for mulching, composting, or digging into the soil.

☐ If weather is mild, feed pansies, snapdragons, and other winter flowers.

☐ Cover strawberries with a floating row cover—they'll fare better over winter and bear earlier next spring.

☐ Have row covers or burlap ready to protect camellias, Confederate jasmine, and fig trees, if temperature threatens to drop below 20°F.

☐ Add a second layer of row cover to protect leafy vegetables, such as spinach, lettuce, and collards (remove the covers during the day, and they'll continue to produce).

☐ Place a few plastic jugs filled with water between rows to collect heat during the day and radiate it back at night.

☐ Plant bareroot trees.

Zone 8

☐ Continue planting onions, chives, spinach, mustard, peas, beets, and radishes.

☐ Plant more lettuce in the coldframe.

☐ Plant petunias, calendulas, annual candytuft (*Iberis umbellata*), pansies, sweet alyssum (*Lobularia maritima*), cornflowers (*Centaurea cyanus*), stocks (*Matthiola incana*), scabiosa (*Scabiosa atropurpurea*), verbena, pinks (*Dianthus* spp.), and daisies.

☐ Plant bulbs, corms, and rhizomes of iris (*Iris danfordiae, I. histrioides, I. reticulata*) amaryllis, anemone (*Anemone coronaria, A. sylvestris*), calla, and liriope.

☐ Clean up garden debris to eliminate over-wintering areas for diseases and insect pests.

☐ Start to build beds for spring by adding lots of compost.

☐ Plant bareroot trees, shrubs, roses, and vines.

Zone 9

☐ Apply lime-sulfur spray to peaches and nectarines to combat peach leaf curl.

☐ Apply a dormant oil spray to fruit trees to kill insects and eggs.

☐ Sow winter cover crops, including annual rye grass (*Lolium multiflorum*), fava beans (*Vicia faba*), oats, barley, pearl millet (*Pennisetum americanum*), or proso millet (*Panicum miliaceum*).

☐ At month's end, plant perennials, shrubs, and trees.

☐ Also at the end of the month, begin to prune established deciduous trees and shrubs to remove crossed and diseased branches and to open up the center to light and air.

Zone 10

☐ At the beginning of this month, start cold-loving veggies, such as brussels sprouts and English peas.

☐ Most citrus fruits ripen now—remove and compost old fruit or use for slug traps.

☐ Feed mangoes a shot of compost tea as soon as flower spikes appear.

☐ If rainfall is scarce, provide at least 1 inch of water per week.

☐ If frost threatens, be prepared to protect plants with row covers.

☐ Keep harvesting beans, beets, broccoli, carrots, greens, onions, potatoes, radishes, and melons.

Sunflower Power

I've tried unsuccessfully to use soap to repel the deer that love to eat my strawberries from my garden. But thanks to birds (yes, birds!), I was able to eat strawberries this year!

I planted a row of sunflowers on the outside of the garden for the birds. Strangely enough, the deer still walk up to the garden, but when they get within 15 feet of the sunflowers, they stop, shake their heads, sniff, and then back off. They eat weeds up to that distance, but go no farther. I had a new row of strawberries on the other side of the garden that the deer had already found and nibbled. So I laid sunflower stalks on the row of berries, and they stayed away (but still ate weeds in other parts of the yard).

Dorothy M. Holland
Laporte, Minnesota

The Best Birds for Your Garden

Birds will eat insect pests year-round in your garden, if you provide a few of the basic necessities to attract and keep them nearby. Here's how to attract 10 of the best birds for controlling garden pests.

Bluebirds

Bluebirds sing for spring and for their supper of garden pests. The spring diet of the western bluebird (which ranges from southern British Columbia down to central Mexico and from the Pacific to west Texas) is entirely insects, especially grasshoppers! Beetles, weevils, crickets, and caterpillars—sprinkled with the occasional ant, fly, centipede, sowbug, and snail—are the meals of choice for most bluebirds.

They prefer to nest in sunny, open areas. Their perfect nest box would be mounted on a post within 50 feet of a tree (facing it, if possible), fence, or other structure away from bushy hedgerows.

Chickadees

Don't let their sweet song fool you. Chickadees and their cousins, titmice, are pest-control champions throughout the United States and Canada. As much as 90 percent of their diet consists of insects—moths, caterpillars, flies, beetles, bugs, plant lice, scale, leafhoppers, and tree hoppers.

In winter, chickadees stay on patrol, searching bark crevices for hibernating insects and the eggs of moths, plant lice, pear psylla, and katydids.

To keep chickadees and titmice on patrol in the winter, provide some suet in a mesh bag or a feeder full of sunflower seeds. In spring, provide a nest box packed with wood chips. If possible, place the nest box at the edge of a wooded area.

Nighthawks

They aren't hawks, but they are insect-eating superheroes that swoop over cities, fields, woodlands, and deserts, sucking up flying ants, flies, leaf chafers, mosquitoes, moths, and grasshoppers. Nighthawks even eat Colorado potato beetles, cucumber beetles, and squash bugs!

Although there isn't much you can do to attract nighthawks (they don't build nests), you can be on the lookout for their eggs and be careful not to harm them. Look for one to three whitish olive eggs with dark blotches on sandy soil (sometimes at the base of a shrub), on gravel (especially on rooftops), on a stump, or in an old robin's nest. Their breeding range extends from the southern Yukon to southern California down to Honduras and Nicaragua.

Nuthatches

Hopping headfirst down a tree isn't just nutty behavior—nuthatches are searching crevices for ants, scale, beetles, moth eggs, caterpillars, and cocoons. Nuthatches feed on seeds and nuts (hence their name) during the cold months, but in summer they're 100 percent insectivorous. They raise their young exclusively on insects. Three different species of nuthatches are found in various regions of North America.

Also woodland natives, nuthatches are more likely to settle into nesting boxes that are located in clearings in or along the edges of wooded areas. Fill the boxes with wood chips; cover the boxes with strips of bark to make them even more attractive to the birds.

Nuts and Bolts of Nesting Boxes

Putting up nesting boxes is the best way to keep birds in the garden in spring and summer, when they're eating the most insects. But remember that one size nesting box doesn't fit all birds. If the dimensions aren't right for the birds you want to attract, the wrong birds will move in and displace the ones you want to nest. For specific dimensions of nesting boxes, check the website of the Cornell Lab of Ornithology (see Resources on page 236 for the address). Make your nesting box from unpainted cypress, cedar, or pine, or use a hollowed-out bottle gourd. The box should have good ventilation and draining. But it shouldn't have a perch! A perch is an invitation to predators.

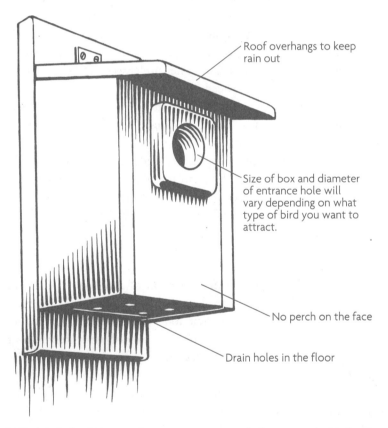

Roof overhangs to keep rain out

Size of box and diameter of entrance hole will vary depending on what type of bird you want to attract.

No perch on the face

Drain holes in the floor

Making a simple birdhouse is a fun winter project. And when you make birdhouses during the winter, you'll be ready to hang them around your yard in very early spring, when the first birds are looking for nesting sites.

GARDENER TO
GARDENER

Save Your Cracked Birdbath

When my cement birdbath developed a crack in the bowl, I thought it would be impossible to fix—until I figured out how to cover the crack with an inexpensive aluminum liner.

First I measured the bowl of my birdbath, then I bought a similar-sized disposable aluminum serving tray at a party supply store. I placed the tray on the bowl and, using a hammer, gently shaped the aluminum until it fit into the bowl. This liner has turned out to be better than the original bowl. It's easy to clean algae off of in the summer months. And when the water in the bowl freezes during winter, I just pick up the tray, pour some warm water over the outside, and the ice slides right out. I fill the pan back up with warm water and the birds drink it up as if it were a cup of warm cocoa.

Kathy Landis
Tulsa, Oklahoma

Phoebes

These stealthy hunters wait on low tree branches, slowly lowering and raising their tails, then swoop out to snap up insects with loud clicks of their beaks. Phoebes (whose name comes from their characteristic FEE-BE song) feast on everything from flies, mosquitoes, small moths, flying ants, and small beetles to grasshoppers, crickets, and caterpillars.

Because these fearless flyers especially like to swoop down over water to scoop up insects, try using water (a small pool, pond, or water garden) to entice them to your yard. Since phoebes prefer to build their mud-made nests in, on, or around manmade structures, you can attract them by providing a nesting shelf or two under your eaves (located in a quiet spot, away from busy doorways, porches, or decks).

Native Sparrows

These include the song sparrow, chipping sparrow, and field sparrow (but not the so-called house sparrow, which is actually a weaver finch). Although most of the sparrows' diet is seed, it consists of more than one-third insects, especially during the nesting season. Sparrow seed eating is even garden friendly. They prefer weed seeds, such as from crabgrass, ragweed, and pigweed.

Their insect choices include grasshoppers, caterpillars, beetles, leafhoppers, true bugs, ants, and beetles. One warning, though: In warmer parts of the country, sparrows sometimes supplement their diet with winter garden crops—clipping off seedlings and sprouts. In these areas, just protect young seedlings with row covers or mesh screening.

To make it easy for the birds to nest along the perimeter of your yard, provide nesting materials like straw, bark, and pieces of string. Sparrows raise two or three broods per year.

Swallows

In spring, insects make up 99 percent of a swallow's diet. These graceful birds (which include the famed, insect-eating purple martin) are excellent flyers and much of their food—flies, beetles, winged ants, moths, grasshoppers, and dragonflies—is caught while they're on the wing. A few species occasionally feed on the ground, chomping on ants, beetles, and other insects.

Swallows often nest in dead trees, in holes in the face of a cliff, or in banks along streams and roads. They also have a real affinity for man-made structures. Barn and cliff swallows build their characteristic muddy nests under eaves, in barns, and under bridges and culverts. To encourage this, build a nesting shelf under an eave and make a patch of mud near your garden. Tree swallows and violet-green swallows (a

Northwest native) will also come to bluebird boxes (in fact, they're probably easier to attract there than bluebirds). You can buy houses specifically for purple martins, but make sure there's a pond or other body of water nearby, because purple martins prefer to feed on insects that live near water.

Vireos

Vireos prefer wooded areas, with most living their summers in the North and their winters in the warm South. In spring, 99 percent of their diet is caterpillars (their favorite), snails, moths, bugs, beetles, ants, and flies.

Vireos are most likely to venture into yards where clumps of dense shrubs and tangles of blackberries surround the perimeter, especially if it borders on a wooded area.

Woodpeckers

These well-known woodsy dwellers are more easily coaxed into your backyard than vireos. Of the 21 species found in North America, the downy, hairy, and red-bellied woodpeckers are most likely to drop by for a meal. The downy and hairy woodpeckers get up to 85 percent of their food by chowing down on wood-boring beetle and moth larvae, ants, caterpillars, adult beetles, millipedes, and aphids.

Woodpeckers might use a nest box packed with wood chips in a clearing along the edge of the woods. But they're even more likely to nest in old dead trees (or "snags")—so if you have one on your property, trim off most of the branches, and leave the trunk for woodpecker nests. These snags also attract and house other native creatures.

Woodpeckers will eagerly venture into your yard for suet or sunflower seeds in the off-season and eat your pests spring through fall.

If you have a dead tree in your yard, turn it into a deluxe woodpecker feeder by drilling holes in the wood and filling them with suet.

Wrens

Brown or gray plumed, lively and vocal, 10 species of wrens call North America their home, living everywhere from brushy woodlands, shrubbery, and marshes to rocky canyons and even deserts.

The Carolina wren is almost exclusively an insect eater in the summer. The widespread house and Bewick's wrens also have insect-rich diets. Most wrens search trees, shrubs, and vines for caterpillars, ants, millipedes, grasshoppers, flies, snails, and beetles.

Wrens generally raise more than one brood during the season, with six to eight eggs per brood. It takes a lot of bugs to fill all those beaks, so it's fairly easy to get these prolific birds to nest in your yard. They'll take up residence in nest boxes; in empty gourds, cans, and jars; and even in clothespin bags left on the wash line!

Winter Gardens for Wildlife

Have you ever really noticed what happens in your yard on a crisp fall day? While you're doing your final garden chores, observe the many wild creatures that are also preparing for winter: a gray squirrel stashing acorns in a dead tree limb; a tiger swallowtail caterpillar forming a chrysalis on a branch; a thrush growing fat on spicebush berries. You can help them by creating a winter wildlife garden. Come spring, you may be rewarded by seeing a luna moth that spent the winter as a pupa in a cocoon hidden beneath fallen leaves, or a toad emerging from its snug site under a rock pile to devour a fat worm in the compost.

Numerous Niches

Each animal prefers a certain kind of habitat, whether it's high in the tree canopy or deep in blackberry brambles. By providing a variety of landscape niches—different plant heights and topography—you'll attract a greater variety of wildlife.

"A layered landscape is the key to wildlife diversity," says Adrian Binns, head of the landscape design firm Wildlife Gardens in Langhorne, Pennsylvania. "If there are canopy trees in a neighboring yard, you can fill in with understory, shrubs, and herbaceous plants. If you have trees surrounded by lawn, then it's time to eliminate some of the lawn in favor of the other layers."

Replace the lawn beneath existing trees with shrubs and smaller trees, such as redbuds (*Cercis* spp.) and serviceberries (*Amelanchier* spp.), to create a small grove. Extend the plantings to neighboring trees or woods to offer corridors for small animals. These are important in winter, when a hovering hawk has a clear view of the ground.

Plant a Feast

If you think of winter as an unattractive season in the garden, you'll be happily surprised by the color and form of the many plants that attract wildlife. Simply remember to plant a mix of regionally native plants that are suited to your site, and your garden will be host to many wildlife species.

Berries. Plenty of native trees and shrubs have gorgeous berries. Some, such as sassafras (*Sassafras albidum*), have berries so tasty they are stripped clean by fall-migrating birds before cold weather arrives. In your winter garden, aim to add trees and shrubs that produce less-favored berries, such as chokeberries (*Aronia* spp.), hackberries (*Celtis* spp.), American cranberry-bush (*Viburnum trilobum*), sumacs (*Rhus* spp.), inkberries (*Ilex glabra*), snowberries (*Symphoricarpos albus*), and winterberries (*Ilex verticillata*). High in carbohydrates, they can be lifesavers when there's nothing else to eat.

Evergreens. Trees such as pines, firs, spruces, junipers, and cedars provide important roosting and nesting sites for many birds, and game birds and small animals seek shelter under the trees' branches. The cones and berries of evergreens feed numerous small animals, including squirrels and the small birds that glean the seeds they drop.

Grasses. Ornamental grasses not only look spectacular in the winter but also feed and shelter a number of animals. Choose natives such as Indian grass (*Sorghastrum nutans*), big bluestem (*Andropogon gerardii*), and switchgrass (*Panicum virgatum*). Sparrows and blackbirds eagerly consume their seeds. The caterpillars of skipper butterflies feed on switchgrass and big bluestem, and they overwinter in leaf nests on the plants.

Nectar producers. Aim to provide an early nectar source—such as hawthorn (*Crataegus* spp.), crabapple, or willow—for the native bees and flies that appear in late winter to early spring.

Thickets. If you have space, reserve a corner for a thicket-forming plant, such as snowberry (*Symphoricarpos albus*), red-osier dogwood (*Cornus sericea*), sprawling rose, or willow. Or plant a hedgerow, a living

Cagey Bird Perch

After I harvest my tomatoes in the fall, I take my concrete wire mesh tomato cages and group them together near a freestanding bird feeder. The birds enjoy the multilevel perches as they wait their turn at the feeder, and I don't need to bother storing the cages. Just be careful not to place the cages too close to the feeder or you'll create a springboard for squirrels—as we all know, they definitely don't need any help in finding their way onto your feeder!

David Long
Lexington, Kentucky

You'll attract more birds by setting up a bird-feeding station. Erect a low tray feeder and a simple birdbath. Also set up a tube feeder and a hopper feeder.

fence of thorny shrubs and vines. It provides safe travel, shelter, nesting sites and food; and its abundant edge draws wildlife to eat and to seek a mate. Include such plants as currants (*Ribes* spp.), huckleberries (*Gaylussacia* spp.), elderberries (*Sambucus* spp.), hawthorns, roses, black haw viburnum (*Viburnum prunifolium*), crabapples, blackberries, native honeysuckles such as Southern bush-honeysuckle (*Diervilla sessilifolia*), junipers, and pines. Put plants close together so they can tangle.

The size of your yard will determine how many plants to buy. Many wildlife-attracting plants, such as hollies, have male and female flowers on separate plants, and both are required for female plants to produce berries. Take a walk around your neighborhood to see whether a mate plant is close by. (Males have no berries.) If not, increase your chances of getting both sexes by planting three or more of the same species.

In your vegetable garden, let some parsley, fennel, carrots, and broccoli go to seed, providing winter food for goldfinches and chickadees. Also, leave a few cornstalks standing to provide shelter for foraging birds and field mice.

Go-Easy Maintenance

Whatever you choose to plant, use a light hand in garden cleanup. Globe thistles (*Echinops* spp.), coneflowers (*Echinacea* and *Rudbeckia* spp.), milkweeds, and other perennials still are useful to birds through the winter. Remove just enough seeds to replant next season, and leave the rest for the birds. Seeds that aren't eaten might be used for nesting material, such as the downy fluff of the milkweed. Tiny butterfly larvae overwinter on leaves and stalks of such plants as lupine and mullein, waiting for spring's fresh growth to begin.

Allow spent goldenrod stems to stand. Bumps on their stems, known as galls, host many insects: the wasps that form the galls, the wasps' parasites, and other opportunists looking for a warm home. In winter, birds perch on the stalks and tear open the galls, seeking an insect meal.

Allow a section of grass to remain unmowed, serving as a protected corridor for still-active frogs, snakes, mice, and insects. In winter, birds will search in the grass for seeds and insects.

GARDENER TO GARDENER

Deer—Slip 'Em Some Soap

Every summer the deer come down from the hills to enjoy our apples and string beans. We repel them by hanging deodorant soap (wrapped in cheesecloth) every 12 feet, either in trees or from fence posts. You don't need large pieces of soap, and you don't have to worry about replacing the soap after rain—a shower actually renews the aroma.

Enid Berne
Albany, Oregon

Free Bean Salad

As we live in an area surrounded on three sides by woods, deer have been a continuing problem—they like our fresh vegetables as much as we do. Last year we purchased a bulk bag of year-old bean seeds and planted a row near the woods along the entire length of the garden, where the deer appear most frequently. All summer they grazed on the beans and left the rest of our garden alone.

Rita and Peter Cole
Prospect Harbor, Maine

Bloodmeal: A Deterrent and a Fertilizer

We tried almost everything (including fences, radios, and dogs) to keep the deer from ruining our crops—especially sweet potatoes and young tomato plants. Finally we found something that works: We sprinkle dried bloodmeal very lightly on the leaves of crops we especially want to protect and the deer (and woodchucks) don't touch them. Rain washes the dried blood off, of course, but the smell remains at the base of the plants (and as an added benefit, the dried blood adds nitrogen to the soil).

After several rains we sprinkle a bit more dried blood. We see deer tracks right alongside the bloodied sweet potatoes, but the plants remain untouched.

Nancy and Gus Carlson
Alma, West Virginia

What's That Smell?

I've found that planting garlic around my garden keeps rabbits out.

Justin Smith
Indianapolis, Indiana

To repel rabbits (and squirrels, deer, and raccoons): Crush garlic (cloves, stems, and seeds), put the mash in a jug, fill it with water, and let the jug sit in the sun for several days. The concoction will ferment and become quite potent. Strain the mixture and pour into plastic squirt bottles; in the evening, squirt it around the perimeter of the garden. Sometimes I have to apply it several nights in a row, but it definitely works for me.

Frank Daley
Menomonie, Wisconsin

GARDENER TO GARDENER

Pepper Sends 'Em Packing

I had turned my ankles more than once in the holes that gophers made. I dumped ¹/₂ teaspoon of black pepper in all the holes I could find. The result? No more gophers. I fill the holes with dirt and renew the pepper if any gophers return.

Duane Rymenams
Racine, Wisconsin

Groundhogs Tune into Talk Radio

The best method I've found for keeping critters, namely one large groundhog, from eating my garden is to put a portable radio inside a couple of plastic bags (to keep out dew and moisture) in a shady spot. I turn it on, tune in to a local news station, and turn it up—and that groundhog doesn't come near my garden. On days when I forget to put the radio out in the garden, I find things nibbled up.

Virginia O. Ansbergs
Cohasset, Massachusetts

Baffle the Buggers

I've finally banished woodchucks from my flower and vegetable garden. Initially, I had a 3-foot-high wire fence whose bottom was buried 6 inches deep in a trench filled with large rocks. For a few years, the rock-filled trench stopped the burrowing woodchucks. Then some of them learned to climb the fence. (Yes, we actually saw this!)

Last spring I added a baffle using 7-inch-wide strips of the same fencing—it hangs out at a 90-degree angle from the top of the existing fence. To build such a baffle, wrap the cut ends of one side of the baffle around the top wire of the existing fence. Join the ends of the strips together (except at the gates) to form a continuous baffle (every 8 to 10 feet, use a bent wire garden stake or a wire coat hanger to hold up the overhang).

We haven't had a woodchuck problem all season—they can't seem to climb up past the baffle. This idea may also work for raccoons, too.

Rochelle Paris
Yonkers, New York

Mix a Little Salsa

I mix 3 ounces of cayenne pepper with 1 gallon of water, and use a sprinkling can to wet all the leaves of munched-on plants. The only rabbits that return to dine are either crazy or experiencing short-term memory loss.

Laura Stone
Granger, Washington

A Garden of Their Own

I learned by experience that rabbits don't eat gourds, tomatoes, and peppers, but they love lettuce. So I planted some lettuce for myself amongst the crops that the rabbits don't like, and then I planted a second garden of what they love (mostly lettuce) about 100 feet closer to the woods. The lettuce in the rabbit garden got munched on, but the lettuce in my garden didn't. I saw ten little ones munching on that lettuce at one time, but they never visited my other garden. I think they like having an organic garden of their own.

Adrienne Diotte
Matapedia, Quebec

GARDENER TO GARDENER

Rabbits? Grow "High-Altitude" Beans

I garden near the local wildlife refuge, so it's inevitable that some critters will find their way to the garden for a free meal. For a number of years, rabbits destroyed my bush beans by eating all the leaves and tender young beans. So I began growing pole beans, which quickly grow out of the rabbits' reach. I also use a double fence—lining the inside of my green vinyl fence with fine chicken wire to keep those baby rabbits from squeezing through.

Jan Goodland-Metz
Newport, Rhode Island

Beheaded Tulips? Try This

For years I was unable to enjoy my tulips because the neighborhood squirrels would decapitate every single one of them just as they began to open. Finally, a friend told me that she had had good luck deterring rabbits by sprinkling black pepper on her crocuses. So I decided to try her remedy, but took it a step further. I steeped 2 tablespoons of cayenne pepper in a quart of water, strained it into a spray bottle, added a teaspoon of horticultural oil (to make the pepper-spray stick to the plants), and sprayed the tulips periodically as they grew. The cayenne did the trick: For the first time in years, I had a gorgeous, full tulip display.

Diana Jones
Baltimore, Maryland

Give Birds a Drink

I tried everything to keep birds out of my garden—and away from my tomatoes and strawberries. Finally, an older gardener told me that the birds ate my tomatoes and strawberries because they wanted the water in them. Provide those thirsty birds with a birdbath, he said, and they'll leave the produce alone. I took his advice and it worked. As long as I keep water in the birdbath, the birds leave my vegetables alone.

John C. Lowe Jr.
Warrenville,
South Carolina

Tansy Repels Rodents

A chicken wire fence kept most animal pests out of my garden, but it never stopped the voles. Then I read how people used to scatter the herb tansy on earthen floors to deter mice and ants. (Tansy is a pretty, lacy perennial with yellow flowers and a very pungent smell.) So I started gathering and drying the tansy that grows around our old house. When we closed up our house for the winter, I left dried branches of tansy on the windowsills, in drawers, under sofa cushions, and along the mouse runs. And when we returned in the spring, there was barely a trace of the mice that had bothered us before.

Then I decided to try the tansy on the voles in the garden. I scattered tansy branches all around onions and shallots after planting. In the past, voles would dig the sets up within 24 hours of planting. But no more—the tansy seems to have stopped them in their tracks.

Elizabeth Nichols
Mt. Vernon, New York

GARDENER TO GARDENER

Counting Crows?

If crows have been eating your corn seed, plant some garlic in your patch three to four weeks before you plant your corn. The garlic will be an unpleasant surprise for any crows that get too curious! My brothers discovered this trick many years ago, when they returned home from WWII and wanted to grow their favorite garden crop—corn. But it was only March (a bit too early to plant corn on Long Island, New York), and so they satisfied their immediate urge to plant by setting out some garlic cloves that had already begun to sprout.

Soon, whenever our mother went out to hang up the laundry, she would find two or three cloves of garlic pulled up out of the ground, so she replanted them. This kept up for about a week then stopped. Shortly thereafter, my brothers planted their corn seed amidst the garlic sprouts. The corn thrived and, in due course, produced a bountiful and delicious harvest, much to the amazement of our neighbors whose corn sprouts were all pulled up and eaten by the crows. The crows must have thought my brothers' corn sprouts were more garlic and left it alone.

Dorothy C. Moses
Northport, Long Island, New York

Mouse Moat

The tastiest carrots in the garden are those that have survived a few frosts. Unfortunately, the straw mulch that we use to cover our carrots during late fall and winter attracts mice, who also like to feast on the carrots. Last year we found a solution to this carrot conundrum: We dug a ditch the depth of a shovel all around the carrot bed, then covered the bed with mulch and the mice do not cross that line. Honest! So far the score is us: 100, mice: 0.

William Wolfgang
Sellersville, Pennsylvania

Stop Crows with Grass Clippings

I'd tried just about every repellent I could imagine to protect my sweet corn from the red birds, blackbirds, robins, and starlings that ate the newly emerging seedlings. Undaunted, the birds still decimated my plantings. Finally, I discovered that spreading fresh grass clippings over my patch did the trick! Apparently the birds can't distinguish the thin leaves of the seedlings from all the green grass clippings. I've had good corn patches ever since. I guess you still can learn new things after 75 years.

Pete Dilg
Terre Haute, Indiana

GARDENER TO GARDENER

Deer Deterrent That Works

We planted dozens of ornamental trees and shrubs around our new home in the mountains, but for the first three years, deer destroyed all of our hard work. The commercial repellents and homemade scare devices we tried were ineffective. Finally we discovered a simple recipe that works.

Mix 2 teaspoons of beef bouillon and two well-beaten eggs into 1 gallon of water. Place the mixture in an out-of-the-way spot and leave it there for several days until it starts to smell bad. Pour the mixture into a sprayer, then apply it to the trees. You'll need to respray after a heavy rain. Our plants have been thriving since we began using this repellent and, as an added bonus, it seems to ward off grasshoppers too.

Alta Wilhelm
Enterprise, Oregon

Forks Foil Cats

Thanks to a friend, I've finally found a way to keep cats from rolling around my favorite garden plants. I was visiting her organic garden when I noticed a plant completely surrounded by plastic forks, their tines pointed toward the sky. Hearing me laugh out loud, she explained that the tines of the forks kept the neighborhood cats from romping and rolling over the plant. Thanks to those forks, the plant (previously unable to grow larger than a stub) was large, lush, and healthy. I was so impressed that I tried her method in my own garden, where it worked equally well.

Barbara Mraz
Chelsea, Vermont

Tie a Red Ribbon

I'd been bothered by birds eating berries and tree fruits. But I found something that keeps them away from the fruit—shiny, red-and-silver mylar ribbon (called BirdScare Flash Tape). I just string it in the trees and bushes before the fruits ripen, and I'm rewarded with bird-free fruit! (Note: Remove the tape after harvest so birds don't get used to it.)

Linda Hayes
Bellingham, Washington

Part 2
Your Gardening Journal

Your garden is a unique reflection of your personal style, and so is the way you keep your garden records. Some gardeners like to keep detailed notes on the planting and progress of their crops. Others enjoy recording events like the first time they spot a butterfly in their perennial garden. A garden journal can become a personal diary, too, if you include some of the thoughts and feelings you have while working in or sitting and relaxing in your garden.

No matter how you like to keep notes, the journal pages that follow should work for you. You set the pace because you fill in the date and year yourself. So if you only take garden notes during the active gardening season, you can date the first journal page from your first day in the garden. And if you go on vacation for a couple of weeks in the summer, you can pick right up where you left off.

MONTH _____ YEAR _____

_____

_____

_____

_____

_____

_____

_____

_____

_____

_____

_____

_____

_____

_____

_____

To own a bit of ground, to scratch it with a hoe, to plant seeds,
and watch the renewal of life—this is the commonest delight,
the most satisfactory thing a person can do.
—Charles Dudley Warner, from *My Summer in a Garden*

MONTH _____ YEAR _____

MONTH _____ YEAR _____

_____

_____

_____

_____

_____

_____

_____

_____

_____

_____

_____

_____

_____

_____

_____

_____

_____

*To be a part of summer one must feel a part of life, but to
be a part of winter, one must feel a part of something older
than life itself.*

—Joseph Wood Krutch, from *Twelve Seasons*

MONTH _____ YEAR _____

_____

_____

_____

_____

_____

_____

_____

_____

_____

_____

_____

_____

_____

_____

_____

Now draw the plan of our garden beds,
And outline the borders and the paths correctly.
We will scatter little words upon the paper,
Like seeds about to be planted.

—Amy Lowell

Our vegetable garden is coming along well, with radishes and beans up, and we are less worried about the revolution than we used to be.
                                                                —E. B. White

We turn the soil, another season's crop
Growing from seed, from rain, and last year's rot.
                    —Wyatt Prunty, from _The Vegetable Garden_

_____

_____

_____

_____

_____

_____

_____

_____

_____

_____

_____

_____

_____

_____

_____

_____

_____

_____

_____

_____

The whole year is beginning. All nature, with bud and seed and egg, looks forward with optimism.
—Edwin Way Teale, from *Wandering Through Winter*

The opening of the first buds and the resurrection of plants that looked to be dead fill the garden with an enthusiasm that is as perennial as the season.
                    —Elizabeth Lawrence, from _A Southern Garden_

MONTH _____ YEAR _____

I like trees because they seem more resigned to the way they have to live than other things do.
                                                    —Willa Cather, from _O Pioneers!_

_____

_____

_____

_____

_____

_____

_____

_____

_____

_____

_____

_____

_____

With butterflies 'tis etiquette
To keep their wings from getting wet,
So, when they knew the storm was near,
They thought it best to disappear.
          —Frank Dempster Sherman, from *Blossoms*

Spring makes its own statement, so loud and clear that the gardener seems to be only one of the instruments, not the composer.
—Geoffrey B. Charlesworth

Life begins the day you start a garden.

—Chinese proverb

MONTH _____ YEAR _____

_____

_____

_____

_____

_____

_____

_____

_____

_____

_____

_____

_____

_____

_____

_____

_____

_____

_____

From December to March, there are, for many of us, three gardens—the garden outdoors, the garden of pots and bowls in the house, and the garden of the mind's eye.

—Katherine S. White

MONTH _____ YEAR _____

March brings breezes loud and shrill, stirs the dancing daffodil.
—Sara Coleridge, from _Pretty Lessons in Verse_

MONTH _____ YEAR _____

_____

_____

_____

_____

_____

_____

_____

_____

_____

_____

_____

_____

_____

_____

_____

_____

_____

_____

I have found violets. April hath come on,
And the cool winds feel softer, and the rain
Falls in the beaded drops of summer time.
—Nathaniel Parker Willis, from *April*

I love spring anywhere, but if I could choose, I would always greet it in a garden.

—Ruth Stout

MONTH _____ YEAR _____

_____

_____

_____

_____

_____

_____

_____

_____

_____

_____

_____

_____

_____

_____

_____

_____

Pleasures lie thickest where no pleasures seem:
There's not a leaf that falls upon the ground
But holds some joy of silence or of sound,
Some spirits begotten of a summer dream.

—Laman Blanchard

Gardener's Glossary

Acid. Soil pH that's less than 7.0 (neutral); acid soils tend to be deficient in phosphorus and sometimes contain excess manganese and aluminum.

Alkaline. Soil pH that's above 7.0 (neutral); alkaline soils tend to lack manganese and boron.

Annual. A plant that flowers, bears seed, and dies within one growing season.

Backfill. To fill in a planting hole around a plant's roots with soil.

Bareroot. Plants (usually woody ornamentals, such as roses, shrubs, or young trees) sold without soil on their roots.

Beneficials. Insects considered helpful in the garden because they prey on pest insects. Examples: lady beetles, ground beetles, tachinid flies.

Blanch. 1. To mound soil around stems or leaves of growing plants, especially leeks and asparagus, so that they become white and tender. **2.** In food preservation, the process of boiling vegetables for a specific time period in order to slow deterioration during storage.

Bolt. To produce flowers and seed prematurely (often due to hot weather).

Broadcast. Scatter seed by hand in a random pattern.

BT (*Bacillus thuringiensis*). Naturally occurring pathogen that's toxic to insect larvae but not harmful to other organisms; various strains are sold commercially.

Cell pack. Thin plastic or peat containers that have several compartments, used for starting individual seedlings.

Clay. Soil type that absorbs and drains water very slowly, due to lack of air space between particles.

Coldframe. Low, enclosed structure for protecting plants from cold; clear cover lets in sunlight.

Compost. A humus-rich, organic material formed by the decomposition of leaves, grass clippings, and other organic materials. Used to improve soil.

Cover crop. Plant grown and then turned under to improve soil texture and fertility. Examples: clover, rye, buckwheat, vetch.

Crown. The point where a plant's roots and stem meet, usually at soil level.

Cultivar. A cultivated variety of a plant, usually selected for a special trait, such as compact growth or disease resistance.

Cutting (hardwood). Mature wood (deciduous or evergreen) taken at the end of the growing season or during dormancy in order to start new plants.

Deadhead. To remove faded flowers.

Determinate tomatoes. Tomatoes that have vines that grow to a given height and then stop. Most of the fruit is produced and ripens at one time.

Diatomaceous earth. The fossilized remains of ancient marine organisms, sold as a control for soft-bodied insect pests, such as aphids and slugs.

Direct seed. To sow seeds outdoors in garden soil (as opposed to starting seed indoors for later transplanting).

Double dig. To work soil to a depth that is twice the usual by digging a trench, loosening the soil at the bottom of the trench, then returning the top layer of soil to the trench. This produces a raised bed that contains a deep layer of very loose, fluffy soil.

Drip irrigation. A type of irrigation in which water seeps slowly into the soil via hoses or pipe systems. There is less evaporation and more control than with overhead watering.

Drip line. Imaginary line on the soil marking the outside circumference of a tree's canopy.

Flat. Shallow tray for starting seeds indoors; does not have individual compartments.

Force. To bring dormant plants (especially bulbs and cut branches) into bloom by manipulating temperature.

Frass. Insect excrement; can be used to help identify garden pests.

Friable. Having a crumbly texture. Desirable for garden soil.

Green manure. A fast-maturing leafy crop—such as buckwheat, rye, or clover—that adds organic matter to the soil when it's turned under.

Harden off. Gradually expose a plant to outdoor conditions before transplanting it to the garden.

Hardiness. Ability to survive the winter without protection from the cold.

Humus. The complex, organic residue of decayed plant matter in soil.

Hybrid. The offspring of genetically different plants.

Indeterminate tomatoes. Tomato varieties that produce vines that continue to grow for the life of the plant.

Interplanting. Combining plants that have different bloom times or growth habits so that bloom lasts longer and chance of disease is lower.

Leaf mold. Decomposed leaves. An excellent winter mulch, attractive to earthworms.

Loam. An ideal garden soil: contains plenty of organic matter and a balanced mix of small and large particles.

Medium. Soil mix or potting mixture.

Microclimate. Local conditions of shade, exposure, wind, drainage, and other factors that affect plant growth at a given site.

Mulch. Material layered over the soil's surface to hold in moisture, suppress weeds, and (if organic) improve soil.

Open-pollinated. Varieties whose seeds come from plants pollinated naturally.

Organic matter. Materials derived from plants and animals, such as leaves, grass clippings, and manure.

Overwinter. To keep a plant living through the winter so that it can continue growing the next year, may require the use of coldframes, row covers or hoop houses.

Pathogen. Disease-causing microorganism.

Peat pot. Commercially available seedling container made from compressed peat moss. Gradually breaks down, so both pot and seedling can be planted without disturbing roots.

Perennial. Any plant that lives for at least three seasons; can be woody (trees and shrubs) or herbaceous (those that die back to the ground in winter).

Perlite. Lightweight expanded minerals added to potting mixes to improve aeration.

pH. Measure of soil acidity or alkalinity; 7.0 is neutral.

Pinching. Periodically removing the newest growth of a leafy plant to encourage a more "bushy" form.

Pot-bound. A containerized plant whose roots have completely filled the potting soil inside the container, making it difficult to remove the plant from the container.

Pot up. To plant in a container or to move a containerized plant into a larger container.

Row cover. Translucent polyester fabric placed over garden plants or beds to protect them from pests. Heavier types also used to protect plants from cold. Lets in water and light.

Side-dress. To spread a layer of compost or other fertilizer on the soil surface, next to growing plants.

Succession crop. To follow early-maturing crops with other plantings so that beds continue to produce throughout the growing season.

Thin. To remove excess seedlings or fruits to ensure best spacing for plant health, yield, and size.

Tilth. Soil texture and workability.

Top-dress. To apply a layer of fertilizer to the soil surface (not working it in).

Umbel-shaped. Plants with flower heads shaped like an umbrella, including dill, fennel, anise, yarrow and coriander. Attractive to beneficial insects.

Underplant. To plant short plants, such as ground covers, below taller plants, such as shrubs.

Vermiculite. Lightweight mineral added to soil mix to improve aeration.

Wallo'Water. A product sold to protect plants from cold; water-filled plastic walls retain heat around plants.

Zones. Geographic regions; hardiness zones marked by a range of lowest temperatures in an average winter for a given area. Example: 0° to –10°F.

Resources

Use the listings below to find companies that sell seeds, plants, and organic gardening supplies, as well as organizations that offer expertise in birdwatching. When you contact associations or specialty nurseries by mail, please enclose a self-addressed, stamped envelope with your inquiry.

Vegetable and Flower Seeds

Bountiful Gardens
18001 Shafer Ranch Road
Willits, CA 95490
Phone: (707) 459-6410
Fax: (707) 459-6410
Web site: www.bountifulgardens.org

W. Atlee Burpee
300 Park Avenue
Warminster, PA 18974
Phone: (800) 888-1447
Fax: (215) 674-4170
Web site: www.burpee.com

The Cook's Garden
P.O. Box 535
Londonderry, VT 05148
Phone: (800) 457-9703
Fax: (800) 457-9705
Web site: www.cooksgarden.com

Fedco Seeds
P.O. Box 250
Waterville, ME 04903
Phone: (207) 873-7333
Fax: (207) 872-8317

Gurney's Seed & Nursery
110 Capital Street
Yankton, SD 57079
Phone: (605) 665-1671
Fax: (605) 665-9718
Web site: www.gurneys.com

Johnny's Selected Seeds
1 Foss Hill Road
RR 1, Box 2580
Albion, ME 94910
Phone: (207) 437-9294
Fax: (207) 437-2759
Web site: www.johnnyseeds.com

Nichols Garden Nursery
1190 Old Salem Road NE
Albany, OR 97321
Phone: (541) 928-9280
Fax: (800) 231-5306
Web site: www.nicholsgardennursery.com

Park Seed Co.
1 Parkton Avenue
Greenwood, SC 29647
Phone: (800) 845-3369
Fax: (864) 941-4206
Web site: www.parkseed.com

Pinetree Garden Seeds
P.O. Box 300
616 A Lewiston Road
New Gloucester, ME 04260
Phone: (207) 926-3400
Fax: (888) 527-3337
Web site: www.superseeds.com

Seeds of Change
P.O. Box 15700
Santa Fe, NM 87506
Phone: (888) 762-7333
Web site: www.seedsofchange.com

Southern Exposure Seed Exchange
P.O. Box 17
Earlysville, VA 22936
Phone: (804) 973-4703
Fax: (804) 973-8717
Web site: www.southernexposure.com

Stokes Seed Inc.
Box 548
Buffalo, NY 14240
Phone: (716) 695-6980
Fax: (716) 695-9649
Web site: www.stokeseeds.com

Tomato Growers Supply Co.
P.O. Box 2237
Fort Myers, FL 33902
Phone: (888) 487-7333
Fax: (888) 768-3476
Web site: www.tomatogrowers.com

Fruit

Bear Creek Nursery
P.O. Box 411
Bear Creek Road
Northport, WA 99157
Phone: (509) 732-6219
Fax: (509) 985-2282

Henry Field's Seed & Nursery Co.
415 Burnett
Shenandoah, IA 51602
Phone: (800) 798-7842
Fax: (800) 357-4149
Web site: www.henryfields.com

Johnson Nursery, Inc.
1352 Big Creek Road
Ellijay, GA 30540
Phone: (888) 276-3187
Fax: (706) 276-3186
Web site: www.johnsonnursery.com

Lewis Nursery & Farms, Inc.
3500 NC Hwy 133
Rocky Point, NC 28457
Phone: (910) 675-2394, (800) 453-5346

Raintree Nursery
391 Butts Road
Morton, WA 98356
Phone: (360) 496-6400
Fax: (360) 496-6465
Web site: www.raintreenursery.com

St. Lawrence Nurseries
325 SH 345
Potsdam, NY 13676
Phone: (315) 265-6739
Web site: sln.potsdam.ny.us

Strawberry Tyme Farms
RR 2, #1250, St. Johns Road
Simcoe, Ontario N3Y 4K1
Phone: (519) 426-3009
Fax: (519) 426-2573
Web site: www.strawberrytyme.com

Perennials

Andre Viette Farm & Nursery
P.O. Box 1109, Rt. 608
Fishersville, VA 22939
Phone: (800) 575-5538
Fax: (540) 934-0782
Web site: www.viette.com

Bluestone Perennials
7211 Middle Ridge Road
Madison, OH 44057
Phone/fax: (800) 852-5243
Web site: www.bluestoneperennials.com

Busse Gardens
17160 245th Avenue
Big Lake, MN 55309
Phone: (800) 544-3192
Fax: (320) 286-6601
Web site: www.bussegardens.com

Canyon Creek Nursery
3527 Dry Creek Road
Oroville, CA 95965
Phone: (530) 533-2166
Web site: www.canyoncreeknursery.com

Carroll Gardens
444 E. Main Street
Westminster, MD 21157
Phone: (800) 638-6334
Fax: (410) 857-4112
Web site: www.carrollgardens.com

Forestfarm
990 Tetherow Road
Williams, OR 97544 -9599
Phone: (541) 846-7269
Fax: (541) 846-7269
Web site: www.forestfarm.com

Gardens North
5984 Third Line Road N
North Gower, Ontario K0A 2T0
Phone: (613) 489-0065
Fax: (613) 489-1208
Web site: www.gardensnorth.com

Heronswood Nursery Ltd.
7530 N.E. 288th Street
Kingston, WA 98346-9502
Phone: (360) 297-4172
Fax: (360) 297-8321
Web site: www.heronswood.com

Kurt Bluemel, Inc.
2740 Greene Lane
Baldwin, MD 21013-9523
Phone: (800) 248-7584
Fax: (410) 557-9785
Web site: www.bluemel.com

Niche Gardens
1111 Dawson Road
Chapel Hill, NC 27516
Phone: (919) 967-0078
Fax: (919) 967-4026
Web site: www.nichegdn.com

The Perennial Gardens
13139 224th Street
Maple Ridge, British Columbia
V4R 2P6
Phone: (604) 467-4218
Fax: (604) 467-3181
Web site: www.perennialgardener.com

Plant Delights Nursery
9241 Sauls Road
Raleigh, NC 27603
Phone: (919) 772-4794
Fax: (919) 662-0370
Web site: www.plantdel.com

Plants of the Southwest
Agua Fria, Route 6, Box 11A
Santa Fe, NM 87501
Phone: (800) 788-7333
Fax: (505) 438-8800
Web site: www.plantsofthesouthwest.com

Shady Oaks Nursery
P.O. Box 708
Waseca, MN 56093
Phone: (800) 504-8006
Fax: (888) 735-4531
Web site: www.shadyoaks.com

Siskiyou Rare Plant Nursery
2825 Cummings Road
Medford, OR 97501
Phone: (541) 772-6846
Fax: (541) 772-4917
Web site: www.wave.net/upg/srpn

Wayide Gardens
1 Garden Lane
Hodges, SC 29695-0001
Phone: (800) 845-1124
Fax: (800) 817-1124
Web site: www.waysidegardens.com

White Flower Farm
P.O. Box 50
Litchfield, CN 06759-0050
Phone: (800) 503-9624
Fax: (860) 496-1418
Web site: www.whiteflowerfarm.com

Gardening Supplies/Soil Testing

A-1 Unique Insect Control
5504 Sperry Drive
Citrus Heights, CA 95621
Phone: (916) 961-7945
Fax: (916) 967-7082
Web site: www.a-1unique.com

ARBICO
P.O. Box 4247 CRB
Tucson, AZ 85738
Phone: (800) 827-2847
Fax: (602) 825-2038
Web site: www.goodearthmarketplace.com

Gardener's Supply Co.
128 Intervale Road
Burlington, VT 05401
Phone: (888) 833-1412
Fax: (800) 551-6712
Web site: www.gardeners.com

Green Spot Ltd.
93 Priest Road
Nottingham, NH 03290
Phone: (603) 942-8925
Fax: (603) 942-8932
Web site: www.greenmethods.com

Harmony Farm Supply
3244 Gravenstein Highway N
Sebastopol, CA 95742
Phone: (707) 823-9125
Fax: (707) 823-1734
Web site: www.harmonyfarm.com

Peaceful Valley Farm Supply
P.O. Box 2209
Grass Valley, CA 95945
Phone: (888) 784-1722
Fax: (530) 272-4794
Web site: www.groworganic.com

Woods End Research Laboratory
Old Rome Road, Box 1850
Mt. Vernon, ME 04352
Phone: (207) 293-2357
Fax: (207) 293-2488

Worm's Way
7850 N. Highway 37
Bloomington, IN 47404
Phone: (800) 274-9676
Web site: ec2.wormsway.net/ecom/mechant.mv

Bird-Watching Organizations

Cornell Lab of Ornithology
159 Sapsucker Woods Road
Ithaca, NY 14850
Phone: (607) 254-2473
Web site: www.birds.cornell.edu

National Bird Feeding Society
P.O. Box 23L
Northbrook, IL 60065-0023
Phone: (847) 272-0135
Fax: (847) 498-4092
Web site: www.birdfeeding.org

National Wildlife Federation
8925 Leesburg Pike
Vienna, VA 22184
Phone: (703) 790-4000
Web site: www.nwf.org

Books and Periodicals

Bradley, Fern Marshall, and Barbara W. Ellis, eds. *Rodale's All-New Encyclopedia of Organic Gardening.* Emmaus, PA: Rodale, 1992.

Bradley, Fern Marshall, ed. *Rodale's Garden Answers: Vegetables, Fruits and Herbs.* Emmaus, PA: Rodale, 1995.

DiSabato-Aust, Tracy. *The Well-Tended Perennial Garden.* Portland, OR: Timber, 1998.

Gilkeson, Linda, Pam Peirce, and Miranda Smith. *Rodale's Pest & Disease Problem Solver.* Emmaus, PA: Rodale, 1996.

Hodgson, Larry. *Perennials for Every Purpose.* Emmaus, PA: Rodale, 2000.

Nick, Jean M. A., and Fern Marshall Bradley. *Growing Fruits & Vegetables Organically.* Emmaus, PA : Rodale, 1994.

Ondra, Nancy J. *Soil and Composting.* (Taylor's Weekend Gardening Guides.) Boston: Houghton Mifflin, 1998.

Organic Gardening magazine, Rodale Inc., 33 E. Minor Street, Emmaus, PA 18098

Phillips, Ellen, and C. Colston Burrell. *Rodale's Illustrated Encyclopedia of Perennials.* Emmaus, PA: Rodale, 1993.

Powell, Eileen. *From Seed to Bloom..* Pownal, VT: Storey Communications, 1995.

Rodale Organic Gardening Basics: Roses. Emmaus, PA: Rodale, 2000.

Roth, Sally. *The Backyard Bird Feeder's Bible.* Emmaus, PA: Rodale, 2000.

Sombke, Laurence. *Beautiful Easy Flower Gardens.* Emmaus, PA: Rodale, 1995.

Index

USDA Plant Hardiness Zone Map

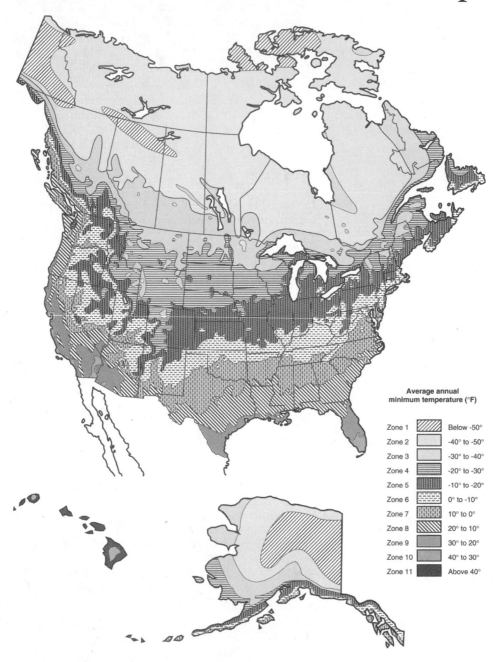

Average annual minimum temperature (°F)

Zone 1		Below -50°
Zone 2		-40° to -50°
Zone 3		-30° to -40°
Zone 4		-20° to -30°
Zone 5		-10° to -20°
Zone 6		0° to -10°
Zone 7		10° to 0°
Zone 8		20° to 10°
Zone 9		30° to 20°
Zone 10		40° to 30°
Zone 11		Above 40°

This map was revised in 1990 and is recognized as the best indicator of minimum temperatures available. Look at the map to find your area, then match its color to the key. When you've found your color, the key will tell you what hardiness zone you live in. Remember that the map is a general guide; your particular conditions may vary.